The Encyclopedia of
CLASSIC CARS

The Encyclopedia of
CLASSIC CARS

A CELEBRATION OF THE MOTORCAR FROM 1945 TO 1975

Martin Buckley

HERMES
HOUSE

For Catherine and Sean

This edition published by Hermes House
an imprint of

Anness Publishing Limited
Hermes House, 88-89 Blackfriars Road, London SE1 8HA

A CIP catalogue record for this book is available from the British Library

Publisher: Joanna Lorenz
Project Editor: Joanne Rippin
Designer: Alan Marshall
Additional text supplied by Paul Hardiman

© Anness Publishing Limited 1997
Updated © 1998, 1999, 2000, 2001, 2002
1 3 5 7 9 10 8 6 4 2

The publishers would like to thank *Classic and Sportscar* magazine, Haymarket Specialist Motoring, for
supplying most of the pictures in the book. Additional pictures supplied by:
BFI Stills, Posters and Designs: 58mt; 59tl/mb. Don Morley: pp 54; 67bl; 68tm/bm/br; 69t; 72 all;
91br; 92bl; 94bl; 128tr; 140t/bl; 150t/ml/mr/br; 151t/ml/b; 157bl; 172m; 182b; 190t/m/b;
191t/ml/bl/br; 192ml; 194t/m/b; 195ml/b; 196t; 197mr; 200bl/br; 201t/mt; 202br; 204bl; 205tl;
206bl/br; 207tr; 209tr; 218ml/br; 219t/m; 230t; 241tl/l/m; 243mtl; 248m; 249m.
John Colley: pp 1; 14m; 177tl; 200mr; 216bl; 234bl; 244t; 251tl/tr/ml/mr/bl; 102bl.
National Motor Museum, Beaulieu, England: pp 3 (N Wright); 44; 82m; 82bl (N Wright); 94tr/m/br;
98tr/m/bl; 99tr/mr/b; 100t (N Wright); 101tl/tr (N Georgano); 101mr; 104t; 118tr/m (N Wright);
119m/br; 142t; 162br; 166b; 178b; 208t; 210mr.
Quadrant Picture Library: pp 187m; 208br; 221t; 132tr/bl/br; 210ml; 211b.
b=bottom, t=top, l=left, r=right, m=middle.

Contents

SECTION ONE

Introduction   6

The Classic Era   8

The Growth of an Industry   20

Building the Pedigree   44

Classic Culture   54

SECTION TWO

The A-Z of Classic Cars   64

Index   254

INTRODUCTION

As government regulations threaten to engineer much of the character out of modern cars, as our roads become more congested and dangerous and the air we breathe gets more contaminated, we can look back to the "classic" era of the 1950s and 1960s as the romantic Golden Age of the motorcar. In Europe, more and better mass-produced cars were seen as a liberating force for families previously restricted to public transport. In North America, cars simply got bigger, reflecting the wealth and confidence of the most powerful nation on earth. Traffic was yet to reach its often gridlocked state of today, petrol was much cheaper and, in Britain at least, there were no speed restrictions on the newly-opened motorways.

Before the mergers and close-downs of the 1970s, buyers could choose from a far wider range of makes reflecting national identities. The Japanese motor industry, later so dominant, was not even a speck on the horizon in the 1950s and 1960s. In engineering and styling, too, cars tended to be more varied and individual – you could tell an Austin from a Morris, a Vauxhall from a Volvo without having to look at the badge. Safety was optional: it was speed, glamour and style that sold cars, and in the 50s and early 60s nobody had even begun to think of the exhaust-emission regulations that would strangle power outputs in the 70s. Back then, the motorcar was our servant. Now, through its very proliferation, it has become our master. In this book, we celebrate the glory days and beyond and the marvellous machines which rode through them, fixing in our cultural consciousness a picture of the ideal motor – the classic car.

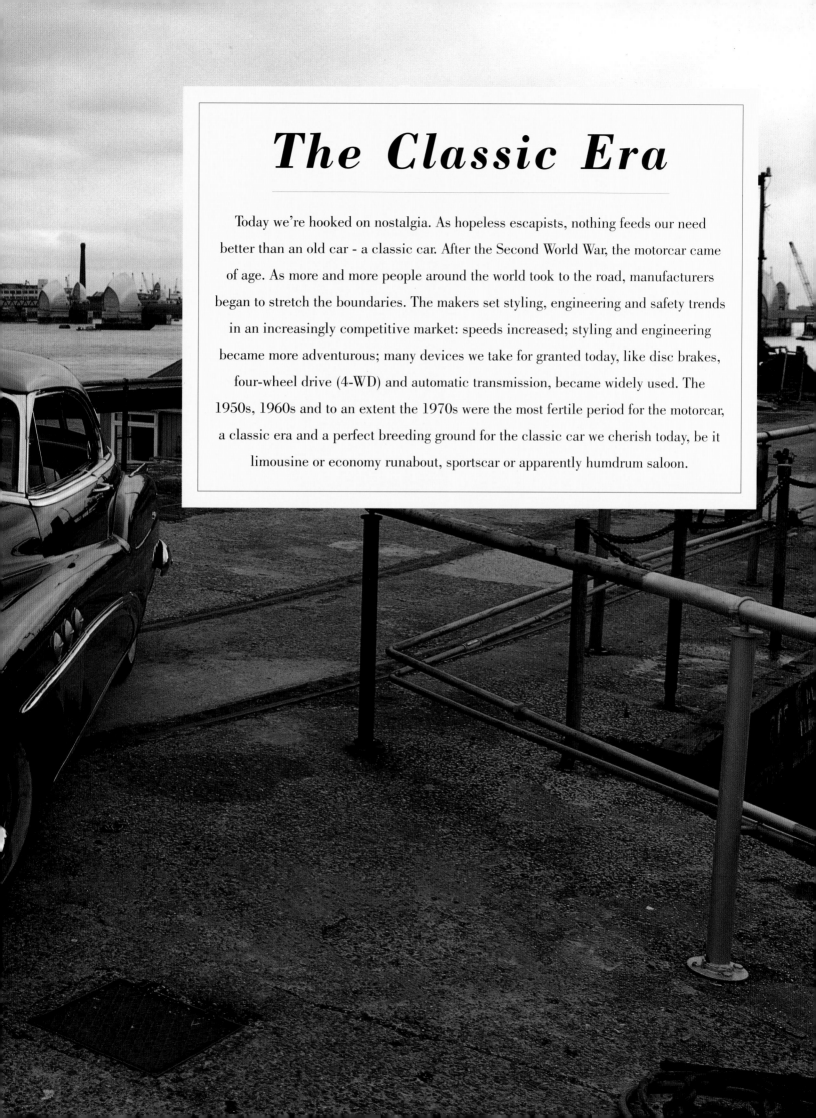

The Classic Era

Today we're hooked on nostalgia. As hopeless escapists, nothing feeds our need better than an old car - a classic car. After the Second World War, the motorcar came of age. As more and more people around the world took to the road, manufacturers began to stretch the boundaries. The makers set styling, engineering and safety trends in an increasingly competitive market: speeds increased; styling and engineering became more adventurous; many devices we take for granted today, like disc brakes, four-wheel drive (4-WD) and automatic transmission, became widely used. The 1950s, 1960s and to an extent the 1970s were the most fertile period for the motorcar, a classic era and a perfect breeding ground for the classic car we cherish today, be it limousine or economy runabout, sportscar or apparently humdrum saloon.

EVOLUTION OF THE MOVEMENT

As the 20th century draws to a close, we seem to look back as much as forward, pining for what were, as we see it, better times. We can't revisit our Golden Age, but at least we can own and experience the material objects that evoke it: clothes, music, films and cars – classic cars. Glamorous, kitsch, humble or high bred, these mobile time warps powerfully conjure up a particular period.

New Vintage

The hobby of preserving and collecting cars built after the Second World War began to take shape in the early 1970s. Veteran (pre-1905), Edwardian (pre-1919) and Vintage (pre-1931) cars – as defined by Britain's Vintage Sports Car Club – have always been easy enough to categorize but, by the end of the 1960s, post-war motorcars of the better kind were coming of age. To call them simply "old cars" no longer seemed appropriate: whether beautiful, fast or technically pre-eminent, the post-1945 car had at its best all the gravitas of the pre-war machinery. Slowly, quietly, the "new Vintage" had arrived, filling the gap between Vintage and

■ ABOVE *Classics so evocative of their period as these – the AC Ace, Ferrari 166 and C-Type Jaguar – have always been in strong demand and are priced at a premium.*

■ BELOW *Racing cars with some historic significance are eagerly sought by collectors and achieve astonishing prices at auction.*

modern for a new generation of enthusiasts.

One-marque clubs for well-bred sporting marques such as Aston and Bentley had been around for years, but as enthusiasts for the less exalted makes felt the need to huddle together around a common banner, many new guilds and registers sprouted. Traditionalists had long complained that modern cars all "looked the same", but in the 70s there was a gut feeling that the motorcar had seen its best years as safety and pollution regulations made inroads into designers' freedom. Styling, particularly in Britain, seemed to be losing its way.

No wonder older cars began to look increasingly attractive. They were plentiful, cheap, easy to work on and still very usable on increasingly busy roads. Drive an old car and you made a statement about your individualism: you weren't prepared to become just another faceless, sterile tin can on the bypass to oblivion or obsessed with keeping up with the Joneses in the yearly new-model scrum. It all came together in 1973 when a UK magazine, *Classic Cars*, was launched.

The name "classic" stuck, a useful catch-all term for a sprawling, ill-defined genre that in

■ ABOVE *High prices obtained by auction houses for high-grade classics had a knock-on effect on the rest of the industry.*

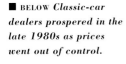

■ BELOW *Classic-car dealers prospered in the late 1980s as prices went out of control.*

just 20 years or so has blossomed from an eccentric pastime in to a multimillion-pound industry. Not much happened for about ten years, until about 1982-83 when the nature of the hobby began to change dramatically. Slowly, under the noses of true enthusiasts, market forces took hold as it dawned on investors that really prime machinery could prove a fine hedge against inflation or an appreciating asset. Suddenly, the market hardened as Americans came to Europe seeking prime collectables.

At first, gilt-edged pre-war hardware – Bentley, Bugatti, etc. – set the pace in auction rooms but, by mid-decade, supercars of the 50s, 60s and 70s were hyped on their coat tails. Once affordable Ferraris, Astons and Jaguar XKs and E-Types became "investor" cars,

commodities too expensive and precious to be driven (which was rather missing the point).

As the auction houses pulled even bigger numbers, hype went into overdrive. Banks and finance companies offered loans to buy classics. The increasing ranks of classic-car magazines bulged with advertizing. Enthusiasts' gentle hobby was turned into an ugly brawl driven by greed. Many found themselves with cars that were worth more than their houses, machinery they were now too nervous to use. The boom couldn't last, fortunately. The recession hit in 1989 and demand quickly fell.

A hobby again

Today, the investors are long gone, the market is stable and the cars are where they should be – with enthusiasts. Though we are unlikely to see such madness again, rare and high-calibre thoroughbred cars – especially those with a racing pedigree or an interesting provenance – will always be in strong demand. Fashion still has its part to play in the lower echelons of the market, but those who bought Citroëns and Jaguars have learnt about the dedication required to run an old car. Some went back to their moderns, others caught a lifelong bug.

TECHNICAL DEVELOPMENTS

In the beginning, cars were motorized horse carriages or, in the case of the three-wheeled Benz of 1889, relied heavily on cycle technology. Most cars were braked only by the rear wheel; steering, often by tiller, was slow and ponderous. A shoulder-high centre of gravity threatened to tip the car over. All this was containable at the 4mph (6.4kph) first allowed in Britain for motor vehicles and not too scary at the 14mph (22.5kph) allowed by 1896, but as speeds rose, something had to be done. Makers who introduced each refinement created classics along the way.

Technology filters down

Excellence began with high-class cars such as the Rolls-Royce and Bentley. Steadily, the technology filtered down to such humble transport as the Austin Seven. By the start of

■ LEFT *Cord's 810 used a supercharged V-eight Lycoming engine with revolutionary front-wheel drive.*

■ BELOW *The Chrysler Airflow was one of the first cars designed with an eye to aerodynamics.*

■ LEFT AND BELOW *The Lancia Aprillia was a groundbreaking saloon of the mid-1930s.*

the Second World War, bodies were generally made of steel, sat on a separate chassis, and there were brakes all round. Jaguar brought disc brakes to the world's notice at Le Mans in 1953; five years later they appeared on Jaguar's road cars and soon every maker used them.

Refinement follows

Four-wheel drive, with antilock brakes, was pioneered by Ferguson Formula. It first appeared in a passenger car on the Jensen FF of 1966, along with Dunlop Maxaret anti-lock brakes derived from aircraft technology. It was expensive and complex – only 320 were built.

Overhead camshafts allow more direct

operation of valves and a better combustion-chamber shape. They were used on specialist racing cars such as the Alfa Romeo and Bugatti from the 20s onwards and were introduced to the mainstream in the straight-six XK engine in the 120 of 1948. Soon, makers realized they could run double overhead camshafts and multivalve layouts.

Self-levelling was a standard feature of the futuristic DS launched in 1955 by Citroën. Even the cheaper 2CV had a modicum of levelling, because front and rear suspension were interconnected by springs. The British Motor Corporation (BMC) 1100 and 1800 of the 60s – and Minis of the period – are interconnected hydraulically. Self-levelling was used at the tail end of the Range Rover from its launch in 1970.

Front-wheel drive, used by BSA, Cord and Citroën since the 30s, did not hit the mainstream until the Mini appeared in 1959. While scorned by purists, this layout makes for

■ ABOVE *A 1956 Chevy: crude - but comfortable and well equipped.*

■ RIGHT *The Citroën 2CV: quirky, uncomfortable and poorly equipped. So who cares!*

■ BELOW RIGHT *The revolutionary Mini, a masterpiece of packaging.*

■ BELOW *The boxy body design of Lancia's Flavia an expensively-engineered, superb-handling car.*

safe, predictable handling and better packaging – more interior room for a given size – than rear-driven counterparts.

All the while, chassis improvements and tyre technology shadowed each other: Citroën's *Traction-avant* was the first car to use radial tyres, the narrow and distinctively treaded Michelin X.

America thinks big

In America, spacious cars with powerful, six- and eight-cylinder engines were common, even before the war. Makers loaded cars with every device to take the work out of driving: automatic transmission, power steering, power brakes, air conditioning, self-dipping headlamps. Engines, generally understressed by large capacity, showcased maintenance-free features such as hydraulic tappets (initially used for quietness).

MILESTONE MODELS

The following are technically important cars that made history from the 1930s to the 1970s, and had a lasting impact on the industry.

Citroën *Traction Avant*

Front-wheel drive and monocoque construction – in 1934! All this and unrivalled ride and handling from low centre of gravity and all-independent-torsion bar suspension came from the fertile mind of André Citroën.

Fiat 500

Dante Giacosa's master-stroke, the Italian car for the masses, was the Topolino. It was a full-sized car scaled down, with a tiny four-cylinder engine but all-steel unitary construction and independent suspension. (John Cooper plundered this for rear-engined racers.)

■ LEFT *The Citroën Traction Avant was a brave move but teething troubles nearly broke the company.*

■ BELOW *Spaceship: just imagine the effect of the Citroën DS's shape on the public in 1955.*

■ BELOW *Fiat 500: poor man's transport, now the darling of the trendy.*

Citroën DS/SM

When launched to a stunned public in 1955, the DS looked like a spaceship. Its incredible other-worldly body style by Flaminio Bertoni used easily-removable outer panels; it had a glass-fibre roof and tail-lamps like rockets. A pressurised, self-levelling gas and oil system replaced suspension springs, and also pwered the brakes, steering, clutch and even gear change. Its complexity scared off many buyers.

Mini

Alec Issigonis's revolutionary Mini of 1959 set the convention for every small car since and is a strong candidate for the most significant car of the 20th century. By mounting the engine transversely and making it drive the front wheels (not a first: Alvis, sundry American companies and Fiat had tried it before), Issigonis fitted space for four adults into a package 10ft (3m) long.

To keep the driveline package very short, the gearbox sat under the engine, in the sump. The use of a 10 in (25.5cm) wheel at each corner not only minimized the encroachment of

■ LEFT *Lotus Seven, the greatest-handling road classic, designed in 1956 and still in production today.*

Jaguar E-type

With its gorgeous, curvy, phallic shape derived from Malcolm Sayers's Le Mans-winning D-Type racer, combined with a 3.8-litre version of the classic XK engine, this is the car that epitomized the racy end of the Swinging 60s. It was fantastic value at its 1961 launch price equivalent of only four Minis – and early versions really would come near the alleged top speed of 150mph (241kph). Forget the crunchy gearbox and unpredictable brakes, this is one of the world's most desirable cars.

Datsun 240Z

The Japanese had really arrived in 1969 with this "Big Healey" beater. Its classic fastback shape has never been bettered by Japan, and the strong, 2.4-litre straight-six engine made all the right noises. Good handling came from its all-independent strut suspension and super performance from its relatively light weight. Later cars – the 260 and 280Z – became heavier and softer. As is so often the case, first is purest. This is Japan's first classic and the world's best-selling sportscar.

wheel-arch space into the passenger compartment but, together with the direct rack-and-pinion steering and firm, rubber suspension, took handling to new standards of "chuckability". The Mini is still made to the same familiar specifications, although big changes are predicted for the model in the new millenium.

The Mini has competed since it first appeared; most notable performances were ace Paddy Hopkirk's wins in Alpine rallies in the 60s, his finest moment being victory in the 1965 Monte Carlo Rally. Minis still hold their own in historic rallying in the 90s.

■ ABOVE *The 246 Dino, one of the most gorgeous shapes ever, although it never badged Ferrari.*

■ RIGHT *Datsun's 240Z took on the mantle of the "Big Healey" - a lusty six banger for the 1970s.*

LEADING ENGINEERS

These are some of the most innovative and imaginative engineers from the world motor industry.

André Citroën

A true innovator, Citroën followed his own direction to produce cars that led the world for refinement and technical innovation. His engineeering tour de force, the *Traction-avant* of 1934, was followed up by his utilitarian masterstroke, the 2CV of 1948.

Ferdinand Porsche

Porsche designed the world's best-selling car, the VW Beetle which became the basis for the Porsche 356 designed by his son Ferry, forerunner of the immortal 911.

Alec Issigonis

Issigonis's masterstroke was the Mini, a brilliant piece of packaging whose layout – transverse engine, front-wheel drive and an

■ ABOVE *André Citroën carried a torch for innovation; much of the detailed design work was done by others.*

■ ABOVE RIGHT *Ferry Porsche, son of the man responsible for the world's best-selling car, himself made a vital contribution – the 356.*

■ LEFT *Alec Issigonis left his legacy in the shape of two brilliant small cars, the Morris Minor and the immortal Mini.*

independently-sprung wheel at each corner – has been copied for every other small car in the world. But people forget he was also reponsible for the Morris Minor, the best-handling and most modern car of its generation.

Antonio Fessia

Engineering supremo behind the classic Lancia Fulvia – and its bigger siblings the Flavia and Flaminia – Professor Antonio Fessia joined Fiat in 1925. By 1936, at only 35, he was director of the central technical office. Under him, Dante Giacosa designed the Topolino. A demanding, sometimes difficult boss, Fessia approached design scientifically. His 1960 Lancia Flavia, harking back to the 47 Cemsa Caproni, was the first Italian car with front-wheel drive. He followed up with the smaller V-four Fulvia which shared many components. He stayed with Lancia until his death in 1968.

William Lyons

Lyons was responsible for the beautiful styling of his Jaguars, from SS through MkII to XJ6 –

all classics. Another achievement was to keep prices low without sacrificing quality – Lyons's Jaguars were always superb value. An autocratic boss, he started Swallow Sidecars in the mid-1920s, at first building sidecars, then fitting more luxurious bodywork to Austin Sevens. The first SS Jaguars, brilliantly styled saloons and a beautiful SS100 sportscar appeared in the mid-1930s, all-time styling greats from Lyon's fertile pen. After the Second World War, his company became Jaguar.

■ ABOVE LEFT *WO Bentley was a gifted engineer, but he soon left the company that bore his name and went to Lagonda.*

■ ABOVE RIGHT *Colin Chapman, a brilliant and innovative designer, produced some of the best-handling cars ever.*

■ LEFT *Sir William Lyons, a great designer and an intuitive stylist: his cars always looked like a million dollars but represented superb value for money.*

Colin Chapman

A truly gifted structural engineer whose radical designs changed the face of racing – the road-car operation was intended only to shore up the racing effort. His first self-built car and the legendary Lotus Seven hit the road in 1953 and 1957 respectively. Chapman's weight-paring efforts, all for agility and speed, sometimes earned criticism for risking driver safety. He was devastated by the death of his star driver and friend Jim Clark in 1968.

Dante Giacosa

Dante Giacosa studied mechanical engineering at Turin Polytechnic and joined Fiat in 1928. From 1933 he was involved in the design of a small car. He put his watercooled Topolino against an aircooled design and won. More than four million Topolino's were made, taking their rightful place as one of the world's great small cars beside the Austin 7, the VW Beetle and the Mini.

Giacosa then created most archetypal small Italian cars, including the Fiat Nuova 500, 600, 127 and 128, and the masterpieces 8V and Cisitalia racer. He died in 1996.

MASS PRODUCTION

Henry Ford started it all with his Model T Ford. Production began in America in 1908 and later began in Britain. By 1913, Ford's plant at Old Trafford, Manchester, was making 8,000 cars a year by mass production whilst traditionalist Wolseley could manage only 3,000.

Where English cars were largely produced by hand, with chassis parts being individually made, drilled, reamed and assembled, Ford invested in huge machine tools that would

■ BELOW LEFT AND RIGHT *Henry Ford's automated production lines speeded car making, here a row of Model T's, beyond belief. He took his new methods to England, setting up a factory in Old Trafford, Manchester. In 1913 it could make 8,000 cars a year.*

stamp out parts by the hundred, exactly the same every time, which did not need skilled labour to assemble.

The cost of these tools was huge, so selling the resulting cars cheaply in huge numbers was the answer. Where car bodies had traditionally been made by hand, all to slightly different specifications, Ford's T's were, with a few variations on the theme, all the same and had pressed and welded bodies, like today's cars. Spray painting saved hours over the traditional multicoat process with its laborious rubbing down by hand between coats.

■ LEFT *A test track was built on the roof of Fiat's factory at Lingotto, Turin.*

Conveyor-belt cars

To achieve this huge production, Ford installed its first moving-track assembly operations in Detroit, Michigan, the world's largest car-manufacturing centre, and in Trafford Park, Manchester, England. Instead of men moving to the cars to complete their specialist operation, or pushing cars by hand from one assembly station to another, the cars came to the men for each additional operation to be completed, with components fed in from overhead conveyors. Each man would walk beside the chassis until his task was completed and repeat the exercise on the next chassis. By the end of the line, the car was complete. Ford's basic T two-seater, the runabout, was produced in 1913. A classic was born.

Gradually, all other makers followed, although luxury cars were still largely hand built, just as prestige classics always have been. Morgan still hand builds cars in the same way it has since the 1920s, rolling partially-completed cars from one station to another. Yet by 1927, Citroën was producing a car every 10 minutes.

■ ABOVE *Fiat 850 coupés on production lines at Turin.*

■ BELOW *Ford Anglias being sprayed on a moving line at Dagenham, Essex. In time, robots replaced people.*

Robots lend a hand

Even greater speed and productivity were achieved by the use of power tools, suspended from the ceiling so they could be manhandled more easily. The next step was to cut manpower. First, spray painting was robotized, then the welding of bodyshells. To show how production methods continue to progress, of cars made today the one needing the most labour-intensive welding on its bodyshell is the Mini, first seen in 1959.

It was through mass production that cars such as the MG were born. The first MG Midget of 1929 used simple components borrowed from the Morris saloon cars in a more sporty body, just as all MGs since have done, right up to the F of 1995. Thanks to mass production, classic sportscars were made available to the general buying public.

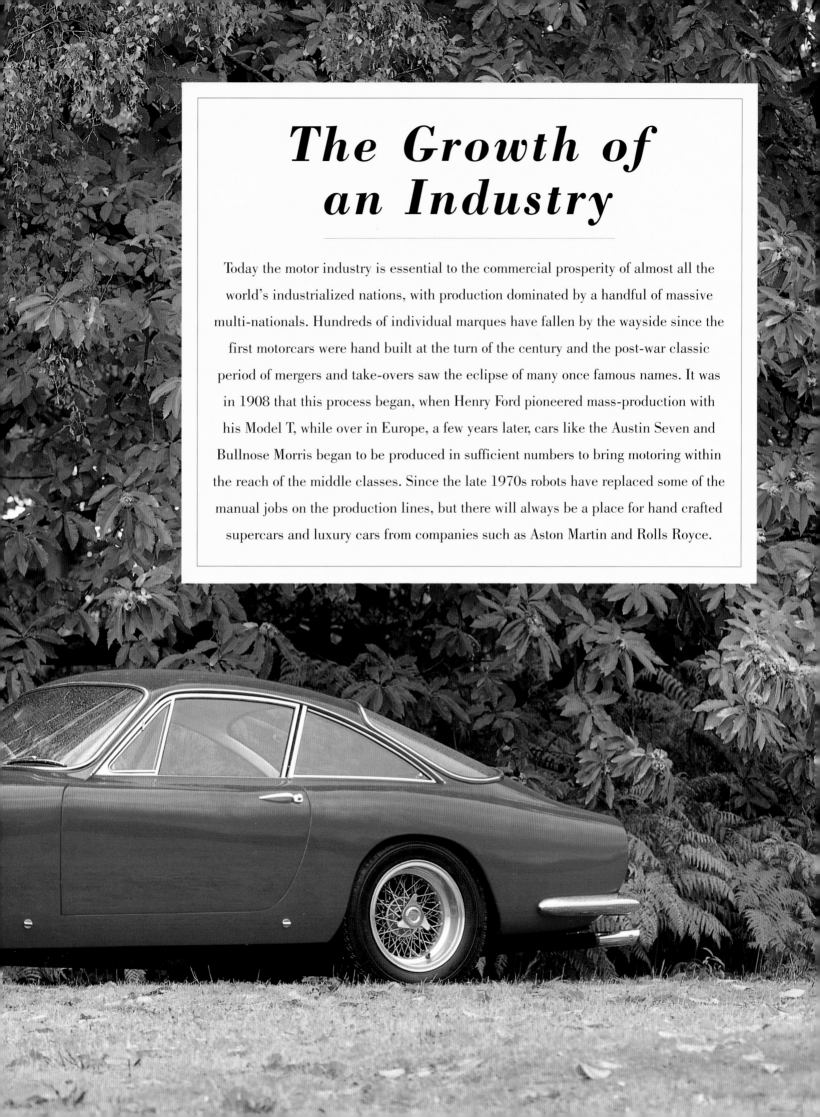

The Growth of an Industry

Today the motor industry is essential to the commercial prosperity of almost all the world's industrialized nations, with production dominated by a handful of massive multi-nationals. Hundreds of individual marques have fallen by the wayside since the first motorcars were hand built at the turn of the century and the post-war classic period of mergers and take-overs saw the eclipse of many once famous names. It was in 1908 that this process began, when Henry Ford pioneered mass-production with his Model T, while over in Europe, a few years later, cars like the Austin Seven and Bullnose Morris began to be produced in sufficient numbers to bring motoring within the reach of the middle classes. Since the late 1970s robots have replaced some of the manual jobs on the production lines, but there will always be a place for hand crafted supercars and luxury cars from companies such as Aston Martin and Rolls Royce.

WHAT MAKES A CLASSIC?

"Without a certain amount of snobbery, efforts would be hopeless ... A motorcar must be designed and built that is a little different from and a little better than the product of the big quantity manufacturer."

Cecil Kimber, founder of MG, had it right. He sensed a need and virtually invented the concept of the classic – but MGs have never been particularly special or mechanically innovative. What they do have, however, is that little extra desirability, so that owners and onlookers alike *see* them as classic cars. MGs are instantly recognizable, even to many non-enthusiasts, in much the same way that Jaguars, Ferraris and Bentleys are – all of them true classics.

Most enthusiasts would categorize a classic car as one whose design is inalienably right: it must look good, handle well, probably be possessed of higher performance or equipment

■ BELOW LEFT *BMW 328: a timeless classic, lithe, lean and light.*

■ ABOVE *Performance, grace - and a competition classic. NUB 120 is the most famous Jaguar XK120 ever.*

levels than were normal for its day – but overall it must be desirable.

Age alone cannot make a classic, even though a common definition given today is "any car more than 20 years old". Those who use that definition would say that Avengers and

Marinas are classics; most enthusiasts with other criterior would not.

Beauty is in the eye of the beholder but there is no disputing the beauty of a real classic. Who cannot be moved by the shape and form of a Bugatti Type 35, Alfa Monza,

■ ABOVE *The basic shape of the Porsche 911 endured for nearly 35 years from launch in 1964.*

■ LEFT *Bugatti Type 35,*
a GP racer for the road
- a model of sparse
functional character.

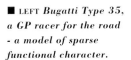

Duesenberg, Jaguar XK120 or early E-Type,
Ferrari 250 GT, AC Ace, Citroën DS and
Mercedes Gullwing, by the stark efficiency of
an early Porsche 911 or the simplicity of the
Austin Seven or Mini?

Then there were the "firsts", each with its
claim to classicdom: Colin Chapman's Lotus
Seven, a racer for the road; the Mini Cooper 'S'
which further defined the small car and was
the first "pocket rocket"; the Hispano-Suiza
and Pegaso, Spain's only, exquisitely made
supercars from the 20s and 50s respectively;
the Reliant Scimitar GTE which introduced a
new concept – the sporting estate car; the Golf
GTi, which spawned a whole new breed of
enthusiasts' car. Each of these counts as a
classic for defining a new niche in car-lovers'
hearts. That each one of these cars – and many
more like them – is notable in its own field
helps reinforce its claim to be a true classic.

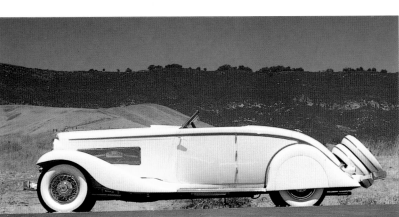

■ ABOVE *Duesenberg:*
coachbuilt elegance,
American style. It could
achieve more than
100mph (160kph).

■ RIGHT *The straight*
eight engined Alfa
Monza: epitome of the
classic vintage racer.

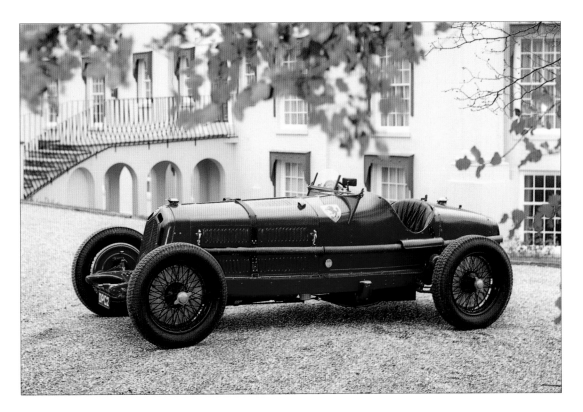

CLASSIC ENGINES

Once a classic is in motion, the engine does more than any other feature to give it character. The 1945–75 period started with almost universal use of sidevalve power, except on the most costly and exotic cars, and ended with multiple camshafts and valves, fuel injection and unusual materials becoming the norm. Most of these advances were first developed for racing, then refined for road use as they showed the way to efficiency.

Progress had meant more performance. Where 1940s power outputs were small, by the 70s, engines in better sportscars were up to 80bhp per litre. Efficiency came from ideally-shaped combustion chambers, usually hemispherical, for which a more complex valve arrangement is usually needed. The simplest way to operate these is by overhead cams, first seen on a Clément of 1902 and used by Alfa Romeo, Bentley and Bugatti in the 20s, MG in the 30s and Jaguar since the 50s, but not used on non-classics until the 80s. It's costly to develop but usually leads to better breathing.

Further advances included fuel injection,

■ ABOVE *The 16-cylinder powerplant used in the racing BRM: fantastically powerful, but too complicated to live.*

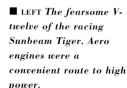

■ LEFT *The fearsome V-twelve of the racing Sunbeam Tiger. Aero engines were a convenient route to high power.*

■ BELOW LEFT *The light-alloy 3.5-litre Rover V-eight, beloved of specialist sportscar makers, is derived from an unwanted Buick unit of the 1960s.*

which did away with compromises forced by carburettors. It was first used on production cars, in rather basic form, by Chevrolet on its Corvette in 1954 and by Mercedes-Benz on its technical tour de force 300SL in 1955. In the early 70s, Bosch's Jetronic systems began to appear on performance classics such as the Porsche 911. Since 1993, with universal fitment of catalytic convertors, fuel injection has become a necessity, along with electronic ignition, which began to appear at the end of the 60s. For convenience, the hydraulic tappet was designed by Bollée in 1910. General Motors began to fit them in the 30s, leading to extra mechanical refinement and less servicing.

Hydraulic tappets were universal in America by the 60s; now almost all cars use them. These are the milestone power units:-

Jaguar XK

The XK was designed in the Second World War by the nicknamed "Firewatchers" Walter Hassan, Harry Mundy and Bill Heynes when they were on evening fire duty. It is the epitome of the classic in-line twin-cam engine and was sorely needed as an alternative to the pedestrian Standard engines Jaguar was forced

to use before and immediately after the war. Launched in the XK120 of 1948, displacing 3.4 litres and producing 160bhp, it enjoyed its finest moment in a road car as the 265bhp 3.8 which propelled the 1962 E-Type coupé to 150mph (241kph). In 3.0- and 3.4-litre dry-sumped form it took D-Types to Le Mans wins and powered Jaguar saloons right up to 1987.

Rover V-eight

A cast-off from Buick (the Americans had found themselves good at thin-wall iron casting so there was no need for fancy light-alloy stuff), this 3528cc engine was discovered by Maurice Wilks on a visit to America in 1966. Realizing

■ ABOVE *Classic Italian – the Maserati 250F V-twelve racing engine with twin camshafts and a separate carburettor choke for each cylinder.*

■ LEFT *Alfa Romeo's 2.9-litre engine of the 1930s used a twin double-overhead-camshaft, straight-eight layout.*

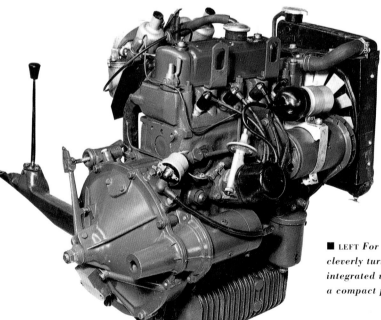

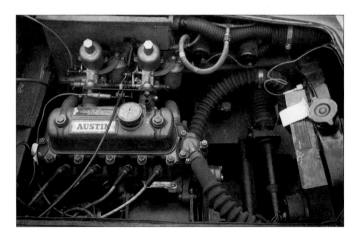

■ LEFT *For the Mini, the engine was cleverly turned sideways and integrated with the gearbox to produce a compact powerplant.*

■ ABOVE *Here's the same A-series engine, which first appeared in 1952, as it started out, mounted longitudinally.*

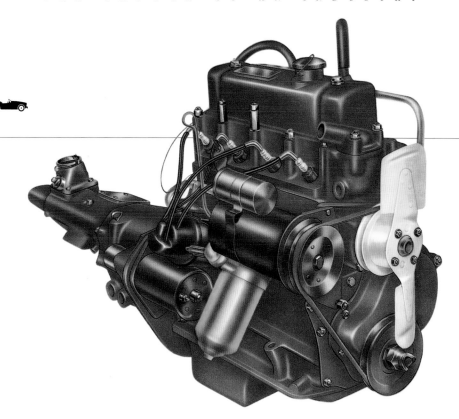

■ ABOVE *The B-series – bigger brother to the Mini engine – as used in the Wolseley 1500. It grew up to be a 1798cc unit powering the MGB.*

this compact unit would be perfect for powering Rover's big P5 saloon, he quickly acquired the rights. It was a good move: the staid, heavy saloon was transformed into one with a top speed of 110mph (177kph) and 0–60 (96) in 10 seconds. The engine did sterling service in the Rover 3500 before proving itself ideal for the Range Rover of 1970. Light and tunable, this engine has also found favour with MG, TVR, Marcos – and survives in 4.6-litre form in the Range Rover of 1996.

Ferrari V-twelve

Complex, beautifully made and exquisitely finished, Ferrari's engines are expensively engineered for big power at huge revs. The V-twelve was first seen in 1946 as the tiny Colombo-designed two-litre V-twelve 166. The larger Lampredi-designed engine appeared in 1951, in the 340 America. In front-engined Ferrari V-twelve parlance, the model number gives the displacement of one cylinder; multiply by 12 and you have the engine size. The four-camshaft layout arrived with the 275GTB/4 of 1966. This classic sports-car power unit looks as good as it goes: almost always with twin oil filters nestling together at the front of the vee and black crackle-finish cam covers cast with the legend "Ferrari".

Porsche flat-six

One of the longest-lived engines ever, this air- and oil-cooled flat six was derived from the flat four first seen pre-war in the VW Beetle. It grew from the 120bhp two-litre of 1963 to a turbocharged 3.3-litre, punching out a seamless

■ LEFT *The Cosworth DFV. Funded by Ford, this engine won over 100 Grands Prix.*

■ RIGHT *Lessons learned with the DFV spawned a whole series of Cosworth race engines. This is a four-cylinder BDA, showing the cogged belt which drives the twin camshafts.*

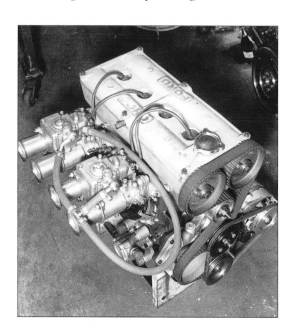

■ ABOVE *The rotary engine, used by Mazda and NSU, is so compact that it is almost hidden by its ancillaries.*

■ RIGHT *The mighty Cobras were all powered by the Ford V-eight of 4.2, 4.7 or 7 litres, producing up to 400bhp.*

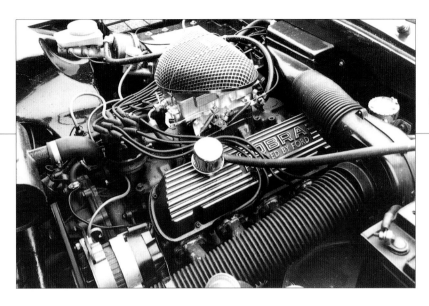

output with the low engine weight he needed for his small sportscars, it made sense to base this hitherto prohibitively expensive arrangement on existing engine technology. Ford's simple, light and tough 1340cc Kent engine from the short-lived Capri was the ideal candidate. For it, *Autocar's* then technical editor Harry Mundy designed a light-alloy twin-cam head with hemispherical combustion chambers and near-perfect valve angles. When Ford announced that the base pushrod engine would be enlarged to 1600cc form Chapman's new engine displaced 1558cc and produced 105bhp on twin carburettors. It has appeared in the Elan, the Europa, Lotus Cortinas and even early Escorts and inspired many followers.

300bhp with so much torque that only a four-speed gearbox was needed. Pioneering the Nikasil cylinder lining that did away with iron liners, and always with a single camshaft per cylinder bank, these exactingly engineered powerplants have a Germanic reputation for reliability and longevity. In the most classic 911 of all, the RS Carrera of 1973, it produces 210bhp at 7000rpm on mechanical fuel injection – accompanied by raw exhaust snarl that tingles the spine. A derivative still powers the current 911.

■ ABOVE *The two-litre four-cylinder Standard engine used in the Triumph TR3 also powered Vanguards, Morgans and, in modified form, the Ferguson tractor.*

■ RIGHT *The other side of the B series, as used in twin-carburettor 68bhp form in the Riley 1.5. The carburettor and exhaust are on the same side as the engine.*

Lotus/Ford twin-cam

When Colin Chapman realized in the 60s that twin camshafts were the way to achieve higher

SUSPENSION

The first suspension for cars – the most classically simple arrangement of all – was copied from horse-drawn carts. The beam axle, held to the chassis by leaf springs, is the simplest form of springing. It's still used, in little-modified form, on many of today's trucks. The system was used on the most basic cars until the 50s, and at the rear end of many cheaper cars until the 80s.

Soon, however, with increasing engine sophistication and speed, cart springs put limits on a car's ability to ride well and handle safely. By 1924, makers like Frazer Nash were trying extra links to control the axle's movement better while still springing it by leaf. The next big move was to independent suspension – where the movement of one wheel does not affect the other. Most of the world's favourite classic cars have this in some form but the way suspension is arranged seems to be national preference.

Americans were keen on independent front suspension by wishbones from the 1930s. An American invented the now universal MacPherson strut, although it was first used on a British car, the Ford Consul, in 1950.

Germans pioneered independent suspension

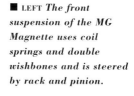

■ LEFT *The front suspension of the MG Magnette uses coil springs and double wishbones and is steered by rack and pinion.*

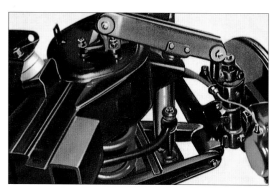

■ LEFT *Rover used a similar but larger system for its P4, this time with an anti-roll bar and separate, telescopic shock absorbers.*

■ LEFT *Mercedes used air suspension to provide a supple ride on its big 600 and 300SEL 6.3 saloons. A compressor inflates rubber bags incorporated between suspension members.*

■ LEFT *No springs! In fact the Riley 1.5 uses torsion bars – like a coil spring straightened out – to provide suspension.*

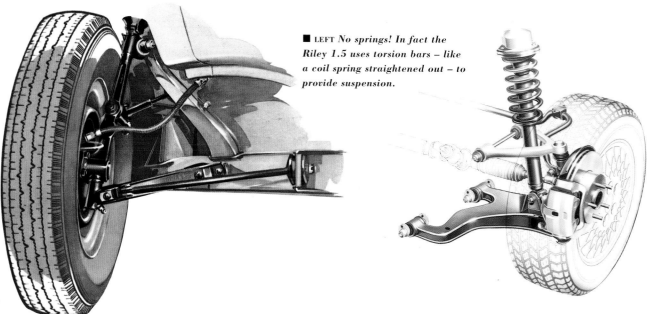

■ LEFT *Mounting the coil spring and damper concentrically solves a space problem but makes removal more complicated.*

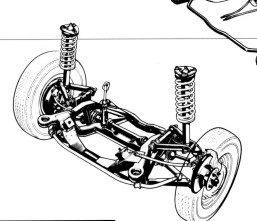

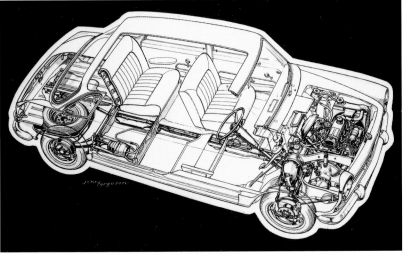

■ ABOVE AND LEFT *Struts can be used to provide independent suspension at the front or rear.*

■ ABOVE *The Austin/Morris 1800 used Hydrolastic (fluid/air) suspension. One Hydrolastic unit can be seen under the cut-away rear seat.*

■ OPPOSITE *The modern solution is to suspend the car on struts, which incorporate both spring and damper. A MacPherson strut also locates and steers the wheel.*

by swing axles with the Mercedes, which lasted into the 60s. VW used a pair of trailing links, in parallel on each side of the car, for independent front suspension for the Beetle, which had a semiswing axle rear suspension. The typical set-up to be found on a performance saloon of the 60s and 70s consisted of MacPherson struts at the front and semitrailing arms at the rear. With liftoff or extreme power oversteer (tail slides) easily available, this produced what most enthusiasts would count as "classic" handling. The tail-heavy Porsche 911 and all BMWs of the 60s and 70s that were equipped with semitrailing arms tended to oversteer.

The Italian Fiat Topolino was ingeniously sprung by lower wishbones, transverse leaf springs, forming the upper links. Lancia used the same set-up in the 60s at the front of its

Fulvia and Flavia models and it could be found under Fiat-drive Seats of the 80s.

The purest and most classic suspension system of all, however, is the double wishbone set-up, used by practically all single-seat racing cars since the 50s and on most supercars thereafter. It's costly to make and can be tricky to set up correctly but offers the best fully-independent wheel control thanks to its ideal geometry and acceptable unsprung weight.

MacPherson struts

Ford's slab-sided new Consul of 1950 broke new ground with its full-width body hiding a new suspension system that revolutionized the way cars were built. An American Ford engineer, Earle S. MacPherson, came up with a new design for independent suspension whose beauty lay in its simplicity. MacPherson struts were used on every new small Ford – including the Classic of 1961 – and are the most common front suspension system used today.

Air suspension

Air suspension was tried by Cadillac on the 1958 Brougham and by Mercedes on its 300 and 600 saloons of the 60s. Air suspension provides a truly supple ride but air-bag durability, a fall in handling precision and the fact that modern, computer-controlled suspension is better made it a blind alley.

BRAKES AND TYRES

The first brakes were blocks of wood made to rub against wheel rims by a system of levers. This is how Trevithick's steamer of 1804 was slowed. As a method of stopping, it was woefully inadequate even for horse-drawn transport.

The 1886 Daimler used a wire hawser wrapped around a wooden ring mounted to the wheel hub. Pulling a lever tightened the wire, which slowed the rotating drum. A refinement of this was the use of a flexible steel band lined with wooden blocks or a strip of leather. This increased the brake's efficiency by extending its friction area.

In 1901, Maybach introduced the internally-expanding drum brake. It used a ring of friction material pressed against the inside of a brake drum by rollers. This was used on the 1903 Mercedes 40hp. Meanwhile, in 1902, Louis Renault designed the definitive drum brake still used today.

Renault's brake used two curved shoes fixed to a backplate, each pivoted at one end. The other ends rested on a cam. When the brake pedal was pressed, the cam forced the shoes

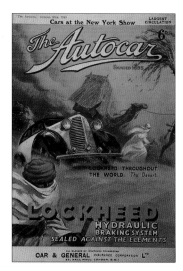

■ ABOVE *Disc brakes work by squeezing the rotor (the round bit) between a pair of friction pads which are fixed into the caliper (the lumpy bit).*

■ ABOVE LEFT *A very early Girling disc brake, as fitted to the TR3 from 1956. The pads were bolted in place.*

■ ABOVE *Power brakes were something to shout about in the 1940s; now nearly all cars have servo assistance.*

■ ABOVE *The next development was easier replacement of brake pads. On this 1959 Lockheed caliper, the pads are retained by pins.*

■ ABOVE *Drum brakes work by forcing the curved shoes against the inside of a drum, which rotates with the road wheel. They do not stand up to repeated stops as well as disc brakes.*

apart and against the inside of the drum.

Drum brakes served for 50 years. Initially, they were used on rear wheels only, for it was feared front brakes could cause skids. Mercedes was the first maker to fit four-wheel brakes, but only as an option, in 1903. All-wheel braking did not become a universal fitting until the 20s. Ever-increasing power and speed demanded more powerful drum brakes, which meant larger and wider. The ultimate form was the huge twin-leading shoe drums used by the Auto-Union and Mercedes "silver arrows" racing cars just before the Second World War. These incorporated scoops and fins

for maximum ventilation to keep temperatures moderate and reduce brake fade. When friction material becomes too hot, it stops working.

Discs take over

Nothing bettered these until Jaguar turned the brake world on its head with the disc brakes it pioneered on its C-Types at Le Mans in 1953. Crosley in America had tried discs in 1949 but soon stopped production. Jaguar gave discs worldwide acceptance. These brakes, borrowed from the aircraft industry, use a pair of friction pads to grip and slow a disc mounted to and spinning with the wheel hub. Because they dissipate heat better and are far more resistant to fade, they give much more powerful stopping for longer than drum brakes. Jaguar won the race that year. There was no going back. By 1956, Girling disc brakes were a standard fitment to Triumph's new sportscar, the TR3,

■ ABOVE *The Dunlop Road Speed RS5 – a crossply that was the performance choice if you had a big, powerful car in the 1950s.*

■ ABOVE *The Michelin XM+S – a "mud and snow" radial designed for severe winter conditions. It was fitted as standard to early Range Rovers.*

■ ABOVE *The Pirelli P600, an update of the legendary P6, was the performance tyre of the 1980s – here it's on a Golf GTi wheel. As well as having superb grip, its classic tread pattern also looked good.*

and the Jensen 541 had Dunlops. Jaguar offered Dunlop disc brakes as an option that year on its XK140. Every model since has had all-round discs as standard.

By the time four-wheel drum brakes were standardized at the end of the 20s, they operated by cables, rods and levers, or hydraulics, or a combination of both. Austin's Hydro-mechanical system, used on its small cars of the 40s and 50s, operated front brakes by hydraulics and rear by a system of rods. The MG Magna sportscar of the 30s had brakes operated by a system of cross-linkages and cables which needed frequent adjustment. The Americans had been using hydraulics since the Chrysler 58 of 1926. Citroën had its own ideas. Since the revolutionary DS of 1955, its cars have had fully-powered disc brakes all round. This gives powerful braking with light pedal pressure. Rolls-Royce used Citroën's high-pressure braking system for its Silver Shadow first seen in 1965.

The classic supercar brake setup, of servo-assisted, multipiston calipers gripping a ventilated disc brake at each wheel, has not been bettered. Antilock brakes – derived from aircraft technology – were pioneered in production on the four-wheel drive Jensen FF in 1966. They were not generally available until the 80s.

Tyres

The classic tyre always seems to be a bit wider and fatter than those on a modern car. Since cars began, the trend has been for fatter and stickier tyres. But it's the high-performance, most costly cars – the classics – that get them first. Crossply tyres, tall, unstylish, inflexible and short on grip, hung on into the 60s, but the classic tyres have all been radials.

CLASSIC STYLE

Body styling, the car's skin, is the emotional trigger that attracts most of us to a motorcar: driving it comes later, to seal the love affair – or end it. A pretty but underachieving car will always have more followers than one that drives like a dream but doesn't look like one.

1945–55

Many mass-produced cars were still tall and spindly. They had separate headlights and mudguards and narrow, letter-box screens.

In Italy, however, coachbuilder Battista "Pinin" Farina (later Pininfarina) had not been idle. His pre-war aerodynamic bodywork on the Lancia Aprillia chassis hinted at the disappearance of the separate wing profile within fully enveloping sides. With the Cisitalia 202 and Maserati 1500 Berlinetta, the theme found full expression. Simple and slender, these cars inspired a generation to come, including the beautiful Lancia Aurelia B20 of 1950, the first of the modern Gran Turismo coupés and a masterpiece of its period. Pininfarina styled many of the great Ferraris too, but it was Touring's classic 166 Barchetta, a model of elegant simplicity, that got the ball rolling in 1948. It directly influenced the AC Ace of

■ ABOVE *The 1951 Hudson, nicknamed "Step-down" for its low-slung construction.*

■ RIGHT *The classic Pininfarina-styled Cisitalia 202 coupé, a landmark.*

■ BELOW *The BMW 503 had clean, well-balanced lines that influenced BMW coupés of the 1960s and 1970s.*

1954, another stunningly pretty shape later tarnished by the bulging arches of the hybrid Cobra in the early 60s. There was nothing so radical going on in Britain, though few could argue with the perfect poise and elegant purity of Jaguar's XK120, inspired by the pre-war BMW 328s.

It was in America that some of the most influential, if not the best, styling would be created over the next decade or so. By 1948, the Americans were starting to shake off the pre-war left-overs and were shaping some radical cars: Ford's Custom series brought with it the new all-enveloping styling – later imitated on the British MkI Ford Consul/Zephyr series – while the "step-down" Hudson Super Six looked rakishly low and modern. The first tiny rear fins were beginning to appear on the Series

■ BELOW *A Studebaker by industrial designer Raymond Loewy.*

■ BELOW *An Austin A40, one of the Farina-styled British cars of the 1950s and 1960s.*

■ BELOW *Big American cars of the 1950s could retain elegance, as with this Cadillac.*

62 Cadillacs, a taster of what was to come.

It was Europe's sportscars that Americans were developing a real taste for by the early 50s: the 1953 Healey 100/4 was undeniably attractive, with a simple, perfectly balanced shape that was to survive 15 years. The TR2 was bug-eyed and awkward by contrast, yet enormously successful.

1955–65

The American influence was still strong during this period as the seperate mudguard all but disappeared in the name of full-bodied, all-enveloping modernity. The trend was towards lower, wider cars. Chrome was still used in abundance but glass areas increased, hand in hand with half-framed doors and dog-leg wrap-around screens. In Britain, coach-building was

■ ABOVE *Bertone's Alfa Guilia, an early GT car.*

■ BELOW *Pininfarina was also responsible for the clean, elegant styling of the Lancia Flaminia coupé.*

still a lively trade as big luxury cars – mostly those of Rolls-Royce and Bentley – still had separate chassis construction, but this decade was to see many famous old names – even Rolls-Royce – switch to unitary construction which didn't really allow for coachbuilt bodywork.

Pininfarina took the styling initiative in the second half of the 50s with the Lancia Florida show car. Like the Cisitalia nine years earlier, here was a true turning point in design. The Florida's taut, chisel-edged architecture was set to influence big-car styling for decades (the 1957 Lancia Flaminia saloon came closest to original expression). An even more radical big saloon was Citroën's DS of 1955, a car that was as futuristic in looks as it was in technical detail. Another frontrunner in the beauty stakes was the 507 of 1955 from BMW, styled by Albrecht Goertz. Created to capture American sales and to challenge the 300SL Mercedes, it was always too expensive, but its slender,

was never designed to win catwalk prizes. Yet the boxy shape was so right and so eternally fashionable (and has changed so little) that it surely deserves a styling accolade.

Pininfarina – a big fan of the Mini – was virtually Ferrari's official stylist by the end of the 50s, shaping such classics as the Spider California, the 250 GT and countless show-stopping one-offs. He never got it more right

pinched-waist design remains one of the greats.

The Americans were on the verge of the tailfin craze at this point, particularly General Motors designs. Under styling supremo Harley Earl, everything from the humble Chevrolet Bel Air upwards had rocket-inspired fins by 1957.

In Britain the second half of the 50s brought MG's pretty A roadster, the best-looking car they ever built, while Lotus was about to break into the mainstream with the delicate Elite, a timelessly elegant little coupé. Meanwhile, Bertone of Italy built the first of its memorable, long-lived Guiletta Sprint Coupés in 1955, offered with a Pininfarina Spider version.

Form came second to function with the revolutionary Mini Minor of 1959, so the car

■ ABOVE *One of the most mouthwatering Ferraris ever, the 250 Lusso.*

■ RIGHT *The Facel Vega combining Italiante good looks with V-eight power was French.*

■ BELOW *Lancia Stratos, brutal but beautiful, derived from a Bertone show car. Fewer than 1,000 were built.*

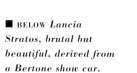

than with the 250 Berlinetta Lusso: here was a compact two-seater with perfect proportions.

Much the same could be said of Jaguar's sensational E-Type roadster and coupé launched at Geneva in 1961. Malcolm Sayers's slim and sensual design was a lesson in motorcar architecture, derived from his D-Type racer of the mid-50s. American styling was finding its way again in the early 60s with clean, well-proportioned cars like the Corvair, the Studebaker Avanti and the Buick Riviera coupé. The 1961 Lincoln "Clap door" Continental was Detroit styling at its most elegant.

1965–75

The tailfin had all but disappeared by 1965 and even the Americans were cleaning up their act with handsome, clean-lined, if still huge, cars. The fuss and clutter of 50s saloon cars was being swept away by cleaner, classier styling,

■ RIGHT *The Lotus Europa combined a svelte glass-fibre body with super-sharp handling. This is a later, twin-cam car with a more pleasing, lower rear roof line.*

boxy at worst (e.g. the Fiat 124), elegant at best.

In Europe, Bertone was a force in the mid-60s, its crowning glory the magnificent mid-engined Miura. Bertone made waves with the Lamborghini Espada, too, although it was cleverly conceived rather than beautiful in the conventional sense, a big four-seater coupé with a bold, uncompromising profile. With the introduction of the Ghia-styled Ghibli in 1965, Maserati finally had a supercar to challenge Ferrari. Conventionally front-engined, it was every bit as beautiful as the Miura, cleaving the air with a sharply-profiled snout.

The Ferrari Dino 206 of 1967 was the finest-looking car Pininfarina had launched for some time, a jewel-like mid-engined coupé that survived well into the 70s. The 1967 NSU Ro80 was certainly the most futuristic production saloon of the decade, its rising waistline, tall glasshouse and low prow prophetic of aerodynamic saloons yet to come.

Jaguar proved they could still build a good-looking car with the wide, curvy XJ6 of 1968, a classic shape that was to prove very durable: it was still being made in 1990. The trendsetter of 1968, however, came from Staffordshire, in the English Midlands, in the shape of the Reliant Scimitar GTE, the first sporting estate car.

Citroën made a dramatic start to the 70s with a swoopy glass-nosed coupé called the SM.

Here was a real piece of automotive sculpture with presence and enormous class. Fiat's classic 130 coupé was more chisel-edged, its glass-to-steel areas perfectly balanced with wonderful detailing and fine, sharp lines.

Though many beautiful cars have been made since the mid-70s, it is only when the passage of years has allowed us to see them in the context of their time and ours that the truly classic shapes will emerge.

■ ABOVE LEFT *Alfa Romeo Montreal - a front-engined supercar with mid-engined looks.*

■ ABOVE RIGHT *Spen King's Range Rover was the first luxury offroader in 1970. Its classic lines remained in production for 25 years.*

■ LEFT *Alfa's 2000 coupé was an enduring design by Bertone.*

BODYWORK CONSTRUCTION

Car bodywork followed horse-carriage procedure until the 1920s – in style and construction. With the first cars and until the start of the 50s on prestige cars like Rolls-Royce and Bentley, the customer chose throughout – buying first the rolling chassis from the maker, then having it bodied in a selected style by a chosen coachbuilder.

A typical light or sporting car of the 20s would have had fabric body panels stretched over a wooden frame – with aluminium used to form the bonnet and wings. Notable examples were Weymann bodies and classic Vanden Plas

■ LEFT *Fiat's Topolino featured an all-steel one-piece body. It was one of the first small cars so built.*

■ ABOVE *Le Mans Bentley: ash frame, fabric covering and an aluminium bonnet.*

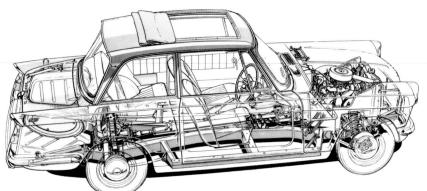

■ ABOVE *A cutaway of the Triumph Herald showing its separate chassis.*

■ LEFT *The Citroën Traction Avant's monocoque (one-piece) body exposed. Front outriggers supported the powertrain.*

■ BELOW LEFT *"Skeleton" of a unitary-construction steel body. Outer panels will be welded or bolted in place.*

open-tourer bodies used on Bentleys. Even when aluminium was later used for all the outer panels, the traditional ash frame remained underneath until the advance of machine-pressed steel panels which could be welded together. The BSA of 1912 was one of the first cars to use this construction. Soon, it was adopted for all small cars, leading to a standardization of body styles. But bodies were still built separately and then mounted on to a chassis which held all the mechanicals. Surely, it would be simpler and more efficient to build the body and chassis as one? Vincenzo Lancia thought so and his beautiful Lancia Lambda of

■ **RIGHT** *Superleggera (superlight) bodies are made by clothing a lightweight tubular frame in steel or aluminium panels.*

■ **FAR RIGHT** *The Lotus Elan's backbone chassis holds all major mechanical components. The glass-fibre body slips over the top.*

■ **BELOW** *The Lotus Elite was the first glass-fibre monocoque body. It had steel strengthening bonded in at all key points to mount the suspension.*

1923 was the world's first monocoque passenger car. Monocoque means all or most of the loads are taken by the car body's skin. It took a while, however, for other makers to catch up. The VW Beetle of 1938 was a half-way house, relying on the body being bolted on top to provide full rigidity. It was Citroën's revolutionary front-wheel-drive *Traction-avant* of 1934 which popularized the monocoque. Full unitary construction, where the chassis and body are made in one shell with openings for doors and windows, came along with the Ford Consul in 1950. This is the way nearly all cars have been built since.

Superleggera

In this construction, thin steel tubes are built up from the floorpan or chassis, into the shape of the finished body. Aluminium panels are then painstakingly formed by hand (rolled between shaped wheels, or beaten over a suitable wooden former, often a section of tree stump) until they fit the shape. They are then welded together over the frame. Most Ferraris and Maseratis were built this way until the end of the 1950s; the Aston Martin DB4, 5 and 6 were Superleggera cars, too.

Glass fibre (Lotus and Corvette)

Glassfibre is light and easy to work with but usually needs a separate chassis underneath to carry all heavy mechanicals. The Lotus Elan of 1962 is a good example: the one-piece glass-fibre body of this classic small sportscar sits over a simple Y-shaped pressed- and welded-steel backbone. Originally, the Elan was intended to have a much more complicated chassis, but designer Ron Hickman drew up the simple steel chassis as a temporary measure so development on the rest of the car could continue. It stayed. The first glass-fibre-bodied car was the classic Chevrolet Corvette of 1953.

Lotus Elite (glass fibre monocoque)

This car has no steel in the body and chassis, except for localized strengthening. All the stresses are taken through the one-piece (monocoque) body and floorpan unit. Production and budget troubles almost caused Lotus to go under, and Chapman's next car was the more conventional Elan.

THE INDUSTRY, 1945–55

After the Second World War, factories that had been used to make aircraft, aero engines and munitions were turned back to car making. Such had been the industry's preoccupation with war work, however, that there were no new car designs. If you could afford a new car, a pre-war design was what you got, such as Ford's Prefect, which started production in 1938. Even these were in short supply on the home market, for the Government's message to put the economy on its feet was "export or die".

In Germany, production of the KdF Wagen, or "Strength through Joy" car, which became known as the VW Beetle, had got under way again after a faltering pre-war start. Hitler's pre-war dream was for Germany to make a car that every family could afford; in a shattered post-war country, it took the British Army's Royal Electrical and Mechanical Engineers, under Major Ivan Hurst, to get Ferry Porsche's inspired design back into production in post-war Germany.

Later in the 1950s, former aircraft producer Messerschmitt made its own idea of cheap transport for the masses, an alternative to the motorcycle, in its KR200, a tandem two-seater with an aircraft-style canopy and a tiny two-stroke engine in the rear. Today, these cars,

which look like fighter planes on three wheels, are much prized. BMW, trying to keep its head above water now that few of its aircraft engines were needed, tried a different but equally humble route: the Isetta "bubblecar".

Britain thought it needed to earn money after the war with a "world car" for export. A first all-new British design was the Standard Vanguard of 1947, intended to take on the Americans and Australians in their markets. But the most successful export was the Land-Rover of 1948, designed by Rover's Maurice Wilks as a farm runabout and based on a Jeep

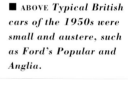

■ ABOVE *Typical British cars of the 1950s were small and austere, such as Ford's Popular and Anglia.*

■ LEFT *This 1953 Buick typifies America and the cars it made in the 50s - big and brash.*

■ RIGHT *The Standard Vanguard was Britain's idea of a "world car".*

■ LEFT *The Wilks brothers' Land-Rover brought utility vehicles to the masses, courtesy of the Jeep.*

■ ABOVE *The "people's car", the VW Beetle, still in production - in Mexico - in 1997.*

chassis, after the Jeep he used on his farm wore out. The Morris Minor of the same year could have been a true world car if it had been marketed as aggressively as the Beetle. Its excellent handling and spritely performance guaranteed it true classic status – and it was Britain's first million-selling car. Ford remained true to its cheap, simple, slightly American-influenced but refined formula first

used for the monocoque-shelled, MacPherson-strutted Consul and continued with its successors through the 1950s.

Rolls-Royce, having taken over Bentley in 1931, continued its line of separate-chassis large saloons, its modern new Silver Cloud and sister Bentley S-Type with classical lines by in-house stylist John Blatchley that still have commanding presence.

In America, less badly affected by the war, car output continued unabated. Exciting, plush new models appeared every year. Even ordinary American passenger-cars offered labour-saving convenience items that would only be seen on luxury cars elsewhere. Citroën stunned the world with its futuristic and technically-advanced DS of 1955, but real innovations were still around the corner, and yet no one took Japan's increasing interest in car production seriously.

■ RIGHT *Messerschmidt 500 - the hot version. Most of these tandem two-seaters were 175 or 200cc.*

■ LEFT *An early advertisement for Maxis, and its Minor, Cowley, Oxford and Isis models.*

■ FAR LEFT *The German DKW had a two-stroke engine and front-wheel drive.*

THE INDUSTRY, 1956–60

A new wave of post-Second World War optimism made the mid-50s an era of exciting new sportscars and saloons.

The "Big Healey" – the Austin-Healey 100, later the 3000 – had been with us since 1952 and the Chevrolet Corvette had appeared the next year. MG slotted its curvy new A in at sub-Healey level in 1955. Aston Martin's fast DB2/4 had metamorphosed into the three-litre DB MkIII by this period but was about to be superseded by 1958's DB4. That year along came a cheeky baby, the Austin-Healey Sprite. At first made with no boot lid and the raised headlamps that gave it the "Frogeye" nickname ("Bugeye" in America), this little car was mechanically an Austin A35.

The AC Ace had been in production from 1953 and a decade later formed the basis for one of the most infamous classics of all – the Cobra which appeared in 1962–63.

The Morgan 4/4 reappeared in 1956. In company nomenclature, this stood for four wheels and four cylinders, using Ford's 1172cc sidevalve engine. Other Morgans were powered by the two-litre TR3 unit. The only significant change was use of a cowled nose, rather than the "flat radiator" style, from 1954.

The big Jaguar news was that the Coventry company complemented its big MkVII saloon with an exciting new compact. Sold initially with 2.4-litre power, it gained its claws as the

■ LEFT *The "fintail" saloons of the 1960s continued to build on Mercedes' reputation for longevity and excellence – the larger 220S in the background first appeared in 1959.*

■ BELOW LEFT *The oddly styled, air-suspended Borgward 2.3 is hardly remembered now, but in its day was a serious rival to Mercedes.*

■ BOTTOM LEFT *Ford's stylish Zodiac MkII was an update of the MkI and helped move technology forward with MacPherson struts and higher-revving engines.*

■ BOTTOM RIGHT *The "Auntie" Rover P4 stuck to traditional wood-and-leather values; later models like this 80 from 1960 were more conservatively styled than the first "Cyclops" 75 of 1950.*

MkII in 1959, with disc brakes and the 3.8-litre version of the XK straight six.

Ford's MkII Consul and Zephyr saloon arrived in 1956, essentially a slightly larger, restyled version of the MkI. Porsche's 356 continued to be improved with better engines. By 1960, 125mph (201kph) was available from the exotic, four-cam 356A Carrera.

In 1959 as American cars were getting bigger and flashier, Alec Issigonis stunned the world with his revolutionary new Mini. Fitting four adults into a 10-ft bodyshell is not easy, but he did it by exemplary packaging – putting in the engine sideways and mounting the gearbox underneath it so the powertrain used the shortest possible space, and fitting a small, 10-in wheel at each corner.

In 1958 the first two-box design and precursor of the hatchback, the Pininfarina-styled A40, appeared. Italian stylists were in vogue: 1959 saw the Michelotti-styled Triumph Herald, which was to give birth to the MG

■ ABOVE *The Austin Healey Sprite lost its "frog eyes" by 1961, and was joined by the identical, badge-engineered MG Midget. This is a 1275cc MkIV Sprite from 1968.*

■ ABOVE RIGHT *Like all proper (pre-Fiat take-over) Lancias, the Flaminia GT was gorgeous, superbly engineered – and expensive.*

■ BELOW LEFT *The Armstrong Siddeley Star Sapphire harked back to a golden age of British luxury saloons, but it was the last car the company made. Production finished in 1960.*

■ BELOW *Even the sporty MG Magnette saloon had its virtues extolled by exaggerated artwork.*

Midget competitor, the Spitfire, in 1962.

In Italy, Alfa Romeo was gearing up for true mass production with its boxy but highly competent Giulietta Berlina. Even more exciting was the Giulietta Sprint, styled by Bertone, a proper little GT that could run rings around many bigger sportscars. The mainstay of Fiat production was still the little rear-engined 500 and 600 models with a wide range of ultra-conventional rear-wheel-drive three-box saloons, from the little 1100 through to the sharp-edged 2100 six-cylinder cars. Lancia, though still losing money because of their obsession with tool-room standards of engineering, produced the most significant car of 1960 – the Flavia. Here was the first Italian car with front-wheel drive, a modern roomy body and superbly insulated suspension.

MAGNETTE MG SALOON

safety fast in airsmoothed style

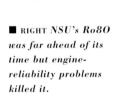

THE INDUSTRY, 1961-75

For the British industry, the 1960s began successfully, but a series of mergers and takeovers and closure of several established British car-makers left it faltering by the decade's end.

The years of triumph had really begun in 1959 when the Mini appeared and, after the E-Type stunned the world at the Geneva Motor Show, other future classics emerged. There was Chapman's new Elan for 1962, closely following the Mini Cooper – a whole new breed of "pocket rocket", or hot small car. By this time, Ford's Cortina had also appeared; larger than

■ ABOVE *Cadillac was still making huge landcruisers in the 1960s but at least the fins were shrinking.*

■ LEFT *The 250 GTO was the last of Ferrari's front-engined racers.*

to improve handling. The Lotus Cortina quickly became the darling of competition drivers. The cars were used successfully for racing and rallying and still compete in historic events.

The 60s were the golden era for muscle cars in the USA. Cheap petrol meant there was no restraint on makers shovelling more and more horsepower into medium-sized saloons, a trend started with the Chrysler 300 series in 1955.

In Germany, NSU pioneered its futuristic new Ro80. Problems with its rotary power unit made it an engineering blind alley but the cars, when running, were amazingly good. Look how

■ RIGHT *NSU's Ro80 was far ahead of its time but engine-reliability problems killed it.*

the Austin 1100, the best-selling car for much of the 60s, it was simple, cheap and light and returned adequate performance from its modest 1200 and 1500cc engines. This car gave birth to a true classic when Colin Chapman got his hands on it, slotting in the twin-cam engine used in the Elan and sorting out the suspension

■ RIGHT *Germanic excellence is epitomized by the 928, a heavyweight grand tourer launched in 1970.*

■ ABOVE *Ford's Cortina 1600E opened up a new class of car, the sporty "executive saloon".*

■ ABOVE *Early 1970s muscle. This Chevrolet Camaro represents the peak years of the American "pony car".*

similar modern Audis are to that car now.

In 1962, the world saw one of the most sensual classics of all: the Ferrari GTO. Lightweight homologation specials and the last of Ferrari's front-engined racers, these cars are possibly the most desirable anywhere in the world today. Despite once being valued at up to £6 million each, many are still racing. Slightly more affordable was the 275GTB/4 of 1966, considered by some to be the best all-round Ferrari. Then in 1968, two of the most important and memorable of Ferrari's cars appeared – the heavyweight 365GTB/4 Daytona and the delicate mid-engined 246 Dino.

When the 1970s began, the British motor industry, was down to three major players: Leyland, Rootes and Ford. By now BMC was

under the control of Leyland. Alvis had become part of Rover, which itself had been swallowed up by Leyland and thus found itself in the same group as its old rival, Jaguar, which had gone under the protective arm of BMC.

Elsewhere, news was brighter. The beautiful, shark-like Ferrari 308 GTB (a Dino replacement) appeared in 1975. In Germany, BMW had taken a lead in aerodynamics to produce one of the the most classic saloon racers of all time, the CSL. Porsche was just putting the final touches to turbocharging its 911. But for Britain, whose industry was by now on a three-day week and would never be the same again, all that emerged at the end of this period was Jaguar's disappointing XJS. 1975 was the dim end of a classic era.

■ ABOVE *The 1970s Wedge Princess showed how styling had lost its way. Such lame ducks helped nearly finish Britain's motor industry.*

■ BELOW LEFT *De Tomaso Panterra, an Italian supercar powered by Ford V-eight muscle.*

■ BELOW RIGHT *MGB - the classic roadster, launched in 1962. Everyone seems to have owned one...*

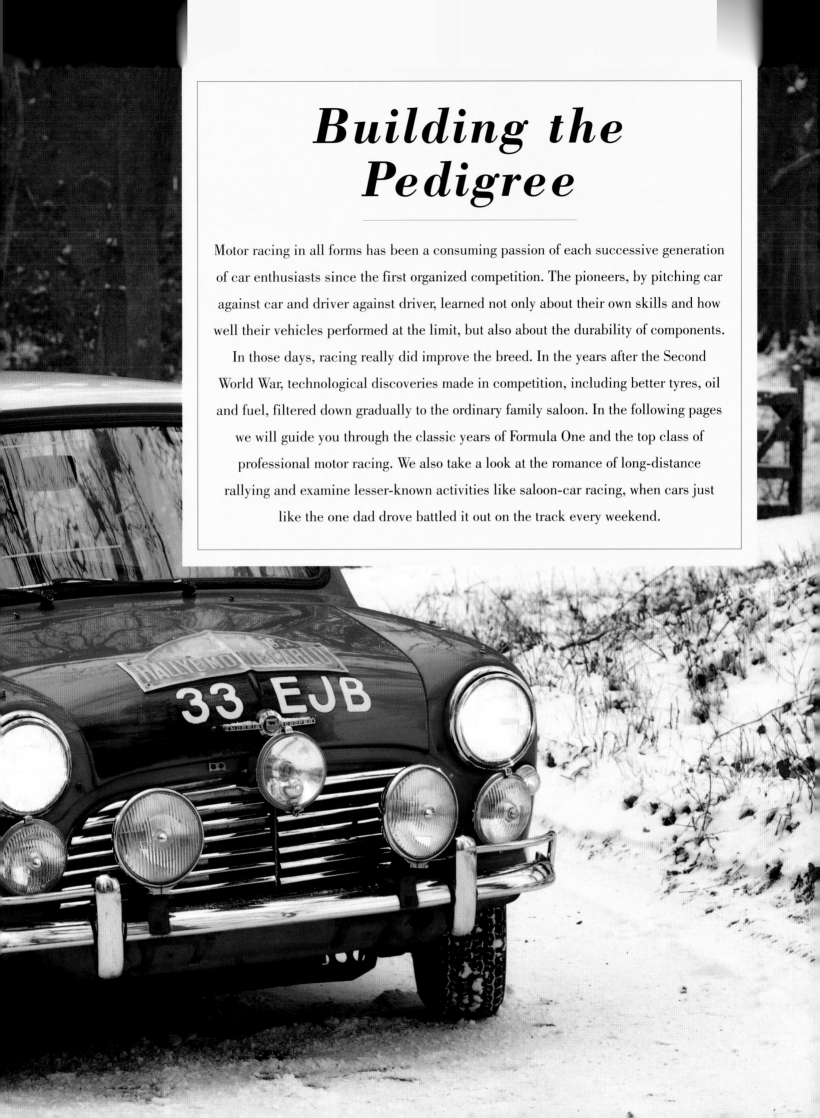

Building the Pedigree

Motor racing in all forms has been a consuming passion of each successive generation of car enthusiasts since the first organized competition. The pioneers, by pitching car against car and driver against driver, learned not only about their own skills and how well their vehicles performed at the limit, but also about the durability of components. In those days, racing really did improve the breed. In the years after the Second World War, technological discoveries made in competition, including better tyres, oil and fuel, filtered down gradually to the ordinary family saloon. In the following pages we will guide you through the classic years of Formula One and the top class of professional motor racing. We also take a look at the romance of long-distance rallying and examine lesser-known activities like saloon-car racing, when cars just like the one dad drove battled it out on the track every weekend.

GRAND PRIX

■ ABOVE *Colin Chapman's revolutionary Grand Prix cars put the driver in a monocoque "tub" with the engine behind him. Here a 25 heads up a Type 23 sports racer.*

As soon as two cars met, motor racing was invented. The first organized competition was the Paris–Bordeaux–Paris road race of 1895, won by Emile Levassor in a car of his own make. The average speed was 15mph (24kph), but by 1900, in a similar race from Paris to Lyons (Lyon), this rose to nearly 40mph (64kph). With little in the way of progress except lack of tyre technology, monster racing cars were soon thundering down dusty, unmade

roads at up to 100mph (160kph).

Racing on public roads did not last long. Fatalities in the 1903 Paris–Madrid and Gordon Bennett Trophy races created the need for dedicated circuits. The world's first, Brooklands, opened in 1907; in the 1920s and 30s heroes such as Birkin and the Bentley boys thundered around here and Le Mans. On these closed circuits, the need for riding mechanics was gone. Single-seater racing was born.

The golden age of racing

Think classic Grand Prix racer and you think 1930s Bugatti. But the greatest era of single-seater racing was the 50s. This was the golden age: with little to separate the crowds from the track apart from rows of straw bales, the racing

enthusiast could actually see his heroes at work, unfettered by high cockpit sides, full-faced helmets or the drivers' need to dress up as mobile billboards. While Fangio was still king of the hill on a good day and a quiet American called Phil Hill took his first drives with Ferrari, greats such as Stirling Moss, Peter

■ ABOVE LEFT *Heroic drivers set off at the start of the 1933 500 miles race at Brooklands, the first purpose-built racing track. The curved banking can clearly be seen in the distance.*

■ ABOVE *Stirling Moss, one of the world's greatest drivers, handles his Cooper 500 around a wet Silverstone in 1954.*

■ LEFT *Mike Hawthorn, one of the most charismatic drivers and Britain's first world champion, in 1958. He retired from racing in 1959.*

■ LEFT *Porsche 917s (20, 21, 22) get a strong start at the beginning of Le Mans, 1970. These cars took over from the Ford GT40s to dominate the 24-hour endurance race for much of the following decade.*

start, Alfa Romeo dominated the scene with the glorious Tipo 158 and 159, but Ferrari, BRM and Mercedes continued to push the tried and tested rear-engined formula, and Maserati's 250F – the classic racing car – won the hearts of drivers and spectators alike. Mercedes used its revolutionary W196 streamliners to steamroller the French Grand Prix at Reims (Rheims) in 1954. But it was Cooper which turned the racing world on its head by the end of the 50s with light, home-built rear-engined single-seaters.

The Chapman revolution

The man who had the greatest influence on Grand Prix cars and took racing-car design into the 60s, having started building his own cars in the 50s, was Colin Chapman. This structural engineer started racing with his Lotus Six and Seven (still with us as the Caterham Seven).

Collins and Mike Hawthorn were at the peaks of their careers – and remained great mates, too. Grand Prix racing had become so popular by the early 50s that crowds of 100,000 flooded to the two big races of the year at Silverstone. This ex-airfield circuit was the home of British motor racing and hosted the British Grand Prix and the British Empire Trophy. Even in those days, you had to be through Buckingham or Bicester by 7.30am to make the start – and little has changed.

This decade and the one after also saw the quickest evolution of racing machinery. At the

■ ABOVE *Mercedes' W154 "Silver Arrow" GP racer. Thorough engineering made these cars nigh-on invincible in the 1930s.*

■ RIGHT *Ford GT40. After Ford had failed to buy Ferrari it built its own cars to win Le Mans. They were successful in four consecutive years from 1966.*

■ BELOW RIGHT *The Lotus 78 Formula 1 car was one of the last of Colin Chapman's innovative designs.*

■ LEFT *One-off V12 version of the Maserati 250F, in six-cylinder form perhaps the greatest front-engined Grand Prix car the world has ever known.*

RALLYING FROM THE 50S TO THE 70S

Rallying in the 50s usually meant long-distance time trials where navigational accuracy and not necessarily outright speed was the criterion. Crews of two or three would battle through adverse conditions against an exhausting time schedule, armed with little more than standard cars upgraded only by extra lights and knobbly tyres. The most famous endurance events are the winter Monte Carlo and Alpine rallies where machinery as diverse as Sunbeam Rapiers, big and small saloons and sportscars, contemporary and vintage, competed against each other. Many entries would be "works" ones, from car makers anxious to prove their model's reliability. Later, in the 1960s, the Porsche 91 made its name as a durable car that withstood all that long-distance rallying could throw at it – and the 911 remains the car to beat in historic rallying in the 90s.

There were rallies at a local level, accessible to anyone who had a car and joined a motor club. These again were tests of navigational and timing accuracy, not speed, often at night.

■ LEFT *Tough hardtop saloons like the Ford Escort dominated rallying from the late 1960s.*

■ LEFT *Alpine rallies were tests of reliability, not outright speed.*

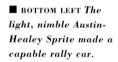

■ BOTTOM LEFT *The light, nimble Austin-Healey Sprite made a capable rally car.*

No helmets or elaborate safety procedures would be needed in those days when even such ungainly machinery as Austin A90 Atlantics would have had a chance.

Stage rallying

By the 70s, rallying to most people had come to mean "stage rallies". These are essentially a series of rough-road sprints. Cars blast sideways in crowd-pleasing power-slides, often on slippery shale or in treacherous ice conditions, through a narrow, twisty course accessible to spectators. The timed sections, or stages, range from a couple of miles to more than 30 (48km), and the object is to get down them as fast as

■ LEFT *The Austin-Healey 3000 in its element. This was one of the rally cars to have in the 1960s.*

■ LEFT *The Mini has been one of the most successful rally cars ever.*

■ ABOVE *A highly-modified Ford Escort being serviced on the 1970 London-Mexico rally.*

■ BELOW *Lancia Stratos, the Ferrari-powered purpose-built rally car, on a special stage.*

possible. The navigator's job is to get driver and car to the start of each stage at the right time, but in the frantic activity of negotiating the stage he is more than mere ballast. Using maps or "tulip" diagrams, he warns the driver of the severity of approaching corners, for advance reconnaissance has often been banned. Shrewd navigation is needed on the road sections between stages: these are subject to strict timing, too, and point loss is possible.

The premier event in Britain has always been the RAC Rally. By the end of the 60s the Ford Escort was king, driven by such stars as Roger Clark and the "Flying Finns", Timo Makinen and Ari Vatanen.

Classic 50s rally car – Austin-Healey

The durability of the powerful, separate-chassis two-seater Austin-Healey, launched in 1954, made it the favourite for long-distance rallies over the Alps. Its first successes were with the Morley brothers. Rally legend Timo Makinen first came to fame driving a "Big Healey". But there was tremendous noise from the bellowing, three-litre straight-six engine,

and lack of suspension movement made for poor ground clearance and a boneshaking ride.

First of the evolution specials – Stratos

With its show-car derived styling and Ferrari V-six engine, the Stratos was conceived with the sole purpose of winning rallies once Lancia's mainstay, the front-wheel-drive Fulvia, had aged. This twitchy, short-wheelbase homologation special (legend has it not even the requisite 500 were built) won the World Rally Championship three times, from 1974–76, and was forerunner of the short-lived, rally-specific Group B cars banned in 1986 for being too dangerous. The Stratos's last win was in the 1979 Monte Carlo Rally.

SALOON CAR RACING

Saloon racing has always been used by car makers – officially or not – to prove the excellence of their products. "Win on Sunday, sell on Monday" is the slogan. If Joe Public saw a car winning that he perceived as being like his own, then brand loyalty was strengthened and could even lead to new sales.

Saloon-car racing began soon after the Second World War, but, even well into the 50s, racing saloon cars were terrifyingly similar to their standard counterparts. Perhaps the tyres would be inflated, the hubcaps removed and a helmet worn, but there would be little safety gear until the 60s.

Professionals such as Graham Hill, who started in saloon cars and continued to race Jaguar MkIIs and Lotus Cortinas into the 60s, might wear overalls or at least matching polo shirt and trousers, but for the rest it would be everyday wear – taking a cue from 50s Grand Prix ace Mike Hawthorn who always raced in a sports jacket and bow-tie.

As new models came on stream, so they would be pressed into service on the tracks, becoming faster as more was learned about their tuning potential. The powerful MkI and MkII Jaguars, first seen in 1957, were naturals, as were to a lesser extent the six-cylinder Ford

■ ABOVE *Modern suspension and a light, stiff unitary body gave 50's Mk1 Ford Zephyrs a chance of success.*

■ BELOW LEFT *The humble Austin Westminster was surprisingly successful in 1950s saloon-car racing.*

■ BELOW RIGHT *Cars were surprisingly standard, hence alarming roll angles.*

Zephyr and Zodiac, but by the early 60s the Mini had started to creep on to the grid, aided by John Cooper of Formula 1 fame. The Mini was a landmark car in this respect; racing people who started their careers in Minis include Ken Tyrrell, James Hunt and the great John Rhodes whose tyre-smoking sideways cornering antics are legend. Others who enjoyed rattling around in unsuitable old cars included Stirling Moss and Jim Clark.

By the 60s, proper championships for touring and modified saloons had become

■ BELOW *Big, heavy Jaguar MkVII saloons were more nimble than they looked.*

■ BELOW *The BMW CSL dominated Group 2 in the 1970s.*

established, leading to exciting racing among Formula 2-engined Escorts, for example, and to the birth of the extensively modified saloons with the Group 2 and 4 BMW "Batmobiles" – and fearsome devices such as the series of Blydenstein Vauxhalls fielded in 70s "Supersaloon" racing by the larger-than-life Gerry Marshall.

America had evolved its own racing for "stock", or standard, saloons. This had started as a 200-mile (322km) sand/Tarmac race at Daytona Beach, Florida, in 1936. By 1959, the course had been transformed into a purpose-built two-mile (3.2km) banked oval track in the same location, and similar tracks sprang up all over the country under the auspices of NASCAR, the National Association for Stock Car Auto Racing. By the end of the 60s, "stock" cars were circulating at up to 200mph (322kph), aided by careful attention to aerodynamics and the rule book.

In Sports Car Club of America racing, where cars had to turn right as well as left, the AC Cobra/Corvette wars of the mid-60s gave way to multiround contests between modified Mustangs and Camaros, making heroes of men like Mark Donohue and Peter Revson.

Farther south, Mexico hosted the maddest road race ever, the 1,864 miles (3,000km) Carrerra Panamericana. This flat-out spectacle, which included a class for saloons among the diverse machinery taking part, was run annually from 1950 until 1954, when the growing number of fatalities forced closure. Since 1991, it has been run again as a retrospective road event.

■ BELOW *"Big Bertha", the V-eight-powered Vauxhall Ventura supersaloon built in the 1970s by Bill Blydenstein for the race ace Gerry Marshall to drive.*

CLASSICS IN COMPETITION TODAY

Classic motor sport has never been more popular. Purists think it's a shame to use up venerable old machinery, but the pragmatic say racing cars were built to race.

Historic motor sport doesn't have to mean big bucks or major track extravaganzas; there are plenty of gentler sprints, hill climbs or rallies populated by more modest machinery. Whatever the car, there's an extra-curricular activity you can do with it. Here are some of the activities that enthusiasts get up to with their classics.

Road runs

Not competition but open to anyone with a suitable classic (usually at least 20 years old) and a road licence, these are run by many clubs as a way of providing their major events with a focal point and also by large organizations such as the RAC MSA which runs the UK's largest annual road run.

Trials

You can enter a production-car trial in pretty much anything with four wheels – but the most stylish trials for classics are the ones operated by the Vintage Sports Car Club (VSCC), for

cars made before 1930. The point of a trial is to arrive at the right place at the right time and to clear certain muddy hill climb sections without stopping. The winner is the driver with fewest errors.

Sprints and hill climbs

Within reason, you can sprint or hill climb any classic, vintage or veteran car you want. Only the most basic safety gear and the cheapest competition licence are needed. Each competitor embarks on two practice and two timed runs on a short, usually twisty course.

■ ABOVE *Historic endurance rallies, following the routes of the classic Alpine rallies of the '50s, are usually for cars made before 1962 and can easily be won in cars like this Jowett Jupiter: accuracy is the key, in both navigation and timing.*

■ ABOVE *Special-built post-war vintage racing combines Napier aero engine and Bentley chassis.*

■ ABOVE *Fast roads tours are available for more rarefied machinery on an invite-only level. Here an Alfa chases an HWM.*

■ ABOVE *Historic sports car racing has never gone away. Here a Cooper Monaco leads at Brands Hatch.*

■ BELOW *The famous paddock shelters at Shelsley Walsh near Worcester, where hillclimbs have been held since 1905.*

■ RIGHT *Historic Grand Prix cars, such as this Lotus, have a strong following, and more are being brought back to the race tracks all the time.*

Navigational rallies

Usually run at night, navigational rallies are tests of map-reading, navigation and time-keeping. Although they aren't speed events as such, an accurate average must be kept.

Stage rallies

There's some navigation in these events, but only to get the car to the beginning of each special stage in good time – and then all hell breaks loose. The stage, often on narrow forest gravel tracks, is closed to traffic, and the object is to get to the other end as fast as possible.

■ ABOVE *A supercharged MG tackles Shelsley, where competitors ascend the hill in less than a minute.*

■ BELOW *Like Lincoln's axe, many historic cars have had parts replaced, but have never stopped racing. Some are going faster than ever.*

Endurance rallies

From the three-day Monte Carlo Challenge over the snowy Alps to the 10-week London-Mexico, run in 1995 as a 25th anniversary of the first event, these gruelling runs demand meticulous car preparation and tremendous self-discipline – but generate fantastic camaraderie between entrants.

Saloon car racing

Back to the glory days, pure and simple, with Anglias, BMW 2000s, Alfa GTAs and Minis scrabbling round on Dunlop racing tyres in scenes straight from the 60s.

Historic single-seater and sportscar racing

From ERA through Maserati 4CM and Alfa Monzas, including Blower Bentleys and Mercedes SSKs, right up to fairly recent Formula 1 material, this evocative, heady mix stirs up memories for everyone. In the sportscar class, glorious packs of Lotus Elevens battle it out with Jaguar D-types, Maseratis, Birdcages and Coopers too. But you have to be rich.

Classic Culture

The first flickerings of interest in classic motorcars made after the Second World War began nearly three decades ago. Now, that interest has grown into an all-consuming passion for millions of men and women all over the world. Some use their classics daily, others just on high days. Some preen them like beauty queens in the concours d'élegance, parades of vehicles to the most elegant, best designed or best turned-out of which prizes are awarded. Many owners are driven by nostalgia, a need to own or recreate a piece of their past; others by simple love of old machinery. As modern cars become ever more amorphous and as image-conscious individuals wear their classics like designer suits, as a statement, the classic is no longer the preserve of bearded, middle-aged men. To own an old car has become trendy. For some, the word classic has become debased down the years, seeming to embrace any number of awful machines. To them, classics, derided by many in their prime, are now dignified merely by rarity. In the early 1970s, however, could the pioneers of the classic-car movement have guessed that the then-new Austin Allegro would one day inspire an enthusiastic owners' club?

WORKING CLASSICS

The attributes that make a vehicle a classic also bring the best cars to the top in the tough world of work. This applies whether services need them to be out in all weathers rescuing stranded motorists, attending a breakdown or accident, pursuing villains and keeping traffic flowing or simply carting goods around reliably.

Each service has its favourites, each vehicle's special abilities suiting it to its chosen job. The Automobile Association (AA) (1905), finding its motorcycle-and-sidecar outfits no longer efficient, bought Land-Rovers almost from inception in 1948 to aid motorists.

■ RIGHT *The "woody" estate, a popular variation on a saloon car which could carry more.*

■ RIGHT *The emergency services found Land-Rovers ideal for rescuing motorists in remote spots. This is one of the AA's first Landoes now restored.*

■ ABOVE *Rare Aston Martin shooting brakes (estate cars) based on the DB5.*

■ RIGHT *The Ford Thames was available in van and pick-up forms. Designed to drive in a similar way to a car, it was ancestor to the ubiquitous Transit.*

Likewise, the Royal Automobile Club (RAC) (1897) used a selection of cars and car-derived vans: Austin Sevens, Morris Minors and then Mini-vans for lighter-duty breakdowns and Bedford CA vans and trucks at the heavier end before they universally adopted the Ford Transit in the 1970s. In the 50s, the RAC ran six Isetta bubblecars in London to reach motorists through the clogged traffic. These tiny two-strokes' towing ability is not recorded!

Policemen and postmen

The police have long used big, powerful and reliable saloons, from the classic, fast, bell-equipped and evil-handling Wolseleys of the 50s to the Rovers and Jaguars of the 70s. Various forces have at times tried to beat the villains at their own game by adopting the same wheels – Jaguar MkIIs in the 50s and Lotus Cortinas in the 60s. The police have also tried out new types of vehicle. In the 60s, forces ran an experimental four-wheel-drive

■ LEFT *The Citroën "H"*
van was the backbone of
many small businesses
in France.

(by Ferguson Formula) Ford Zodiac Mk4, which
may have paved the way for the near-universal
adoption of the classic, big-hearted Range
Rover for motorway patrols.

In the 50s, a Morris Minor van with ugly
rubber wings was a familiar sight. Britain's
General Post Office (GPO) thought the wings
were unbreakable and immune to minor
knocks. Alas, they meant the headlamps sat up
in separate pods and setting alignment was
nigh-on impossible. The GPO then turned to
another car-derived van, the Bedford version of
the first Vauxhall Viva, the HA of 1963. In
France, the entire postal service was served by
a pair of rugged, front-wheel-drive hold-alls,
the Citroën 2CV and Renault 4 vans.

Civilian workers

For "civilian" use, car-derived vans have long
been another way for makers to sell to motorists
unfamiliar with the size and vision difficulties
of the large-panel vans like them. Since the
1920s, panelled-in versions of most popular
cars have been available. They are often

simply an estate version with the windows
filled in and the back seat missing. Before
Purchase Tax applied to commercial vehicles,
this was the cheapest way to own an estate car
– buy a van and fit side windows!

Ford's Transit of 1968 was the trendsetter
whose name became generic for one-tonne
(1,016kg) vans. This much-loved, tough and
surprisingly fast hauler was a natural to carry
everything from parcels to builders' gear. It was
a big hit with criminals, too: they could hide in
it until the coast was clear and carry a lot of
booty. Where there's work to be done, the
chances are you'll find there will be a classic
that has completed it.

■ ABOVE *The Ford V-*
eight Pilot, an
attractive and powerful
chase car in its day.

■ BELOW LEFT *Some*
Dutch police forces
used the Porsche 911.

■ BELOW RIGHT *Many*
forces in Britain used
unusual machines –
such as this MU2 Lotus
Cortina.

CLASSICS ON FILM AND TV

Nothing does more for a classic car's kudos than appearing in a classic film or television series. Who could forget the Volvo P1800 in Britain's *The Saint* series of the 60s or the Alfa Spider in *The Graduate* (1967) with Dustin Hoffman? Both made these cars world-famous and boosted sales. As dynamic and often beautiful objects, motorcars have always looked good on screen as set decoration or the focus of the action. The catalogue of classic-car screen moments is huge.

The Americans have long been masters of putting the motorcar on screen, in everything from Herbie *The Love Bug* (1969) to cult films like *Vanishing Point* (1971), *Two-Lane Blacktop* (1971) or *Duel* (1971). For many connoisseurs it is the 1968 film *Bullitt* starring Steve McQueen that features perhaps the best car chase ever filmed: his Mustang pursues a sinister Dodge Charger at speed through the hilly streets of San Francisco to a superb V-eight soundtrack. The scene lasts 12 minutes,

■ LEFT *MkII Jaguars featured as heavily as getaway cars on film as in real life.*

■ BELOW *An S-Type Jaguar appeared in the 1967 film Robbery.*

■ BELOW *A white Volvo P1800 became a trademark for The Saint played by Roger Moore.*

■ LEFT *Big saloons featured in many British crime films: Richard Burton, Jaguar S-Type in Villain (1971).*

with McQueen, a good driver, doing much of the stunt work himself. In his 1971 film *Le Mans*, McQueen did more driving than acting and added to the list of motor-racing films such as *The Green Helmet* and *Grand Prix* (1966) and *Winning* with Paul Newman (1969) that were neither critical nor box-office successes.

■ RIGHT *What the public did not see – Michael Caine providing extra damage to the red E-Type in The Italian Job (1969).*

Cops, robbers and spies

In British films, the crime genre has long been a fertile hunting ground for classic-spotters. *Robbery* (1967, based on the Great Train Robbery) has a hair-raising pursuit with a police S-Type Jaguar and felons in a silver Jaguar MkII. In *The Italian Job* (1969), a tongue-in-cheek take of an audacious gold robbery starring Michael Caine and Noël Coward, cars outshone actors. The getaway cars are three Mini Coopers that make a cheeky escape along Turin rooftops and drains. Other motorized stars include a Lamborghini Miura, a pair of E-Types and an Aston Martin DB4 convertible. Jaguars provide aura in gangland classics like *Performance* and *Get Carter* (both 1971), while *Villain* (1971), starring Richard Burton, features a payroll heist: look out for the Jaguar S-Type, Ford Zodiac and Vanden Plas three-litre, all wrecked. And look out for the Lamborghini Islero and the Rover 3.5 *The Man Who Haunted Himself*, also of 1970.

James Bond films feature cars heavily as part of 007's equipment. The gadget-laden Aston DB5 caused a sensation when it appeared in *Goldfinger* in 1964 with its ejector seat,

machine guns and radar. Toyota built a special convertible 2000GT for *You Only Live Twice* (1967) but it had no real gadgets. In *On Her Majesty's Secret Service* (1969) new Bond George Lazenby drove a stock Aston DBS and a Mercury Cougar in an ice-racing sequence.

■ ABOVE *A Lotus Elan starred alongside Emma Peel and John Steed in The Avengers.*

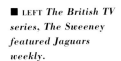

■ LEFT *The British TV series, The Sweeney featured Jaguars weekly.*

■ LEFT *Goldfinger: 007's Aston Martin DB5 featured overrider hooks, machine guns behind sidelights and revolving number plates. Three more were built for Goldeneye (1995).*

CHOOSING & OWNING A CLASSIC

Saloon or estate, two doors or four, open or closed – only you know which type of classic will suit your needs and pocket but, generally speaking, options like power steering, overdrive and air conditioning are always worth searching out if you want the most usable classic in modern conditions. Be prepared in most cases for higher maintenance costs or a lot more unreliability than with a modern car.

Bodywork bother

Rust is the biggest enemy of the older car. Before the 1980s most ordinary – and indeed many expensive – motorcars were only given token rust-proofing, so if you live in a damp climate corrosion will be much more of a problem. Unitary or monocoque construction was coming in across the board by the 60s on mass-produced cars, and any rust in the sills, floor or inner wing areas with this type of bodywork will seriously compromise the car's strength and rigidity.

Cars with separate chassis are generally less of a worry because the bodywork is not self-supporting. That doesn't mean the chassis won't rust eventually, and removing bodywork for restoration is not for the faint-hearted. Aluminium panels – as found on high-calibre

classics like Aston Martins – don't rust in the same way but do suffer from electrolytic action between the aluminium and the steel frame of the car. Aluminium is also more susceptible to damage. Glass-fibre bodywork doesn't rust, of course, and in most cases – apart from the Lotus Elite – features a separate steel chassis, too. However, the passage of time can cause the gel coat to craze, which is a specialist job to rectify. Taking paintwork more generally, look for signs of over-spray on door rubbers and window surrounds, indicating a hasty respray. Brightwork – badges, bumpers, grilles, etc – is

■ ABOVE *The Triumph Spitfire is a relatively easy car to restore because of its separate chassis.*

■ BELOW *A bubblecar could be an ideal project for those with limited space.*

■ LEFT *There are still plenty of unrestored "popular" classics to choose from.*

notoriously costly to refurbish and many pieces are difficult to find for more unusual models.

Mechanical matters

Mechanically, older cars tend to be simpler, although by the end of the 60s fuel injection and complex air suspension was putting many of the more expensive cars beyond the abilities of the home mechanic. Generally, with the engine, you should be looking for signs of excessive smoke from the exhaust and of overheating with watercooled engines, particularly if they are of exotic aluminium construction as with many Alfa Romeo and Lancia models. Gearboxes should be reasonably quiet, though many 50s and even 60s cars featured "crash" bottom gears which give a rather evocative whine. Automatic gear changes won't be as smooth as on a modern luxury car but, even so, changes shouldn't be rough, either. Woolly steering and soggy brakes characterize many big saloons of the classic era, but many sportscars of the 50s and 60s have handling that is rewarding.

Looking inside

Although scruffy interior trim won't stop you driving a classic, a car's interior condition is vital to its feel and ambience. A Jaguar, for instance, with damp carpets, peeling wood

■ **ABOVE LEFT** *The interior of this "woody" station wagon would be complex and expensive to put right.*

■ **ABOVE** *Welding is a useful skill if you intend to tackle restoration yourself.*

■ **ABOVE RIGHT** *It is essential that leather and wood are in good condition. Refurbishment is expensive.*

■ **BELOW** *Rust curses cars of the 1950s and 1960s such as this Jaguar.*

veneer and cracked or split leather seats loses much of its appeal. Retrims are expensive and obscure interior parts difficult to source. The generally far more basic interiors of sportscars are easier to refurbish and, again, for the popular British marques everything is usually available. Hoods are expensive to replace on sportscars – look out for tears – while a hard top is definitely worth paying extra for if you intend using an open classic all year. If you are determined to buy a classic car, do your homework. Join the relevant club, get to know the pitfalls of the model you are after, then go out and look at as many as you can before making a decision.

FUTURE CLASSICS

New "classics" appear all the time. These are cars that, because of sheer appeal, excellence or exclusivity, are instantly memorable and desirable from first sightings at a motor show. Others, cult darlings such as the Golf GTI, have become the definitive cars of their era and have never truly fallen out of fashion with enthusiasts. Others again, such as the Mini, VW Beetle or 2CV, still in or recently out of production, are simply the modern versions of

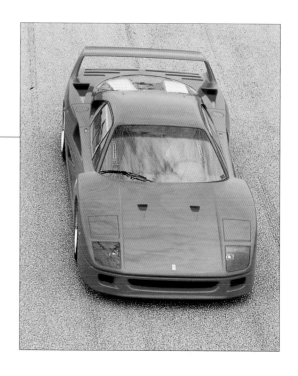

■ RIGHT *All Ferraris will be classics, especially the stunning, 200mph (321kph)-topping supercar F40 of which 1500 were made.*

■ FAR LEFT *Mazda's MX5 aped the Lotus Elan of 20 years earlier – but bits did not fall off.*

■ LEFT *BMW's M3 was a fine-handling supersaloon. Later versions could not quite match its raw appeal.*

acknowledged classic designs. They don't have to be supercars to qualify, although some of the most obvious contenders clearly are: any new Ferrari or Lamborghini is so eagerly awaited that its status upon arrival is guaranteed. In these cases, simply belonging to the right marque is enough to confer immortal desirability.

Porsche 911s all qualify as future classics because of their unique blend of robustnesss and driveability, even if the dashboard design is as confusing as ever. The wide-bottomed 928 will forever hover on the fringes of true classicdom, although some of the early 944 Turbos will be allowed into the hallowed club, and the Speedster-inspired Boxster is clearly on the VIP list from the word go. It's all a question of attitude.

Dodge's awesome eight-litre V-ten Viper has

■ RIGHT *First of the breed – the VW Golf^ GTi. Purists say the first, lightest cars were the best. This is an 1800cc MkI.*

■ RIGHT *The Delta Integrale was a homologation special built so that Lancia could win rallies. It made a scorching road car, too.*

■ RIGHT *Classic coupé, German style. BMW 635 coupés were fine-handling cruisers.*

■ ABOVE *US brutality. The Dodge Viper with its eight-litre V-ten engine is a "Cobra for the 90s".*

■ BELOW *The Peugeot 205GTI, the classic hot hatch, once described as a Mini Cooper for the 1980s. High insurance premiums killed off this breed of car.*

already made a name for itself as the AC Cobra of the 1990s, but its compatriot the Corvette has never been the same since it was emasculated after 1970. Nearly all TVRs occupy the same specialist slot – they are beefy, brutal, British and rear-drive, with that gorgeous V-eight woofle. The Ford Escort RS Cosworth and Sierra Cosworth, both astonishingly fine road cars, have won themselves a place in the hearts of the sort of people who worshipped anything that followed the rally-winning RS Escorts out of Ford's Advanced Vehicle Operation at Boreham, Hertfordshire, in the 1970s. Buying yourself a Lancia Delta Integrale gives the same full-on

driving appeal with even more exclusivity. The first-shape BMW M3 of the late 80s falls into much the same bracket – a rock-hard driving machine – and effectively upgrades the reputation carved out by the 2002 Turbo in 1973, but those in the know say the later cars lack the raw appeal. As ever, the first versions are the purest.

Today's little classics

With cheeky good looks and world's-best handling, Lotus's new Elise, which sadly may not survive a difficult birth, is obviously the Elan of modern times. But for the nearest thing to a real Elan, look no further than Mazda's MX-5, or Miata. Like the original, it's a 1600cc twin-cam rear-driver with sublime handling – it even looks similar – yet nothing falls off it. MGF's, while uninspiring in looks, handles so well that people will always want them; it's also descended from the very first classic sportscar of all.

All Minis will be classics, however feebly powered; its trademark shape, unchanged since it shot to fame in the 60s by winning Monte Carlo rallies, will see to that. And so will that "Mini Cooper for the 90s" – the Peugeot 205 GTI, the best example of that 80s phenomenon, the hot hatch. The choice is huge.

A-Z OF CLASSIC CARS

The A-Z section is a guide to major and minor manufacturers making the world's best-loved and most famous classic cars since the Second World War. It spotlights the models that created their fame. No attempt has been made to detail every make. Rather, the attempt is to reveal a cross section of staple models like the XK120 and Morris Minor that many will have heard of, while giving more esoteric classics like the Iso Grifo and Fiat 130 Coupé a fair crack of the whip. Coverage of the period 1945-76 should provide something for everybody. Some cars were classics from birth. Others earned the title. Some earned it with outstanding dynamic qualities and advanced engineering; some by sheer commercial success (no book on classic cars would be complete without a Volkswagen Beetle, for instance) or conspicuous lack of it. Failures like the Edsel or Austin Atlantic add colour to the motorcar's history. Their stories show how even the top companies can get it wrong – and they make great reading.

AC

■ AC ACE

AC Cars of Thames Ditton, England,
came back to the market after the
Second World War with the staid two-
litre range in 1947, but it was with the
Ace sportscar of 1953 that the company
really made its reputation in the post-
war years. Casting around for a
replacement for the aging two-litre
cars, they took up a design by John
Tojeiro that used a ladder-type tubular
frame, all-independent transverse leaf-
spring suspension and an outstandingly
pretty, open two-seater alloy body,
clearly inspired by the Ferrari Barchetta
of the day.

Early cars used AC's elderly two-litre
overhead-cam straight-six engine (first
seen soon after the end of the First
World War) to give a top speed of
102mph (164kph) and 0–60 (96kph) in
13 seconds. It was hardly a sporting
engine, however, and it was felt that

■ LEFT *The classic
lines of the Ace
were penned by
1950s specials
builder John
Tojeiro, inspired
by Ferrari
Barchetta.*

■ LEFT *All Aces
had a hand-crafted
aluminium body.
This is the rare
Ford Zepyhr-
engined model.*

■ BELOW
*Production of the
Ace ran from 1953
to the early 60s.
Note the minimal
parking protection.*

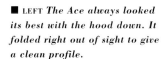

■ BELOW *The AC six-cylinder engine was the least powerful of the trio used in the Ace. The ultimate version has a triple-carb set-up.*

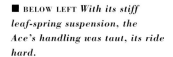

■ LEFT *The Ace always looked its best with the hood down. It folded right out of sight to give a clean profile.*

■ BELOW LEFT *With its stiff leaf-spring suspension, the Ace's handling was taut, its ride hard.*

■ BELOW RIGHT *The Aceca was a sleek coupe version of the Ace, inspired by the Aston Martin DB2.*

something more modern and powerful was required to put the modern chassis to good use. Thus, from 1956, there was the option of Bristol's superb two-litre 120bhp straight-six engine and slick four-speed gearbox. Top speed leapt to 116mph (186kph) with 0–60 (96kph) in the nine-second bracket, and response was much sweeter and more modern. Overdrive was available from 1956, and front disc brakes were an option from 1957, although they were later standardized. With the engine well back in the chassis, the Ace handled well and was successful in competition.

Joining the Ace in 1954 was the Aceca hard top coupé, which had an early form of hatchback rear door but used the same basic timber-framed alloy body. Like the Ace, it came with AC or Bristol power and, with a better drag factor, was slightly quicker in a straight line, although extra weight affected acceleration a little.

From 1961 to 1963 a few Aces were built with Ford's 2.6-litre straight-six to replace the Bristol unit, these new Ken Rudd-modified units; gave up to 170bhp. By then, Thames Ditton were gearing up for the Cobra, an altogether different kind of AC.

Today the pretty AC Ace is much sought after, particularly in its Bristol-engined form.

AC ACE	(1953-63)	
Engine	Straight six (AC, Bristol and Ford)	
Capacity	1991/1971/2553cc	
Power	102/125/up to 170bhp	
Transmission	4-speed optional overdrive	
Top speed	117mph (187kph) (Aceca Bristol)	
No. built	Ace	266
	Ace Bristol	466
	Ace 2.6	47
	Aceca	320
	Total:	1,099

AC

■ AC COBRA 289 & 427

In the autumn of 1961, Texan racer Carroll Shelby approached AC Cars with the idea of fitting a 4.2-litre Ford V-eight engine into their lithe and handsome light alloy Ace sportscar. By early 1962, AC had built the first prototypes and by the autumn had dispatched 100 cars to America for completion. Enter the legendary Cobra, perhaps the most famous muscle-car of them all and certainly one of the fastest.

Using essentially the same tubular steel chassis layout as the six-cylinder Ace, with transverse-leaf springing for the front and rear suspension, this spare

■ LEFT *The seven-litre cars had a stiffer chassis and coil-sprung suspension to handle the power.*

■ BELOW LEFT *With so much power – up to 480bhp and 180mph (290kph) – driving a Cobra at speed is for experts only.*

and handsome two-seater sportscar had electrifying performance thanks to the relatively light weight of the body and the high torque of the pushrod V-eight engines. The first cars used a 4.2-litre unit with the famous top-loader gearbox, but it wasn't long before a bigger 4727cc engine was slotted in by Shelby, boosting power from 164 to 195bhp. Top speed of the 289 car was 138mph (222kph), but even more impressive was the acceleration: 60mph (96kph) came up in 5.5 seconds, the standing quarter-mile in 13.9. It was in this form that the car first became available in Britain in 1964. Naturally, four-wheel discs were

■ LOWER RIGHT *Early 260/289 cars were much prettier and still stunningly quick – 0-60mph (90kph) in 5.5 seconds.*

■ FAR RIGHT *Its arches house massive Goodyear tyres but make the seven-litre Cobra into something of a caricature.*

■ BELOW *289 and 427 Cobras shoulder to shoulder. The bigger-engined cars had alloys, the 289 wires.*

AC COBRA (1962–68)	
Engine	V-eight
Capacity	4261/4727/6997
Power	164/195/345/490bhp
Transmission	4-speed manual
Top speed	136–180mph (218–290kph)
No. built	979

specified and, when the 289 engine replaced the 260, rack-and-pinion steering (rather than Ace-derived cam-and-peg). Even then the Cobra was no car for the novice.

This wasn't enough for Shelby. In 1965 he slotted in the 6989cc engine to produce the seven-litre Cobra. It had claimed 345bhp in its standard form – tuned SC cars gave 480bhp or more – and acceleration that put the Cobra in the record books in 1967 as the world's fastest-accelerating production car: 0–60mph (96kph) in 4.2 seconds. There was a milder Cobra 428 version with the 390bhp 6997cc V-eight from the Ford Thunderbird. In reality the seven-litre was virtually an all-new Cobra and no longer a slim and sylphlike beauty with fat arches front and rear housing huge Goodyear tyres. It shared only the doors and bonnet with the 289. More importantly, the chassis was totally redesigned and much stiffer, while the suspension now used coil springs rather than antiquated leaf springs.

The production of Cobras stopped in 1968 when 4.7 and 7-litre cars were

running concurrently. Since 1965 the "baby" Cobra had been known in Britain as the AC 289 Sports and used the same flared-arch body as the seven-litre. In America, the cars went under the names Shelby Cobra and Ford Cobra and were homologated as Shelby American Cobras.

There are a couple of footnotes to the Cobra story. The chassis lived on under an elegant Italian coupé body designed by Frua and was known as the AC 428, launched in 1966. As recently as 1983 Brian Angliss revived the car as the MkIV Cobra – but that's another story.

ALFA ROMEO

■ BELOW *A 1970s two-litre Alfa Romeo Spider in its natural hunting-ground– the open road. This version had the most torque, but the 1750 was sweeter.*

■ ALFA ROMEO SPIDER

Launched at the 1966 Geneva Motor Show, the Alfa Romeo Duetto Spider was the last complete design by Battista Pininfarina, founder of the Turin-based design house. With sales initially disappointing (the previous Giulietta Spider's best figure of 5,096 in 1960 was not exceeded until after the arrival of the Spider 2000 in 1972), who could have believed that the basic model would remain in production for 27 years? The shape wasn't much admired at first, but the lines matured gracefully over the years through a couple of restyles culminating in the square-tailed cars of the late 80s that ceased production in 1993.

The classic Alfa twin-cam engine grew from 1600 through 1750 and even 1300cc variations to become a fully fledged two-litre in 1971. Experts rate the 1750 highest for its combination of sweetness and refinement, while even the 1600 offers lusty acceleration, and the two-litre offers the most torque. The cars were always highly priced – the 1750 Spider's British price tag in 1969 was not much less than a much faster E-Type – but, with smooth steering, slick gearchange and fine disc brakes, offered

■ ABOVE *In the mid-1980s the Spider gained big bumpers and an unhappy-looking tail spoiler in an attempt to prolong its showroom life.*

■ LEFT *The cars of the 1980s had a chin spoiler and bigger wing mirrors but did without plastic headlamp covers.*

driver involvement and satisfaction that few cars could equal. It was a civilized car too, with a good ride and a watertight hood that could be raised with one hand.

The first-generation Spider's name, Duetto, was chosen after a contest drew 140,501 suggestions. One Guidobaldi

Trionfi of Brescia won a new Duetto for his, which was intended to symbolize the twin-cam engine and two-seater configuration. Rejected names included Pizza, Sputnik, Panther and Al Capone. These early "boat-tail" models gained fame in the 1967 film *The Graduate*.

ALFA ROMEO SPIDER 2000 (1966-93)	
Engine	4-cylinder DOHC
Capacity	1962cc
Power	131bhp @ 5500rpm
Transmission	5-speed manual
Top speed	124mph (199kph)
No. built	82,500

■ LEFT *The rounded lines of the boat-tail or Duetto Spider (nearest camera) alongside the square-tail look of the 1750 of 1970.*

ALLARD

■ ALLARD J2/J2X

South London motor trader Sydney Allard based his famous rugged sportscar on a reliable Ford V-eight engine. His pre-war Special cut its teeth in mud-lugging trails, but it wasn't until after the Second World War that Allard decided to go into production. The K1 and J1 of 1946–48 were spare and primitive but very fast, especially when fitted with the bigger 3.9 Mercury version of the well-tried flat-head Ford V-eight. Production blossomed with the more civilized versions such as the four-seater L Type and M1, with their hallmark waterfall grilles and the best-selling P1 saloon, with up to 4.4 litres, which won the Monte Carlo rally.

Best and most coveted of the breed, however, was the J2/J2X of 1949, a stark, four-wheeled motorbike of a car that, with the more modern type of overhead-valve Cadillac V-eight, could accelerate quicker than the Jaguar

XK120. Nevertheless, it was the Jaguar that spelled the beginning of the end for Allard and many of its ilk. The cars were produced in tiny numbers and could not compete with the mass-market Jaguar on a value-for-money basis. Sales fell sharply after 1953 and the company produced its last car, the Palm Beach, in 1958, in a belated bid for the Austin Healey market.

ALLARD J2/J2X (1946-59)	
Engine	V-eight
Capacity	5420cc
Power	180bhp
Transmission	4-speed manual
Top speed	130mph (209kph)
No. built	173

■ ABOVE *A cross-section of classic Allards: early special, K1, J1 and – furthest from the camera – P1.*

■ FAR LEFT *The evergreen Ford flat-head V-eight engine was at the heart of all classic Allards, giving up to 180bhp in the J2/J2X.*

■ LEFT *Dashboards were Spartan, with parts-bin instruments and a huge steering wheel.*

■ NEAR RIGHT *The J was a short-chassis two-seater with cut-away doors, capable of over 100mph (160kph).*

■ FAR RIGHT *The J2 and J2X, ultimate Allards with minimal creature comforts and stunning performance: 0-60mph (90kph) in 5.9 seconds was sensational in 1949.*

ALVIS

■ ALVIS TD/TE/TF

By the time the Graber-styled cars came out in the late 1950s, Alvis of Coventry had seen its best days with pre-war classics such as the fast and beautiful Speed 20 and 4.3. Post-war car production became something of a sideline to the company's armoured vehicle interests, nevertheless, the TD, TE and TF were fine cars. Developed from the "Greylady" TC21, they were mature motorcars for discerning enthusiasts: luxurious, well built and well mannered yet with a surprising turn of speed.

The TD's shape was the work of Graber, who had licensed Willowbrooks of Loughborough to build the bodies in Britain. These cars, dating from 1956, were known as the TC108G. Quality was

■ LEFT *Alvis of Coventry forged its reputation with cars like this 12/50 tourer in the 1920s.*

■ BELOW LEFT *This Speed 25 of the mid-30s was a supercar in its day with a top speed of more than 100mph (160kph).*

■ BELOW RIGHT *Today the Alvis badge is only to be found on armoured vehicles: car production finished in 1967.*

■ LEFT *The TF was the ultimate Graber-styled car with 150bhp triple-carb engine and five-speed ZF transmission.*

■ OPPOSITE LEFT *Interiors were traditional with large leather seats and walnut veneer. Only Bentley and Rolls-Royce were better.*

■ OPPOSITE RIGHT *Graber-inspired lines were slim and well balanced with a large glass area. Bodywork was coach built at Parkward.*

■ BELOW *Earlier TD models had single front light treatment and slightly less power.*

■ BELOW *Today these cars are highly sought after and have an enthusiastic owners club.*

not all that it should have been, and for the TD of 1958 Alvis commissioned Parkward of London to build its bodywork, while at the same time tidying up the rear of the roof line. Powered by a 120bhp version of the familiar Alvis three-litre straight six, the TD could achieve 100mph (160kph) with ease and looked particularly elegant in drophead form. Series II TDs had disc brakes, and, from October 1962, a desirable ZF five-speed gearbox

of the type used in the contemporary Aston Martin. The four-headlamp 1963 TE had 130bhp and could be bought with automatic transmission or power steering. Best, and last, of the breed was the TF of 1965, which had a triple-carburettor 150bhp engine and a top speed of 120mph (193kph) with the five-speed box. By then the writing was on the wall for Alvis as a passenger-car maker. Rover took a controlling interest and stopped TF production in 1967.

ALVIS TD/TE/TF 21 (1958–67)	
Engine	Straight six
Capacity	2993cc
Power	120–150bhp
Transmission	4/5-speed manual 3-speed auto
Top speed	110–120mph (177–193kph)
No. built	Total: 1528

ASTON MARTIN

■ ASTON MARTIN DB2/ DB2/4 & DB MKIII

Tractor tycoon David Brown, who had bought Aston Martin in 1947, made something of a false start with the underpowered four-cylinder Aston Martin DB1 of 1948. He more than redeemed himself, however, with the DB2 of 1950, a car that set the pace for all subsequent Astons. Here was a luxurious upper-crust coupé with modern performance and old-world charm packing a smooth, powerful six-cylinder twin-cam 116bhp engine from the Lagonda 2.6 saloon (Brown had bought Lagonda too, in 1947). "DB"

ASTON MARTIN DB2, DB2/4, DB2/4 MK II & DB MKIII (1950–59)	
Engine	DOHC straight six
Capacity	2580–2922cc
Power	107–196bhp
Transmission	4-speed manual
Top speed	115–130mph (185–209kph)
No. built	1,728

had his sights held high: there would be no more four-cylinder Astons.

Clothed in handsome open or closed alloy bodywork by Frank Freeley, these cars would top 115mph (185kph) with the standard engine, and more than 120mph (193kph) in high-compression Vantage form, which by early 50s standards represented supercar performance. Underneath, the classic cruciform chassis, with its pre-war belt-and-braces rectangular section tubing, produced thoroughbred handling of the highest order. Coil sprung, the live rear axle was located by trailing links – with

■ TOP *Drophead treatment lent itself well to Frank Freeley's smooth shape.*

■ CENTRE *MkIII models had the most power and could achieve up to 130mph (209kph).*

■ LEFT *The engine was designed by W0 Bentley and was originally intended for a big Lagonda saloon.*

■ LEFT *The DB2/4 had an early form of rear hatch and two extra seats in the back. The body was aluminium.*

■ BELOW LEFT *A functional interior featured a full set of instruments, a big wheel and full leather trim. The build quality was superb.*

a Panhard rod for the high side-loads the car was capable of generating – and damped by Armstrong lever-arms. Front suspension was unusual, a trailing-link design with the main lower locating member running across the front of the car, its shaft turning in widely-spaced bearing with continuous oil-bath lubrication. It had big wire wheels: 15-in (38cm) centre-lockers shod with the best contemporary high-speed Dunlop crossplys.

For the DB2/4 of 1953, Freeley's smoothly contoured fastback shape was made more practical, if not so pretty, by the addition of rear seats and a side-hinged rear hatch which meant stretching the tail by four inches. By the time the MkIII arrived, the tall DB2 grille had evolved into a broad mouth (derived from the DB3S racer) and small fins had sprouted on the rear wings with slim tail lights.

The WO Bentley-designed twin-cam six, in three-litre form since 1954, was upgraded for the MkIII with a stiffer block, beefier crank, and much improved timing chain and intake manifolds. It breathed better, too, thanks to the larger valves and higher-lift camshafts, technology lifted from the latest DB3-S racers. Twin SU carburettors remained, but the "DBA" engine produced 162bhp at 5500rpm.

Mildly tweaked three-litre engines were fitted to a handful of MkIIIs in 1958, of which 10 had a Weber-carbed, twin-exhausted engine giving 195bhp (known as DBB), while a further 47 had a 178bhp running SUs but the hotter cams and twin exhaust of the DBB.

David Brown supplied the gearbox on all models. It had a crash first gear and the option of overdrive on top gear on the MkIII, giving 28.4 per 1000rpm. Girling front discs were another innovation on the MkIII.

The DB MkIII was replaced by the DB4, although production overlapped for some months. The last MkIII was built in July 1959.

■ ABOVE *The MkIII had a bigger, wider grille, a three-litre engine and disc brakes, plus the option of overdrive.*

■ BELOW *All cars featured a separate chassis and unusual trailing-link front suspension.*

ASTON MARTIN

■ ASTON MARTIN DB5

The Aston Martin DB5 was an aristocrat among 1960s sportscars, as exclusive as a Savile Row suit and in Britain on its introduction in 1963, priced accordingly. The same amount of money would have bought you a nice little place in the Surrey stockbroker belt, while Jaguar's faster E-Type was just half the cost. The model's appearance in the James Bond film *Goldfinger* in 1964 put the name of Aston Martin on the lips of the world. Even today Ian Fleming's hero is still synonymous with the marque.

The DB5 was the fifth Aston built

■ LEFT *The lines of the DB5 evolved from the Touring-designed DB4 of 1958, with flared-in lights and a different roof line.*

■ BELOW *The short-chassis DB4 GT was a two-seater intended for competition work. It had a twin-plug engine and always had cowled lights like the DB5.*

under the regime of David Brown. It wasn't a new car, but a development of the sometimes troublesome Touring-styled 3.7-litre DB4 that had been around in one form or another since 1958. By fitting a bigger four-litre version of the twin-camshaft six-cylinder engine – with 240bhp – and a five-speed ZF gearbox, Aston claimed more punch with longer legs. Top speed was 140mph (225kph) – nearer 150mph (241kph) with the optional tuned Vantage engine – with meaty acceleration to match.

■ ABOVE *Made famous in the 1964 James Bond film Goldfinger, this beautiful shape has a timeless appeal.*

■ RIGHT *The standard DB5 was capable of 140mph (225kph), the Vantage version near 150mph (241kph).*

■ LEFT *In its handling the DB5 was well-bred if not quite in the same class as the E-Type*

■ BELOW *Aston Martin boss David Brown had 12 of these shooting-brake DB5s built.*

■ FAR LEFT *The alloy body was beautifully hand-built at Aston's Newport Pagnell factory.*

■ NEAR LEFT *The Volante was the convertible version – one of the fastest open cars of its day.*

■ BELOW LEFT *Early DB5s had three circular lights, later cars had single oblong units.*

Strange to think that in the carefree early 1960s Aston could test its cars on the still new and unrestricted M1 motorway, a spark plug's throw from the Newport Pagnell factory.

Like all Astons before it, the DB5 broke no new technical ground but kept pace with developments. Disc brakes, fitted all round, were becoming the norm on fast cars like the DB5, but Aston were still suspicious of newfangled independent rear suspension and felt they could make their solid axle work just as well. For the most part they were right, although the DB5 was always happier on fast main roads than being chucked about on country lanes. Flared-in lights for Touring's fashionable Italian bodywork, consisting of alloy panels draped over a labyrinth of small tubes, were a nod towards modern aerodynamic

ASTON MARTIN DB5 (1963–65)	
Engine	Straight six
Capacity	3955cc
Power	282bhp @ 5500rpm
Transmission	4/5-speed manual 3-speed auto
Top speed	140mph (225kph)
No. built	1,018

thought, but inside the DB5 retains its club-land feel with rich leather everywhere, electric windows (still rare in 1963) and a push-button radio: switch on and the words "Aston Martin" glowed in red from the tuner. As well as the fastback saloon, Aston built the swish Volante convertible, and David Brown even sanctioned 12 shooting-brake DB5s to sell to his uppercrust country house-owning pals. These were surely the most beautiful estate cars ever built.

With sales of more than 1,000 in a little over two years, the DB5 has to be counted as one of the most successful Astons. It is certainly one of the most memorably beautiful, a slender, sensual machine highlighting how the later, more macho cars from Newport Pagnell lost their way.

ASTON MARTIN

■ ASTON MARTIN V8

The Aston Martin V8 was built in many guises over its 21-year career. The shape, styled by William Towns and fashioned in alloy, was first seen in 1967 as the DBS, but with the old four-litre six-cylinder engine because the V8 was still not ready for production. With its new DeDion rear suspension, the wide, wedge-shaped four-seater DBS handled well but was really a little heavy for its engine, especially when fitted with the power-sapping automatic gearbox. To be fair, a Weber-carbed Vantage version restored the status quo to some extent, but the six-cylinder cars have never been much fancied.

The quad-cam all-alloy 375bhp V8 was thus much welcomed when it arrived in 1969, catapulting the top

■ RIGHT *The Vantage version of the V-eight had a deep chin spoiler and a blanked-out grille. It was good for 170mph (273kph).*

■ BELOW *Like all Astons, the V-eight's body was crafted in alloy. The shape was by English designer William Towns.*

speed up to a Ferrari-challenging 160mph (257kph), although early misgivings about the reliability – and thirst – of the Lucas fuel injection caused Aston to change to Webers in 1973. By then, the shape had already had its first make-over with a new grille and single lamps on either side. Five-speed manual was the standard transmission, but many cars came with the Chrysler automatic gearbox.

A Vantage version of the V8 gave Aston a challenger in the supercar stakes with its 170mph (273kph) top speed and shattering acceleration, while the elegant Volante convertible proved to be a top

seller for this British company. The dramatic Lagonda four-door of 1976 was pure Aston V8 under the skin and appealed to Arab oil sheiks.

The last V8 was made in 1990. By then, the engine had reverted to injection. Large, thirsty, very expensive and fast, the V8 was viewed as a dinosaur yet it had enormous appeal as a traditionally-built high-speed express. Its spirit survives in today's Virage.

■ FAR LEFT *The cabin featured acres of the finest leather, electric windows and air-conditioning.*

■ NEAR LEFT *The standard "saloon" V-eight in Oscar India specification of the late 1970s. By this time many Astons were being built with automatic transmission.*

ASTON MARTIN (1969–90)	
Engine	V-eight
Capacity	5340cc
Power	340–436bhp
Transmission	5-speed manual 3-speed auto
Top speed	160mph (257kph)
No. built	About 1,600

AUSTIN

■ AUSTIN A90 ATLANTIC

Austin was first off the mark into post-war production in 1945, and the A90 Atlantic was Britain's first car designed specifically for the American market. It had a promising start. Launched at the Earls Court Motor Show in 1948, it was a sensation.

While other makers continued with warmed-up pre-war leftovers, here was an all-new 95mph (152kph) British convertible with modern full-width styling: the front wings were bulbous and full, sweeping down across the deep, thick doors to blend gently into the big one-piece rear wings and cowled-in wheel arches, forming a rakish, bold profile. Incredibly for 1948, the Atlantic could be had with a power top and door glasses, unheard-of in Britain: a switch had the top up and latched down in 22 seconds. Other Atlantic luxuries included such rare

■ ABOVE *The dramatic Atlantic dates from the austere late 1940s and was built to woo the Americans.*

AUSTIN A90 ATLANTIC (1948–52)	
Engine	OHV in-line four
Capacity	2660cc
Power	88bhp @ 4000rpm
Transmission	4-speed manual
Top speed	90mph (145kph)
No. built	7,981

refinements as an Ecko radio, adjustable wheel and a heater.

The rugged internals were warmed-up A70 saloon, a long-stroke, overhead-valve 2199cc four-cylinder engine bored out to 2660cc and giving 88bhp on twin SUs: Longbridge rounded the output up to 90 to give the new flagship its name. More telling was the 140lb/ft (190.5 newton metres [N m]) of torque that peaked at 2500rpm. There were four speeds on a very American steering-column shift.

It was the Atlantic's pace, above all, that impressed the pundits. It was one of a handful of cars since the war that could top 90mph (145kph), and of those, the Atlantic was easily the cheapest. 0–60mph (96kph) in 16.6 seconds wasn't hanging about in 1948 either and, with petrol still rationed, up to 25mpg could be obtained. In America, where buyers expected six or eight cylinders, not four, sales never took off. In 1949 an Atlantic broke 63 American stock-car records at Indianapolis over seven days.

The Atlantic was short-lived. Austin tried to sustain interest in it with a $1,000 price-cut in 1949 and then, in 1951, a fixed-head saloon version with hydraulic brakes and a lower axle ratio but the convertible ceased production in January 1951. The saloon struggled on until September 1952, ousted by the BMC merger that year. The final tally was 7,981 cars and of the 3,597 exported, only 350 made it to America.

■ ABOVE *The interior featured white steering wheels and the column gearchange.*

■ ABOVE RIGHT *Twin Austin of England badges and Pontiac bonnet strakes were unusually flash for a British car.*

■ RIGHT *The A90 Atlantic was impressively swift with a top speed of 90mph (145kph). It also featured an advanced power-operated hood.*

AUSTIN HEALEY

■ AUSTIN HEALEY 3000

The original "big" Healey was the Healey 100, first shown at the Earls Court show in 1952 and hastily adopted by BMC as the Austin Healey 100 with the 2.6-litre four-cylinder engine from the Austin Atlantic. Bodies were built by Jensen of West Bromwich, central England, with final assembly at the MG factory at Abingdon, Oxfordshire. In no way was the Healey a sophisticated motorcar: it had a separate chassis, cam-and-peg steering and a solid rear axle sprung and located by half elliptic leaf springs.

In 1956 the six-cylinder BMC series C engine from the Austin Westminster was shoehorned into a stretched version

AUSTIN HEALEY 3000 (1959-67)	
Engine	6-cylinder
Capacity	2912cc
Power	124–150bhp
Transmission	4-speed, optional overdrive
Top speed	114–120mph (183–193kph)
No. built	42,926 all types

■ LEFT *The Healey 100 had the four-cylinder engine from the Austin Atlantic.*

■ BELOW *The last-of-the-line MkIII had opening quarter windows and 120mph (193kph) potential.*

of the car to make the 100/6. However, this wasn't entirely successful: performance was down compared with the torquey old four.

Redemption arrived in the form of the three-litre 3000 MkI in 1959: outwardly the same pretty, shapely, low-slung two-seater but with a 2912cc 124bhp engine. Performance went up to 114mph (183kph), while new front disc brakes improved the stopping power. Overdrive, wire wheels and nominal two-plus-two seating were optional as before. For

■ LEFT *The Austin Healey 100 was originally to be just a Healey.*

■ BELOW LEFT *The MkIII was probably the least pretty but most comfortable of the breed and featured small rear seats.*

■ BELOW *The Healey looks wonderful from the rear. The four-cylinder cars had the best handling.*

■ LEFT *The early cars had a functional dashboard: the MkIII had wood veneer.*

1961 BMC upped the power to 132bhp with triple SU carburettors for the MkII 3000, followed a year later by the MkIIa with wind-up windows, a curved windscreen and a proper, fully convertible hood. From this point the cars were two-plus-two only and can be recognized by a vertical-slat front grille.

Last, and best, of the line was the 1964 MkIII with improved breathing for 148bhp, pushing the top speed to over 120mph (193kph). Brakes were improved by a servo and, inside, the car had a rather opulent wooden dashboard, somewhat at odds with its macho reputation as a rugged driver's car.

North America was always the car's biggest market and it was American

safety legislation that finally ousted the 3000 from production in 1967, after which BMC replaced it with the far less successful MGC. Despite its low ground clearance the Healey was a formidable

works rally car in three-litre form and was never quite the crude and rugged car of legend, certainly in later form. It remains one of the most sought-after British sportscars of the 1960s.

■ ABOVE *The Healey lasted until 1967, when it was ousted by American safety regulations.*

■ ABOVE *The 2.6-litre four-cylinder engine, also found in the Austin Atlantic, had excellent torque.*

AUSTIN HEALEY

■ AUSTIN HEALEY SPRITE

There may have been faster, smaller sportscars than the 1958 Austin Healey Sprite, but few have been more endearing. With its gaping grin and the pop-eyed headlights that gave it its "Frogeye" nickname, this little brother to the big 3000 Healey captured the hearts of enthusiasts the world over. In fact, the trademark protruding lights were an afterthought when the extra cost ruled out Donald Healey's idea for retracting headlights. Taking its mechanics from the well-filled BMC parts-bin (mostly Morris Minor and Austin A35), the 11ft 5in (3.5m) Sprite had a chirpy character on the road, too, with a respectable top speed of 84mph

AUSTIN HEALEY SPRITE (1958–61)	
Engine	In-line four
Capacity	948cc
Power	43bhp
Transmission	4-speed manual
Top speed	84mph (135kph)
No. built	38,999

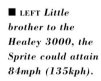

■ ABOVE *The Austin Healey Sprite got its "Frogeye" nickname because of its pop-eyed headlights.*

■ LEFT *Little brother to the Healey 3000, the Sprite could attain 84mph (135kph).*

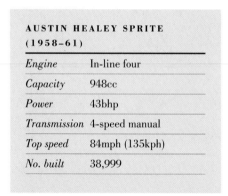

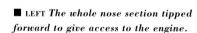

■ LEFT *The whole nose section tipped forward to give access to the engine.*

■ BELOW *Donald Healey's original idea was to give the Sprite pop-up headlights, but this proved too expensive.*

(135kph) and up to 45mpg attainable. Its one-piece front-end lifted up to give excellent access to the 948cc A Series engine, which gave all of 43bhp.

It spawned many variants with increasing levels of ugliness and luxury, though the performance of the last Austin Sprite of the early 70s was way above the original Frogeye. There was a badge-engineered MG variant, too, reviving the old Midget name, that lasted until the late 70s in hideous rubber-bumpered form. The less said about that the better.

■ ABOVE *The Frogeye was unmistakable from the rear too, with its tiny lights and minimal bumpers.*

OTHER MAKES

■ ABARTH
Italian Carlo Abarth launched his firm in 1950 as a tuning concern specializing in the Fiat marque. His first car was the Tipo 207/A Spider of 1955, using Fiat 1100 parts, followed rapidly by the first of the 600-based machines. Through the 1960s, Abarth continued to build cars based on the Fiat 500/600 and latterly the 850, as well as branching out into production of stunning little Simca-Abarth coupés, sports-racers and prototypes with twin-cam engines of entirely his own design. Racing activities pushed the company into liquidation in 1971. Fiat took over the Abarth for its own competition activities.

■ AMPHICAR
Originally the A35-powered Eurocar, this quirky German amphibian was the brainchild of Hans Trippel, creator of the wartime VW Schwimmwagen and various subsequent amphibious cars. An annual production of 20,000 Amphicars was projected, a farcical

overestimate which led to formal production ceasing in 1963, with cars then being assembled from the vast stock of parts at the works.

■ ARMSTRONG SIDDELEY
The firm came into being through the fusion of Armstrong-Whitworth's car-making activities with Siddeley-Deasy of Coventry in 1919. The last products from the firm were distinctly luxurious but were always too expensive compared with the main competition from Jaguar. Car manufacture ceased in 1960 with the big Star Sapphire, and the company concentrated on its core business of aero engines.

■ AUDI
The first cars from the German firm Audi were four-cylinder and were successful in sport, but after the First World War came "sixes" and then the first as a manufacturer of mainly-front-wheel-drive Wanderer-based cars under the umbrella of the Auto-War. The marque remained dormant within the latterly Mercedes-controlled Auto-Union until 1965, when ownership of

the combine passed to Volkswagen. Today, Audi is best known for its Quattro four-wheel-drive system, first seen on the groundbreaking Quattro Turbo Coupé of 1979.

■ AUSTIN
The Longbridge-based company was founded in 1905 by Herbert Austin (later Sir Herbert), whose earliest designs were conventional and reliable, if uninspiring. The Seven of 1922 was a revolution and on this design the firm's fortunes were made. Most products through the inter-war period were dull but worthy, and the trend continued after 1945. The British Motor Corporation (BMC) was formed in 1952 by uniting Austin and Morris, with the former firm emerging dominant.

The most significant post-war BMC was the Mini, and this led to a family of front-wheel-drive models; however, the last of the old line, the Cambridge, survived until 1969. Austin no longer exists as a marque, but its Longridge works is the Rover Group's principal plant.

BENTLEY

■ BENTLEY CONTINENTAL

The Bentley Continental was one of motoring's ultimates in the 1950s. It was not only the fastest genuine four-seater car in the world – it could top 120mph (193kph) with ease – but also one of the most beautiful: big, swoopy and as stunningly elegant as anything from the fashionable design houses of Italy.

Shaped in Rolls-Royce's Hucknall wind tunnel under the direction of styling supremo John Blatchley, this was Crewe's flagship owner-driver super-coupé, its bold, distinctive fastback profile influenced, though no one would admit it, by the Cadillac 62 Series coupé of 1948. The Bentley grille still stood tall and proud, as on the R-Type saloon, but at the rear those hallmark embryonic tail fins kept the Continental tracking straight at high speed. The Continental's alloy bodywork was built in London by HJ Mulliner on a special high-performance chassis.

The gearing was higher than on the saloon, and the 4566cc engine breathed more freely thanks to a higher compression ratio and a big-bore exhaust system. There was a weight-loss regime for this, the first sporting Bentley since the 1930s: bumpers were made of aluminium, not steel, and, inside, the armchair seats of the R-Type saloon had given way to smaller sports buckets with alloy frames.

Even so, the Continental was no Spartan lightweight: four people and all

BENTLEY CONTINENTAL R (1952–55)	
Engine	Straight six
Capacity	4566cc (later 4887cc)
Power	Not quoted
Transmission	4-speed manual
Top speed	124mph (199kph)
No. built	208

■ ABOVE *The distinctive Bentley grille was retained for the Continental.*

■ ABOVE *Its sweeping lines were among the most beautiful of their time and belied the car's bulk.*

■ LEFT *Despite its weight the Continental handled well, especially on fast roads with wide sweeping corners.*

■ LEFT *The Continental shape continued with minor alterations on the new Silver Cloud/S1 chassis.*

■ BELOW *From the rear the sweeping roof line was especially elegant. The shape was evolved in an aircraft wind tunnel.*

their luggage could travel in magnificent comfort in familiar drawing-room surroundings, the driver enjoying a full set of instruments that included a rev counter and an oil temperature gauge, items not normally deemed necessary on the saloon. Out on the road that tall gearing gave the Continental a fantastically long stride with 80mph (128kph) on tap in second, 100mph (160kph) in third and 124mph (199kph) in top, all achieved in fuss-free refinement. For the seriously rich, there was no faster or more stylish way to escape austere, post-war Britain.

Later, the original lightweight R-Type Continental concept was watered down. Tycoons wanted fatter seats, drivers wanted automatic gearboxes, steel bumpers replaced aluminium and before long the Continental was just another heavy coachbuilt Bentley, albeit superbly handsome. The Continental look survived on the "S" Series chassis of 1955, but by then the Continental appellation applied to all coachbuilt Bentleys. Most were desirable, but only that original R-Type will go down as one of the greats, in its time perhaps the finest car in the world.

■ ABOVE *The interior featured a full-width wooden dash with more complete instrumentation. The Continental was at its best as a right-handed manual.*

■ LEFT *The Continental was a genuine four-seater with unbeatable long-distance touring ability. Powered by a six-cylinder engine, it could do 80mph (128kph).*

■ ABOVE *The Continental was for the super-rich only and gradually got heavier and less sporting as it evolved. The body was built by HJ Mulliner in London.*

BMW

■ BMW 507

In search of a flagship glamour car to boost American market sales, as well as their flagging post-war image, in the mid-1950s BMW asked Albrecht Goertz, a German aristocrat with an American-based industrial design agency, to style a new super sportscar.

Using a drastically shortened version

■ ABOVE *The BMW 507 was one of the most beautiful cars of the 1950s. This one has knock-on wheels. The styling was by Albrecht Goertz, later to style the 240Z Datsun.*

■ ABOVE LEFT *From the rear the track looks wide. Vision was poor with the hood up.*

■ ABOVE RIGHT *The 507 even looked good with the hood up. Its lines had near perfect balance.*

BMW 507 (1955–59)	
Engine	V-eight
Capacity	3168cc
Power	150–160bhp
Transmission	4-speed manual
Top speed	125–140mph (201–225kph)
No. built	253

of the big V-eight saloon's box-section chassis as his base, Goertz – later to design the best-selling Datsun 240Z – sketched a slim, pinched-waist roadster that was an object lesson in elegant purity. With its long bonnet, pert tail and impeccable detailing it was an instant classic. Producing 150bhp from a high-compression version of BMW's fine all-alloy V-eight engine (with a four-speed manual gearbox), it went as well as it looked: with the longest of the axle ratios offered, it was capable of 140mph (225kph) and 0–60 (96) in the order of nine seconds. Its exhaust note, a creamy full-blooded wuffle from twin rear pipes,

was almost as memorable as its profile. Torsion-bar suspension front and rear gave a supple ride with confident handling, perfect for its role as a suave high-speed express for the Monte Carlo set. A handsome factory hardtop quickly converted the 507 into a snug, roomy two-seater coupé.

Beautifully crafted in alloy, the 507 of 1955 was aimed squarely at the Mercedes 300SL's market, but somehow it was more of a soft tourer than the complex, difficult-to-handle SL: serious drivers never really took it to their hearts. Its saloon-derived steering was never its best feature, which is probably

■ BELOW LEFT *The 507 was a superb long-legged tourer rather than a sportscar. The longest axle ratio gave up to 140mph (225kph) with the four-speed manual box.*

■ BELOW RIGHT *The stylish vents on the wings were for extracting heat from the engine bay.*

■ RIGHT *The front end was a stylized version of the traditional BMW "kidneys".*

■ BELOW *The alloy V-eight engine came from the 502 saloon but had high compression and up to 160bhp. It was smooth and flexible.*

why its competition pedigree makes short and unimpressive reading. Like the SL, though, it was viciously expensive and each one took a long time to put together, mostly by hand.

There were few uplifting developments in its short four-year career, the most notable being more power – 160bhp – and latterly front disc brakes. Production ceased in 1959, just 253 cars down the line. If anything, it added to BMW's financial problems.

Nonetheless, almost 40 years on, it rates as perhaps the most collectable of all post-war BMWs.

■ BELOW *The typically 50s interior was comfortable and roomy for two people. It featured an excellent hood, and there was the option of a factory hardtop.*

BMW

■ BMW 2002 TURBO

Marketed to bolster the ebbing reputation of BMW's entry-level saloon in its run-out twilight years, the BMW 2002 Turbo lasted only 10 months into 1973. When petrol prices almost doubled overnight, shocked car buyers became acutely aware of the delicacy of oil supply from an Arab monopoly: suddenly this 17-mpg tearaway looked like an anachronism. The first sign of BMW's loss of nerve was the disappearance of the aggressive reversed Turbo lettering on the front spoiler, but by then the Turbo's days were already numbered: it was discontinued by a nervous Munich after only 1,672 had been produced.

BMW 2002 TURBO (1972–73)	
Engine	4-cylinder
Capacity	1990cc
Power	170bhp @ 5800rpm
Transmission	5-speed
Top speed	130mph (209kph)
No. built	1,672

■ LEFT *The 2002 Turbo was based on the bodyshell of the 2002 Tii, itself a quick, yet much more usable and practical car, good for almost 120mph (193kph).*

The Turbo, all left-hand drive because the blower occupies the space normally reserved for the steering column in the right-hand drive car, used the injected two-litre slant-four engine fitted with a KKK turbocharger and made an impressive 170bhp. It did without a wastegate, intercooler or complex electronics and felt much the same as the standard 2002 at low to medium revs, though the turbo boost – from 4500 rpm – tended to cut in rather suddenly and could make the car a handful. Geared for 20mph (32kph) per 1000rpm in the fifth gear of its special ZF five-speed box, the Turbo ran out of breath at 130mph (209kph). Turbos ran a 3.36:1 ratio in their 40 per cent limited slip back ends.

The Turbo had stronger driveshafts and bearings all round, but still used the usual BMW configuration of MacPherson struts at the front and semi-trailing arms at the rear. Spring rates

■ ABOVE *Fat wheel-arch extensions hid bigger wheels. "Turbo" logos raised the hackles of safety campaigners in the 1970s.*

■ OPPOSITE *The tearaway BMW Turbo was a short-lived and unlucky model, launched at the dawn of the fuel crisis.*

■ BELOW *The 2002 shell dates back to the mid-1960s and the 1600-2, an entry-level four-cylinder BMW that survived well into the 70s.*

were increased all round, and there were anti-roll bars at both ends and Bilstein dampers on the back. The tyres – on special 6in x 13in (15cm x 33cm) Mahle alloy wheels – were 185/70x13s Michelin XWXs. The brakes, which were vented discs gripped by four-pot callipers up front, large drums at the rear, had only one servo to the standard 2002's two. Inside, the Turbo featured rake-adjustable buckets. The only other changes were the addition of a boost gauge in a pod tacked on to the centre of the dash and a three-spoke sports steering wheel, while the face of the instrument binnacle became red.

The rare and exciting 2002 is now one of the most collectable 70s BMWs.

■ LEFT *The Turbo, inspired by a factory racer, was a 130mph (209kph) hot-shot with 170bhp.*

■ BELOW *From the front the Turbo was easy to spot – bereft of front bumper and wearing a deep chin spoiler with flashy decals.*

■ ABOVE *The Turbo's cabin featured a thick-rimmed sports wheel, hip-hugging seats and a special instrument pack. All were left-hand drive.*

■ RIGHT *The slant-four engine produced 170bhp with the KKK turbocharger but had somewhat on-off delivery.*

BMW

■ BELOW *The CSL's shape was developed from the less sporting 2800/3.0 CS coupes. Shape harks back to 1965 2000CS.*

■ BMW 3.0 CSL

The CSL was a lightweight version of BMW's flagship six-cylinder coupé, built to homologate the car for European Touring Car Group 2 racing. The first CSLs, announced in May 1971, were real stripped-for-action 135mph (217kph) road racers with thinner body panels, no front bumper, fibreglass rear bumper, racing latches on the bonnet, manual winding side windows made from Plexiglas, and of course the alloy-skinned opening panels, all in the name of weight reduction. BMW even skimped on underbody rust protection and sound deadening, along with some drastically cheaper interior trim (400lb [181kg] was pared off the coupé). Top speed wasn't much affected but acceleration was decisively quicker. Suspension was stiffened by Bilstein gas shock absorbers with advanced progressive-rate springs. Wheels were fat Alpina 7-in (17.8-cm) alloys with chrome wheel-arch extensions to keep them legal. Black accent stripes distinguished the *Leichtgemetal* from the standard CS/CSi. 169 were built, all left-hand drive.

Although the CSL was originally fitted with the 2958cc carburettor version of the in-line six (giving 180bhp), a slight bore increase in August 1972 gave 3003cc which allowed it to slip into three-litre Group 2 competition. At the same time Bosch electronic injection replaced the twin Zenith carburettors and power rose to 200bhp, although brochures of the time quote a carburettor-fed 3003cc engine too. 539 were built.

The British specification RHD car was introduced in the UK in October 1972 and came with the "RHD City package" to appease drivers who wanted the lightweight racer cachet without the discomfort. Most of the excess weight previously stripped off the car was put

BMW 3.0CSL (1971–75)	
Engine	In-line six
Capacity	2985/3003/3153cc
Power	180–206bhp
Transmission	3/5-speed manual
Top speed	133–140mph (213–225kph)
No. built	1,095

back. British importers took 500 CSLs but prices were high – more than an Aston or Jensen – and not everybody liked the Scheel bucket seats, awkward to get into, or wanted easily-damaged alloy panels.

The 3.2-litre CSL – nicknamed Batmobile – was announced in August 1973. It was left-hand drive only and had a bigger 3.2-litre (actually 3153cc) 206bhp engine to homologate the 84mm

stroke used on the 3.5-litre works racing coupé. It was still badged three-litre. The same lightweight shell (initially available only in Polaris silver or Chamonix white with optional motorsport stripes) was used with alloy doors and bonnet, but, to take the weight and downforce of the rear wing, the bootlid was steel with a fitting for the spoiler. The spoiler (racing kit) was packed in the boot on cars sold in West

■ RIGHT *The interior featured special Scheel bucket seats, black trim and a sports steering wheel.*

■ FAR RIGHT *With firmer springs and dampers, the CSL had sure-footed, almost roll-free handling, though oversteer could be a problem in the wet.*

■ LEFT *The standard CSL lines up with the more radical "Batmobile". Note the spoilers, plastic bumpers and slightly lower stance of the later car.*

Germany, where such appendages were illegal. Daft as it looked, the wing was intrinsic to the coupés' success in the European Touring Car (ETC) series, clamping tail to road with massive aerodynamic downforce. It was created in a panic session in a Stuttgart wind tunnel after Jochen Neerspach and Martin Braungart of BMW Motorsport found a loophole in FIA rules that allowed "evolutionary improvements" for existing models. With the works CSL about to return to the ETC, they were looking for a way to eliminate aerodynamic lift at speeds over 124mph (199kph).

It worked. Works CSL coupés easily outpaced Capris first time out at the Nürburgring, cutting lap times by 15 seconds. To use the wing on the track it had be homologated on a production car, hence the Batmobile bits. These also included a deep front spoiler, a roof hoop spoiler just above the rear window, a small lip spoiler on the edge of the bootlid and rubber "spitters" on the front wings. Manual steering and Bilstein gas-pressure shock absorbers with three alternative levels of hardness meant the 3.2-litre CSL didn't need an anti-roll bar. The last CSLs, built in 1974-75, had minor differences such as a three-fin rear batwing and a driver's seat with an adjustable backrest.

■ OPPOSITE *Some CSLs had a deep chin spoiler but panels identical to all-steel CS coupes. "L" stood for lightweight.*

■ RIGHT *The road-going CSL was built to homologate racing coupés like this one for Group 2 Touring Car racing in the 1970s. It remained competitive long after the old-type coupés had gone out of production.*

BRISTOL

■ BRISTOL 401

The Bristol 401, announced in 1949, was only the second model built by the fledgling car builder whose 1946 400 looked much like the pre-war BMW on which it was based. It being a car built by a planemaker, where quality is a matter of life or death, there was no room for penny-pinching compromise in design or construction.

The 401's alloy body was but one example of high-minded extravagance permeating the car's design. Alloy panels, wrapped around small diameter tubes, were graded in thickness according to function, heavier on top of the wings, for instance, where mechanics would lean during servicing. Under the skin was a separate chassis, derived from the first Bristol, which continues in its essentials to this day.

The engine, a throaty straight six appropriated from BMW after the war as reparations, was a gem. Almost 100mph (160kph) from an 85bhp two-litre engine (pulling an opulently trimmed full four-seater) *was* something to write home about in the late 1940s – the likes of Bentley and Jaguar needed double the capacity to do the same job – and to row

■ BELOW LEFT *The steering-wheel was similar to the one used in Bristol aircraft.*

BRISTOL 401 (1949–1953)	
Engine	Straight six
Capacity	1971cc
Power	85–100bhp
Transmission	4-speed manual
Top speed	97mph (155kph)
No. built	650

it along with that beautifully slick four-speed gearbox was a constant delight.

Outright speed, however, was not what this car was all about. Fine handling, especially in the days before motorways, was even more important, and the 401 was well blessed with light precision steering and a general feeling of poised good manners that made the marque many lifelong friends.

The memorable "Aerodyne" body shape, inspired by Touring with its elegant teardrop tail and smooth

contours, was honed on Bristol's two-mile-long Filton runway and was truly aerodynamic for the time. In tests carried out at the MIRAS wind tunnel 20 years after the 401's demise, only four modern cars were found to be more aerodynamic. Low levels of wind noise even at high speed were one side benefit from this attention to aerodynamic detail; another was fuel economy: up to 25 miles (40km) to every gallon of the filthy poor petrol that was still all you could get in 1949.

■ RIGHT *A Bristol 407 with a 411 Series II.*
The size of the V-eight engine, always from
Chrysler, went up from 5.4 to 6.2 litres.

■ BELOW *From the Series SIII onwards, the*
411 had this better-looking full-width
grille. Performance was up to 140mph
(225kph), with automatic transmission.

■ BRISTOL V8s 407–411

The 1961 407, with its Canadian-built
Chrysler 5.2-litre engine, was the first
V8 Bristol, instantly catapulting the big
four-seater into the 130mph (209kph)
class with standing quarter-mile times
equal to the contemporary two-plus-two
Ferrari. Gone was the delicate two-litre
six, and the four-speed Bristol gearbox
was replaced by a Chrysler Torqueflite

■ LEFT *The 410*
shown here was an
intermediate model
with recessed
headlamps and
chrome strips on
its flanks.

■ BELOW *The*
interiors were
always finished to
a high standard.

automatic with flashy push-button
selection and seamless gearchanges.
Though the classic Bristol chassis
remained, the front suspension was new,
coils supplanting the transverse leaf.
Gone too was that lovely rack-and-
pinion steering, replaced by a Marles
worm-type unit which, together with the
sheer weight of the engine, conspired to
make the 407 less nimble than its
thoroughbred predecessors.

The cars were improved through the
1960s. The 408 had the same 5.2
Chrysler engine but new front-end
styling and select-a-ride dampers. The
409, from 1965 on, had rounded corners
on the grille, power steering and better
brakes. The 410 of 1968 had smaller
wheels, floor-shift for automatic gearbox
and twin-circuit brakes.

The 1969 411 had lower ride-height
with clipped fins, less brightwork and a
6.2-litre engine. Series 2 (1970) had

auto self-levelling, Series 3 (1972)
entirely new front-end styling with twin
7-in (17.8cm) lights. Series 4 (1973)
had a 6.6-litre engine, giving 330bhp.
Series 5 411 (1975) had a black grille,
stiffer chassis and improved cooling.
411s could pull 140mph (225kph).

All offered drawing-room luxury with
muscular performance. Later versions'
superb power steering made them
remarkably agile for size. The ride was
excellent, build quality superb. The

BRISTOL 411 (1970–76)	
Engine	V-eight
Capacity	6277cc
Power	335bhp @ 5200rpm
Transmission	3-speed auto
Top speed	140mph (225kph)
No. built	600

relatively narrow build meant that, in
town, drivers could thread through gaps
that would stop most luxury cars and all
from a commanding driving position in
big, armchair seats.

That the little-known Bristol marque
survived into the 90s is an achievement
itself. Rivals such as Aston and Jensen
faced liquidation and disaster in the 70s
and 80s as Bristol plodded on by staying
small (boss Tony Crook has never
planned to make more than 150 cars a
year) and satisfying a small, loyal
clientele.

B U I C K

■ BUICK RIVIERA

The Riviera was a kind of American Bentley Continental. Conceived as Buick's answer to the best-selling Ford Thunderbird, but eschewing the chrome and glitz of its contemporaries, the Riviera was blessed with some of the finest styling to come out of Detroit in

■ ABOVE *The Riviera was the most beautiful Buick of the 1960s, an all-American Grand Tourer.*

■ LEFT *Early cars had a 6.5-litre engine, but this later went up to seven litres, giving a top speed of 130mph (209kph).*

BUICK RIVIERA (1963–65)	
Engine	V-eight
Capacity	6572cc
Power	325bhp
Transmission	2-speed automatic
Top speed	130mph (209kph)
No. built	112,244

the 60s. It was swoopy yet restrained and had presence and gravitas where Cadillacs and Chrysler Imperials were merely big. In a word, it had class.

Under the bonnet was the inevitable V-eight engine, initially a 6.5-litre, later

with 7.0 litres and anything up to 365bhp. Even with the obligatory two-speed automatic gearbox, this huge five-seater was good for 130mph (209kph), although handling was strictly conventional on the separate chassis

and the brakes were never really up to the job, quickly succumbing to the dreaded fade at high speed. Inside, the Riviera driver wanted for nothing, with electric windows and power steering as part of the package and a dashboard that

■ LEFT *In the 1950s Buick was known for its solid, family cars: this is a 1956 Roadmaster.*

■ ABOVE *The Riviera's clean profile was a breath of fresh air after the fins and chrome of its contemporaries.*

■ RIGHT *Later cars had clamshell headlights but, as ever, the original was best.*

looked distinctly tasteful by Detroit standards.

Inevitably, in a land of built-in obsolescence, Buick fiddled with the Riviera's classic styling – most memorably the clamshell-covered lights – and after 1965 the car lost something of its unique personality, sharing its underpinnings and structure with the Cadillac Eldorado. The model redeemed itself in the early 70s with the "boat-tail" version but lost all credibility from 1973 onwards as Detroit's big cars began to lose their way.

■ ABOVE *Under the skin the Riviera was conventional, with a live rear axle and hardly adequate drum brakes.*

■ LEFT *Inside the Riviera had a European flavour with circular dials and a floor-mounted gear-shift.*

OTHER MAKES

■ BERKELEY

The Berkeley was built between 1956 and 1961 by Charles Panter's firm of caravan manufacturers in Biggleswade, Bedfordshire. It was designed by Laurie Bond, who had a particular affection for front-wheel-drive microcars. Technically clever, the cars never really caught on, unsurprisingly, perhaps, given the 1958 advent of the Austin-Healey Sprite. A Ford-based car, the Bandit, never made it to production.

■ BOND

Sharp's Commercials Ltd of Preston, Lancashire, produced Laurie Bond's eccentric three-wheeler Minicar from 1948 to as late as 1966. In 1966, the company diversified into four-wheeler GT coupés based on the Triumph Herald range. In 1969, it was bought out by Reliant, who closed the Preston works and transferred production to its Tamworth factory, Staffordshire, where the only Bond car made was the Bug, an odd sporting three-wheeler.

CADILLAC

■ CADILLAC ELDORADO BROUGHAM

The 1957 Cadillac Eldorado Brougham was a General Motors dream car brought to life. The most prestigious Cadillac out of Detroit since the V-16 17 years earlier, it started life at the 1954 Motorama as the Park Avenue, a four-door town sedan which looked like, but wasn't, a hardtop. It was a minor hit, and in May 1954 Harley Earl, all-powerful GM design supremo, began holding discreet meetings about a super Eldorado, a production version of the Park Avenue for 1956.

The 1955 Motorama Cadillac was the prototype Eldorado Brougham. Curvacious, almost tasteful for this gaudy period, it had pillarless clap-hands doors, restrained knife-edged fins

CADILLAC ELDORADO BROUGHAM (1957–58)	
Engine	V-eight
Capacity	6384cc
Power	325bhp
Transmission	3-speed automatic
Top speed	118mph (189kph)
No. built	704

and a 90-degree wraparound on the front screen. Its stainless-steel roof, narrow white sidewalls and twin headlights were industry firsts. It sat on a new X-frame chassis with air suspension. Steel domes were pressurised by a small compressor regulated by levelling valves. A 6.3-litre 325bhp V-eight engine was hitched to GM's Hydramatic transmission as standard.

The Brougham had power steering, brakes, seats and windows and dripped with electric baubles: automatic headlamp dipper, cruise control, signal-seeking radio, electric aerial and door locks, a drum-type electric clock and an automatic bootlid opener. Other ultra-luxuries included polarized sun vizors, magnetized drinks tumblers in the glove box, cigarette and tissue dispensers, special lipstick and cologne, ladies' compact and powder puff, mirror and matching notebook and comb and an Arpege atomizer with Lanvin perfume. The buyer could choose from 44 trim combinations and between karakul and lambskin carpeting.

The Broughton sold for a fraction of building cost and soon the accountants pulled the plug. It survived two years.

■ RIGHT *From the rear the fins were reasonably restrained. When it appeared in 1957, the Eldorado Brougham was the most expensive and exclusive Cadillac yet built.*

■ FAR LEFT *The Brougham's luxury touches ranged from polarized sun visors to electric seat adjustment – with memory.*

■ LEFT *Twin headlights were still a novelty in the mid-1950s – another industry first on the Brougham.*

■ OPPOSITE *The Brougham had restrained styling for its period, with its clap-hands doors and pillarless roof of brushed aluminium.*

■ LEFT *The rocket-inspired fins on the 1959 Cadillacs were the biggest in the industry and were never surpassed. Cadillac had begun the craze for fins in the late 1940s.*

■ BELOW *The tail lights were shaped like after-burners. The grille across the rear was purely decorative.*

■ CADILLAC ELDORADO BIARRITZ

The American obsession with the tail fin reached its zenith in 1959 and nobody did it bigger, or better, than Cadillac, makers of Detroit's premier luxury motorcar. The 1959 Cadillacs had the biggest fins in the industry, an outrageous 42 inches in height. Their jet-age imagery was accentuated by a pair of bullet-shaped turn and stop lights. Front-end styling was equally distinctive, with twin headlights and double-decker grilles across the board. 20ft long, 6ft wide and scaling two tons in weight the 1959 car came as a two-door coupé de ville, a pillarless four-door hardtop or as an even bigger Fleetwood 75 formal limousine. There was also a high-spec Fleetwood version of the stock four-door saloon. All were based on a simple perimeter frame chassis with drum brakes all round. Best remembered is the Eldorado Biarritz convertible, which had a more powerful 345bhp version of Cadillac's famous 6.3-litre V-eight engine.

All these six-seater land yachts, the ultimate in four-wheeled glamour, came

CADILLAC ELDORADO BIARRITZ (1959)	
Engine	V-eight
Capacity	6384cc
Power	345bhp
Transmission	3-speed auto
Top speed	115mph (185kph)
No. built	11,130

fully equipped with power-operated seat adjustment, electric boot opening and even automatic headlamp dipping over and above the obligatory power steering, automatic transmission, power hood in the case of the Biarritz, and electric windows. Air-bag suspension was one of the few optional extras on the Biarritz, which cost three times the cheapest Chevrolet that year. It was fast in a straight line at 115mph (185kph) but sheer weight and soggy springs gave it handling qualities comparable with a boat. Fuel consumption was in the 8mpg range, but economy was not then an issue in a country where this resource was still cheap.

Nearly four decades on, none of that matters. The 1959 Cadillac has passed into legend, symbolizing an era when the world's most powerful nation was at its most confident.

■ LEFT *The Sedan version of 1959 was not as well balanced as the two-door car, and the handling was awful.*

■ ABOVE *The wild styling of the 1959 Cadillacs was always irresistible to customizers.*

CHEVROLET

■ CHEVROLET STINGRAY

Although the first of the Chevrolet Corvette sportscars were produced in 1953, the marque didn't reach maturity until 1962 and the introduction of the Stingray. Like its ancestors, the new car had a fibreglass body, but the styling, was all new, a mixture of muscular haunches and chisel-edged tension that gave it a unique appeal. The coupé version lost its split rear window after the first year owing to customer resistance: ironically these 1963 cars are now the most collectable Corvettes of all. The convertible looked good with its hood either up or down, the top stowing neatly under a lid. Underneath, the separate chassis remained, but the Corvette was unusual for an American car in having independent rear suspension. Its cheap but effective system used the drive shaft as the upper link, with a simple steel rod as the lower link and a transverse leaf spring.

A range of small-block 5.4 V-eight

■ ABOVE *The mid-70s coupe made quite a practical high-speed express.*

■ LEFT *The Stingray's shape was launched in 1967 and ran through until 1984. It was inspired by the Mako-shark dream car.*

■ RIGHT *1956-62 Corvettes only came with V-eight engines, giving up to 360bhp in fuel-injected form. Manual or automatic transmissions were available, the body was glassfibre.*

engines were offered, from a base model giving 250bhp to a 300bhp unit with a bigger carburettor and the 340bhp L76 with solid tappets and a higher 11.25:1 compression ratio. The latter was available with the famous Rochester fuel injection, unleashing a further 20bhp. The performance of the relatively light

■ ABOVE *The 1963–67 Stingray, seen here as a big-block convertible, was perhaps the best-looking of the Corvettes.*

■ LEFT *The engine was Chevrolet's famous small block of 5359cc. It was strong, torquey and very tunable.*

■ RIGHT *The rare T-top Targa roof model that replaced the full convertible. It was outlawed in America by federal crash protection regulations.*

■ BELOW *The mid-60s Stingray interior shows very complete instrumentation. The twin-cowled effect of the dashboard was inspired by jet-fighter planes.*

Corvette was electrifying, with 0–60 (96) in 5.6 seconds. Transmissions were either three-speed manual (rarely specified), two-speed auto or, more usually, four-speed manual.

Each year of production brought minor cosmetic and technical changes, but the big news for the 1965 model was the big-block 396cu in V-eight engine, packing a colossal 425bhp and 415lb/ft (565.5 N m) of torque at 4000rpm. Now sporting four-wheel disc brakes to keep the huge performance in check, the engine went up to a full seven litres (427cu in) and in 1966 could be had with hydraulic tappets (lifters in American parlance), lower-compression L36 form with a "soft" 390bhp or a solid-lifter, high-compression L72 with 425bhp. The small-block cars, slower but better balanced than the seven-litre machines, remained in production though the fuel-injection version faded away as demand for the big-block took over.

The last year for Stingray was 1967. It was offered with 300 and 350bhp small blocks and big blocks ranging in output from 390 to 435bhp depending on carburation and compression ratio.

For racers, there was the L88 engine, giving 560bhp on 103 octane petrol. With its sky-high 12.5:1 compression ratio, alloy heads and fancy forged

CHEVROLET CORVETTE STINGRAY (1963–67)	
Engine	V-eight
Capacity	5356–7000cc
Power	250–560bhp
Transmission	3/4-speed manual 2-speed auto
Top speed	118–145mph (189–233kph)
No. built	45,456 small block 72,418 big block

crank, this car was virtually unusable on the road anyway. The catalogues rated it at "only" 430bhp to keep GM bosses, safety legislators and unworthy owners at bay. For the 1968 model year the new "Coke bottle" Stingray was announced, a worthy successor that, somehow, never recaptured the sporting spirit of the 1963–67 Stingrays.

■ ABOVE *This is how the Corvette looked from 1984, although many of the mechanical items were carried over. The new body was still glassfibre: this was the only American production car apart from the Studebaker Avanti to use it.*

■ BELOW *Stiff suspension meant that the handling of later Corvettes was roll-free but the ride was harsh. Many had power steering and automatic transmission.*

CHEVROLET

■ CHEVROLET CORVAIR

The Chevrolet Corvair, launched in 1959 as a 1960 model, was the response of General Motor (GM) to the influx of low-priced European economy cars into the North American market in the late 50s and early 60s. In style and engineering it was refreshingly different from the general run of technically very conservative American cars, which makes it doubly disappointing that it fell

■ LEFT *The original Corvair with its clean styling influenced the Hillman Imp and NSU Prinz.*

■ RIGHT *The 1964 restyle made the car look more conventional.*

■ FAR RIGHT *The style was copied for the late 60s Vauxhall Victor.*

so disastrously foul of public opinion and safety hysteria. The controversy surrounding the handling of the early Corvairs inspired consumer rights and safety campaigner Ralph Nader to write a book called *Unsafe at Any Speed*. It was a best seller and began a new era of

government regulations and safety legislation that continues to this day.

With its rear-mounted, air-cooled, flat-six engine and fully independent suspension, the Corvair was far removed from the general run of American cars and its "compact" rivals from Ford and

Chrysler which were really just scaled-down large cars. By European standards, of course, it wasn't compact, with similar dimensions to cars like Ford of Britain's flagship Zephyr.

Enthusiasts loved the car's European flavour, but ordinary buyers weren't so

■ LEFT *The Monza was a sporty coupé with a more powerful version of the flat-six engine.*

■ ABOVE *Though the Corvair was marketed as a compact in Britain, it was actually the size of a Ford Zephyr.*

■ BELOW *The original Corvair saloon. The car earned bad publicity for its handling.*

■ ABOVE *The power output of the first Corvairs was just 80bhp for a top speed of 87mph (139kph).*

■ BELOW *The Monza Turbo was one of the first turbocharged production cars, capable of over 100mph (160kph).*

sure and the Corvair's more conventional rivals comfortably outsold it. It took the introduction of the little Monza coupé with its punchier engine for the Corvair to find its niche in the market as a compact sporty car. Its fortunes took another turn for the better when a convertible version was launched in 1962. There was even a turbocharged version, one of the first on a production car.

Sadly the honeymoon wasn't to last. Bad publicity from Nader's book had given the car a reputation for wayward handling it didn't altogether deserve, and when Ford introduced the Mustang in 1964 the Corvair didn't stand a chance. Buyers gravitated to the Mustang's more conventional, safer engineering and equally sporty image. The Pony car era had begun and the

Corvair was left behind. GM tried a rescue with a restyle for 1964, curing the supposedly oversteer-biased handling with improved rear suspension. But the damage was done. Sales never recovered, though Chevrolet kept the

Corvair in its line-up until 1969.

Although the Corvair is little known in Europe, it has a thriving owners' club in North America. For reasons Chevrolet would probably rather forget, it is an important car in US motoring history.

■ LEFT *Chevrolet ditched the Corvair in 1969. The main reasons for its demise were bad publicity and the arrival of the Mustang.*

CHEVROLET CORVAIR (1959–69)	
Engine	Aircooled flat six
Capacity	2377/2684cc
Power	80–180bhp
Transmission	3/4-speed manual 2-speed auto
Top speed	87–105mph (139–169kph)
No. built	1,271,089

CISITALIA

CISITALIA 202

Cisitalia was founded in 1946 by racing driver and businessman Piero Dusio. His first project, for which he called on the services of Fiat engineers Giacosa and Savonuzzi, was a single-seater racing car with Topolino front suspension and the four-cylinder engine from the Balilla. This was followed in 1948 by the 202 coupé using essentially the same ingredients but with a memorable full-width body on a round-tube frame by Pininfarina. This was a seminal moment in post-war

■ LEFT *The Cisitalia 202 Coupé was a landmark in styling, having no separate mudguards or free-standing lights.*

■ BELOW *One would never guess that this car was introduced in 1948. Only the split screen dates it.*

■ ABOVE *The interior was typically severe, with just the bare minimum of instruments.*

■ ABOVE *Flip-out door handles were a favourite Pininfarina touch.*

■ ABOVE *Pininfarina had begun his ideas on the Maserati AG chassis, and in many ways the Lancia Aurelia was a continuation of this theme.*

■ RIGHT *The clean lines of the Cisitalia were copied on cars as diverse as the Simca 8 and Ferrari 166 Inter.*

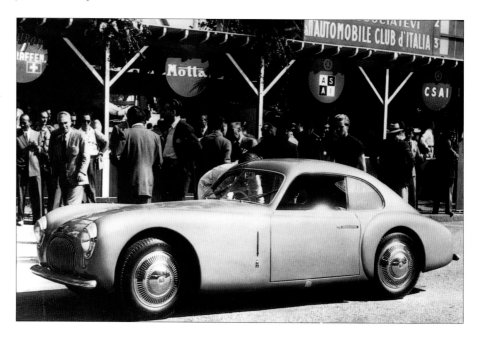

■ RIGHT *Touring made this open Barchetta version not unlike the Ferrari 166 Barchetta of the period.*

■ BELOW *The four-cylinder engine was based on a Fiat design and gave upwards of 50bhp.*

■ BELOW *On just 1100cc the Cisitalia could manage 105mph (168kph) with the most highly tuned road engine.*

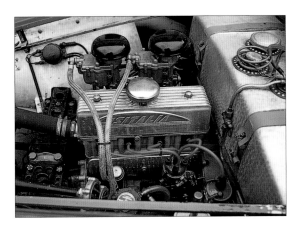

■ ABOVE *Just 485 Cisitalias were built, with bodies by Vignale and Frua as well as Pininfarina.*

styling, the coupé having its bonnet lower than the front wings, headlights blended into the wings (rather than free standing) and smoothly sweeping, simple lines. Farina explored these themes on other chassis but never again to such remarkable effect. The New York Museum of Modern Art has, since 1951, kept a Farina-bodied Cisitalia as an example of "sculpture in movement". Vignale, Frua and Stabilmenti Farina, as well as Pininfarina again, designed convertible variants. Thanks to slippery aerodynamics, the Cisitalia could achieve 102mph (164kph) on just 50bhp from a tweaked Fiat 1100 engine. Competition-tuned variants had up to 120mph (193kph) capability.

As early as 1949, Cisitalia was facing bankruptcy thanks to overambitious

plans for a Porsche-designed Grand Prix car. Dusio upped sticks to Argentina, but the 202 continued in production until 1952.

The marque survived until 1965 under the control of Dusio's creditors but was never to regain the eminence it achieved with the classic 202 coupé. Today these cars are highly sought after.

CISITALIA 202 COUPÉ (1948–52)	
Engine	In-line four
Capacity	1089cc
Power	50 bhp
Transmission	4-speed manual
Top speed	105mph (168kph)
No. built	485

CITROËN

■ LEFT *The Traction-avant in its rare long-wheelbase form. A few were built as "hatchbacks" and called Commerciale.*

■ CITROËN LIGHT 15

The Citroën Light 15, or *Traction-avant* to its many admirers, is a towering reference point in the history of the motorcar, pioneering front-wheel drive on a mass-produced family saloon. It had a three-speed gearbox mounted ahead of the engine in the nose of the car, and the drive went through CV-jointed drive shafts to torsion-bar-suspended front wheels; this was cutting-edge technology in those days. By the standards of 1934, the roadholding of the *Traction-avant* was almost unbelievably good, albeit at the expense of heavy steering.

Sadly, the high development costs sent a penniless André Citroën to an early grave and his company into the arms of

■ BELOW LEFT *The cabriolet had a windscreen that folded flat, and there is a dicky seat in that long, flowing tail.*

■ BELOW RIGHT *Tractions were built for some years in Britain. The British market model had a wooden facia and disc wheels.*

■ BELOW *The pre-war cabriolet used a long- or short-wheelbase chassis and came with four- or six-cylinder power.*

CITROËN LIGHT 15/BIG 15 & 6 (1934–55)	
Engine	In-line 4/6-cylinder
Capacity	1911/2866cc
Power	46–80bhp
Transmission	3-speed manual
Top speed	70–85mph (112–137kph)
No. built	759,123/47,670

■ BELOW *The shape of the Traction saloon is unmistakable. With its front-drive roadholding it was much favoured by the French police – and criminals.*

■ LEFT *Early Tractions had a three-bearing wet-liner engine and three-speed all-synchro gearbox. Not much urge on 32bhp.*

■ BELOW *With the 1.9-litre OHV engine the Traction would do around 75mph (120kph). All-round independent springing by torsion bars gave the car an excellent ride.*

■ ABOVE *The big six-cylinder Traction was fast in a straight line but suffered from heavy steering. A few had an early version of the hydraulic rear suspension later used on the DS.*

Michelin, but the Light 15 and its many derivatives went on to success, selling strongly for 23 years. Front-wheel drive wasn't the whole story. The Light 15's unitary construction was still a rarity in 1934 and the car was both roomy and comfortable to ride in, with torsion-bar independent suspension at the rear too. Top speed with the 45bhp 1911cc four-cylinder engine was 70mph (112kph).

There were many variations on this enduring theme. The Big 15 had an extra seven inches (17.8cm) added to its wheelbase. The *Commerciale* had an early form of rear hatchback. Big families could opt for the eight-seater *Familiale*. For sporty drivers there were rakish coupés and cabriolet models. Top of the range from 1938 was the six-cylinder, 2866cc 15CV, or Big 6, its 77bhp engine pushing the top speed to a respectable 85mph (137kph). Citroën pioneered its hydropneumatic suspensions on the rare 6H version of this model which already featured their self-levelling system on rear wheels only. Styling changed little over the years, but the post-1953 *Traction* has a distinctive projecting boot. From 1938 to 1940 (and, after the Second World War, between 1948 and 1955) these Citroëns were built in significant quantities in the UK. A Slough-built car is recognizable by its wooden dash, leather trim and 12-volt electrics.

It was years before rivals began to catch up with standards set by the Light 15. Only when Citroën had another world-beater, the DS of 1955, did it finally feel obliged to let the *Traction* die. Many examples survive and this stylish, groundbreaking car has a cult following.

CITROËN

◼ CITROËN DS

Never before has a single model embraced so many innovations as the Citroën DS, launched in Paris in 1955. Chief among these was the suspension: eschewing conventional springs, Citroën engineers suspended their new saloon on hydraulic self-levelling hydropneumatic struts, with a unique adjustable ride-height facility that meant the DS could raise itself to negotiate rough terrain. At rest, ignition off, it gradually sank until it sat squat to the floor. The same engine powered a high-pressure hydraulic central nervous system which controlled ultra-sharp

CITROËN DS (1955–75)	
Engine	4-cylinder
Capacity	1911/1985/2175/2347cc
Power	63/84/109/115/141bhp
Transmission	4/5-speed manual and semi-auto
Top speed	84–117mph (135–188kph)
No. built	1,455,746

◼ ABOVE *The trend-setting DS was a commonly seen family car in France. This is the later version, with four headlights in its shark-nose front. The inner pair turned with the steering so that the car could "see" around corners.*

power steering, powerful four-wheel disc brakes (in board up-front) and the clutchless hydraulic gearchange.

Clothed in a beautiful and futuristic windcheating five-seater body (with detachable panels) that made its contemporaries look distinctly stale, the DS was a decade, maybe two, ahead of the game and a true show stopper. With front-wheel drive (as all Citroëns had been since the equally revolutionary Light 15), its handling and stability were almost as sensational as its magic-carpet ride. Only its elderly engine let it down, a clattery 1934 design from the old *Traction-avant* which was unworthy

◼ ABOVE *The high-geared DS was perfect for relaxed long-distance cruising. Its suspension ironed out anything that France's poorly surfaced roads could throw at it.*

◼ RIGHT *The body panels, bolted on, could be removed quickly, making accident damage easy to repair.*

DS 19 or 21 PRESTIGE

■ ABOVE *The interior of the DS had futuristic styling to match the exterior and plenty of room too. Cut-price ID models, without power steering, were much loved by French taxi drivers.*

of such an advanced machine. From the mid-1960s there was a more modern two-litre four-cylinder engine, which was better, but somehow the DS never quite got the kind of smooth, unstressed motor it deserved.

Early reliability problems associated with suspension were soon forgotten and the DS spawned a whole raft of derivatives during the 1950s and 60s. Downgraded models such as the ID19 and, later, the D super, with fewer power-assisted systems and less bhp, appealed to thousands of Paris cabbies; the cavernous Safari Estate cars were the ultimate in family haulers; while the beautiful DS *décapotable* convertibles were expensive and exclusive. High-spec prestige models and the last-of-the line 2.3-litre DS23 cars with five speeds and fuel injection further broadened the appeal in the face of younger rivals. For the true DS connoisseur, meanwhile, there were special coachbuilt coupés by the likes of Henri Chapron, not to mention impressive stretched presidential cars.

The shark-like shape of the basic DS saloon changed little in 20 years – the twin swivelling lights arrived in 1965 – and even when it was finally replaced by

■ LEFT *The main body styles were saloon, estate and flagship convertible, though various French coachbuilders like Chapron built coupes and amazing stretched limousines.*

■ BELOW *The gearchange – manual or semi-automatic – was on the steering column. The single-spoke wheel gave a better view of the instruments. Seats were soft and cosseting.*

the CX in 1975, the competition were only just beginning to catch up with its degree of refinement. Many have now raised the styling of the DS to the level of automotive art – how many other cars have inspired their own art gallery exhibition? Good examples untainted by rust are highly prized.

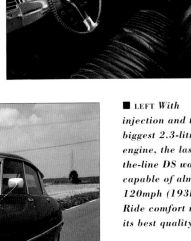

■ LEFT *With injection and the biggest 2.3-litre engine, the last-of-the-line DS was capable of almost 120mph (193kph). Ride comfort was its best quality.*

CITROËN

■ BELOW *It is hard to believe that the futuristic SM dates from 1970. This car wears rare Cabron fibre sports wheels.*

■ CITROËN SM

In the late 1960s, Citroën acquired a controlling interest in the Italian sportscar manufacturer Maserati. First fruit of this marriage was the big Citroën SM of 1970, a prestige GT car utilizing the best from both companies. Power came from a smaller V-six version of Maserati's long-lived quad-cam V-eight engine. At 2.7 litres, it stayed just the right side of the punitive French tax laws that came down heavily on engines over 2.8 litres. Like the DS, the SM had front-wheel drive, with the gearbox/transaxle unit slung out ahead of the compact engine. Its 170bhp through the front wheels was handled by Citroën's now well-tried

hydropneumatic self-levelling suspension, interconnected with the four-wheel disc brakes (in-board up front) and ultra-quick power steering.

Fast and refined, with excellent handling, once a sensitive touch with the steering and brakes had been learnt, the SM was a consummate long-distance GT, superbly stable at speed and with the magic-carpet ride familiar to DS owners.

It was the shape, though, that captured enthusiasts' hearts: crafted inside Citroën, it was dramatic and purposeful with a broad nose fully

■ ABOVE *The SM was a four-seater with a practical hatchback. 12,920 were built before production stopped in 1974.*

■ LEFT *The big, sweeping dashboard was as futuristic as the body. Note the single-spoke wheel.*

CITROËN SM (1970–75)	
Engine	V-six
Capacity	2670cc/2965cc
Power	170–180bhp
Transmission	5-speed manual 3-speed auto
Top speed	140mph (225kph)
No. built	12,920

■ BELOW *The V-six engine was a Maserati unit shared with the Bora. The five-speed gearbox sits ahead of it.*

■ ABOVE *The SM's lights were faired in behind a glass cover on European models: in America they had to be open.*

■ ABOVE *The SM's profile is still stunning today and, like the DS, is very aerodynamic for a 70s car.*

■ LEFT *The five-speed manual SM could do 140mph (225kph), though its weight hampered hot-rod acceleration times. Unfussed high-speed cruising was the car's greatest strength.*

flared in glass and a tapering tail that was as slippery as it looked. It was a four-seater, just, with a futuristic cabin that matched the body.

Sales were initially strong as French enthusiasts flocked to buy their first high-class GT car since the death of the Facel Vega. The love affair was to be short-lived. The fuel crisis hit in 1973, making big 18mpg supercars somewhat unfashionable.

Citroën improved the car with injection, a bigger three-litre version and an automatic option, but it was to little avail. Production ground to a halt in 1975, just short of 13,000 cars down the line.

OTHER MAKES

■ CONNAUGHT

The brainchild of Rodney Clarke and Mike Oliver of Bugatti specialists Continental Cars, the British firm Connaught began as a manufacturer of road and racing sportscars. As racing became ever more important, the Lea-Francis-engined Type A F2 car evolved into the streamlined Type B. In 1955 an unstreamlined Type B became the first British car to win a Grand Prix since 1924; two years later Connaught withdrew from race-car

manufacturing. Their only road car was the Lea-Francis-engined L2 of 1949–51.

■ COSTIN

Building his own car was a bold move by Frank Costin. The Amigo, with its wooden monocoque, was doomed to failure: it cost far too much money when it finally came on sale in Britain in 1972. The eight cars, using Vauxhall Victor engines, were built at Little Staughton, Bedfordshire, backed by Paul Pycroft. Claimed top speed was 134mph (214kph) on two litres.

DAIMLER

■ DAIMLER SP250 "DART"

The SP250 "Dart" was something completely new for Daimler, a company with no tradition of sportscars. The decision to build it came after a change of management in the late 1950s: Daimler was in trouble and the top brass thought a new sportscar would be a fine way to woo American buyers, just as

■ LEFT *The SP250 "Dart" was a complete departure for Daimler: previously its one and only sporty car had been the Conquest Roadster of the mid-50s, which had much less performance.*

■ BELOW LEFT *The body of the Dart was moulded in glassfibre and lacked rigidity: doors on early cars could fly open on bumpy corners.*

Jaguar, Triumph and MG had done before them. Using a chassis and suspension layout hastily copied from the Triumph TR3, Daimler took the then radical step of adding a glassfibre body, a gawky be-finned affair with a guppy-like grille and pop-eyed lights that found few friends.

Its major redeeming feature was its engine, a 2548cc V-eight producing a sweet 140bhp. Designed by Daimler's managing director Edward Turner – famed for his Triumph motorcycle engines – this smooth, torquey free-revving engine with its hemispherical combustion chambers and twin SU carburettors could power the unlovely

■ ABOVE *A rear shot of the SP250 Dart emphasises its then fashionable, but quickly dating, fins. The car's huge steering wheel is evident in this shot too.*

■ LEFT *Styling was done in-house by Daimler and was not deemed a success at the time, but almost 40 years later it seems full of period character.*

■ BELOW *The narrow interior featured a full set of gauges, an outsize steering wheel and a stubby four-speed gear-lever, but few creature comforts.*

but fairly light SP250 to 125mph (201kph). It's acceleration, 0–60 (96) in 9.5 seconds, was not to be sniffed at either, yet the excellence of the performance and the fine, throaty V-eight seemed somehow at odds with the amateurish, hastily designed body and chassis. The critics said as much, but as a niche filler between the cheaper TR and MGs and Jaguar's big XK150, the Daimler SP250 did make a certain amount of sense, especially as it would do a regular 25mpg. Four-wheel Dunlop disc brakes meant that it stopped well too, but its handling never earned top ranking as the steering was heavy, the chassis somewhat whippy: early examples (up to 1961) would pop their doors open alarmingly on rough roads. "B" specification SP250s – the Dart name had to be dropped because Dodge held the patent – had a stiffer chassis

and bumpers as standard, while "C" cars had a few extra luxury touches.

The fate of the SP250 was sealed as early as 1960 when Jaguar took over the ailing Daimler concern to boost its production capacity. Sir William Lyons never liked the Dart, because the styling offended him, but also because it would have been seen as low-level competition for the E-Type. Jaguar made a half-hearted attempt to restyle the car, but it was never really on and Lyons pulled the plug with no regrets in 1964. He was bright enough to see the potential in the SP250's excellent engine, however, and since 1962 had been offering it in a highly successful Daimlerized version of the MkII called the 2½-litre V-eight.

Today the many flaws of the unhappy Daimler SP250 are seen as endearing and characterful, and survivors are highly prized.

■ ABOVE *Priced between the MGA and Jaguar XKs, the Daimler filled a niche in the market but sales were slow – just 2,644 cars between 1959 and 1964.*

DAIMLER SP250 "DART" (1959–64)	
Engine	V-eight
Capacity	2548cc
Power	140bhp
Transmission	4-speed manual 3-speed auto
Top speed	125mph (201kph)
No. built	2644

■ BELOW LEFT *The Daimler's greatest asset was its smooth and flexible V-eight engine designed by Edward Turner.*

■ BELOW RIGHT *Jaguar boss Sir William Lyons had no time for the awkwardly styled SP250 and pulled the plug on it in 1964.*

DAIMLER

■ BELOW *Who would have guessed that this sober saloon could do 120mph (193kph)? The styling was carried over from the previous six-cylinder Majestic.*

■ DAIMLER MAJESTIC MAJOR

The Daimler Majestic Major was one of the most intriguing – and unlikely – high -performance saloons of the early 60s. By fitting a brand-new hemi-head 4.7 litre V-eight (an enlarged version of the unit found in the 2.5 litre Dart) into its biggest executive saloon, Daimler created a 120mph (193kph) hot-rod limousine that was quicker than the contemporary Jaguars – an embarrassing situation given the Jaguar takeover of Daimler in 1960 – and had astonishing acceleration: 0-60 took just 9.7 seconds.

Despite its traditional separate chassis and tall, dignified body, the Majestic Major had good manners to match its performance and was well reviewed in the press.

The Majestic Major was good value too, with automatic transmission, power steering and disc brakes as standard. Busy managing directors could lounge in leather-lined comfort as they were driven around in the Majestic Major, which had an appropriately huge boot too.

For its carriage trade customers there was a limousine version of the Majestic

■ ABOVE *From the front this is unmistakably a Daimler. In its stretched, long-wheelbase form the car was a favourite with funeral directors.*

■ ABOVE *The styling of the Majestic was by the same man who gave the English the FX4 taxi-cab. Spot the resemblance?*

■ FAR LEFT *The Majestic limousine was replaced by the Jaguar MkX-based DS420 Daimler limousine, here in very rare landaulette form.*

■ NEAR LEFT *The Majestic Major's fine, high-revving 4.5-litre 220bhp V-eight engine.*

Major called DR450, with a stretched chassis to accommodate extra occasional seats. It was a little heavier but had scarcely less performance – it was one of the quickest ways of getting to the cemetery.

So impressive was the Daimler's engine that Jaguar briefly toyed with the idea of fitting it to a Daimlerized version of the big MkX. The resulting V-eight prototype was canned when it proved embarrassingly faster than the Jaguar production model.

Production of the Majestic Major was always small scale, so sales were low. Production finished, after 1,180 cars and 864 limousines were built, in 1968. From then on, all Daimlers were destined to be badge-engineered Jaguars.

■ LEFT *Just 1,180 Majestic Majors were built in a 10-year production run. The car's performance embarrassed the Jaguar MkX.*

■ BELOW *The DS420 again, here in early standard-bodied limousine form. They were the last cars to use the famous Jaguar XK engine.*

DAIMLER MAJESTIC MAJOR	
Engine	V-eight
Capacity	4561cc
Power	220bhp
Transmission	3 speed auto
Top speed	122mph (194kph)
0-60	9.7 secs
No. built	1180 (plus 864 DR450 limousines)

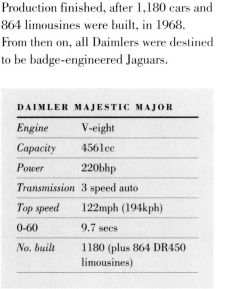

■ FAR LEFT *The Majestic Major had a traditional dashboard with all the instruments grouped in the centre. Power steering was standard.*

■ LEFT *There was room for the tired executive to stretch out in the back on generous leather seats.*

DATSUN

■ DATSUN 240Z

In the 1960s, Japan built its credibility as a sportscar maker with cars like the Honda S800 and the Toyota 2000GT. What it lacked was a high-volume market-leader to sell to the Americans, a car that could step into the shoes of the Austin Healey 3000 whose days were numbered and challenge the aging E-Type Jaguar and Triumph TR in this big, profitable market.

Into the fray, in 1969, stepped the Datsun 240Z, the best-selling sportscar of the 1970s. What the badge lacked in

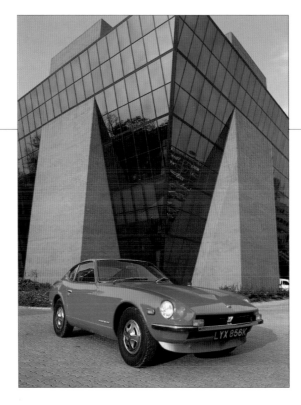

■ LEFT *The original 240Z had svelte European lines by Count Albrecht Goertz, father of the BMW 507.*

■ ABOVE RIGHT *The Datsun badge had little credibility with sportscar drivers before the able and low-priced 240Z.*

DATSUN 240Z (1969–75)	
Engine	Straight six
Capacity	2392cc
Power	151bhp
Transmission	4/5-speed manual
Top speed	125mph (201kph)
No. built	156,076

romance and cachet, the 240Z more than made up for with its well-balanced muscular lines, designed by Albrecht Goertz, father of the beautiful BMW 507. With its long bonnet, recessed lights and flowing, tense rear haunches, the Z clearly took styling cues from the fixed-head E-Type Jaguar; yet it was pure and elegant enough, apart from unattractive wheel trims – a typical weakness of Japanese cars – to have its own appeal. A well-equipped two-seater with a rear hatchback, the 240Z held few surprises under the skin, yet lacked for nothing: the engine was a smooth and punchy straight six, making 151bhp from

■ ABOVE *Its rear hatchback made the Z extremely versatile. These Wolf race wheels are non-standard but look better than the gruesome original trims.*

■ BELOW *It was hard to believe the 240Z was a Japanese car, so pure and elegant was its profile.*

■ BELOW *With all-independent suspension the 240Z had thoroughbred cornering abilities.*

■ RIGHT *The classic appeal of the 240Z was quickly recognized, and there are owners clubs for the cars all over the world.*

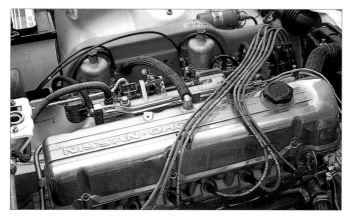

■ ABOVE *The engine was a lusty straight six from the big Cedric saloon. It was smooth and flexible and sounded great.*

■ RIGHT *The Z cars suffered from the cheap-looking finish of the day, but equipment levels were high.*

2393cc. Power went via a five-speed gearbox to a well-sorted strut-and-wishbone rear end. There were struts at the front, too. Precise rack-and-pinion took care of the steering. Butch and meaty in character – not unlike the big Healey – the 240Z was a far superior car even if never offered as a drophead. For the same price, in America, as Triumph's abysmal GT6, the customer received a car that handled superbly, if traditionally, and topped 125mph (201kph) with ease. It even sounded the part, with a gruff straight-six growl that was pure machismo.

Datsun sold 150,076 before the 260Z

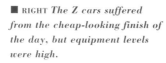

■ ABOVE *There was more than a hint of Ferrari about the front end of the 240Z. The spoiler is a period after-market extra.*

took over in 1975. Seeking more refinement, Datsun made the 260 a softer, less aggressive car and, inevitably, a heavier, slower one. Nevertheless, it was what the public, certainly the American public, wanted. Sales continued to climb. Automatics and a two-plus-two, longer-wheelbase version broadened the Z's appeal, though today's purist enthusiasts turn their noses up at this uglier variant.

With the 280ZX, Datsun finally lost the plot altogether. This unattractive parody of the purebred original was unworthy of the name. A good 240Z is a rare find today. Rust got many.

DODGE

■ DODGE CHARGER

If one car encapsulates the "muscle" era of the 1960s, it has to the Dodge Charger. Made famous by the classic chase sequence in the 1968 Steve McQueen film *Bullitt*, in which it was driven by the villains, the Charger was a full-sized fastback coupé, huge for a two-door four-seater yet gracefully styled by Detroit standards. With its buttressed rear pillars and tastefully simple front end, yet with a hint of menace about its blanked-out grille (twin-headlights were mounted behind electric flaps), it was a far cry from the chintzy, gin-palace American cars of the 1950s.

The first car to bear the Charger name, a bold but somehow bland fastback, had lasted just a season. The 1968 shell was to last, with minimal changes, until 1970, unless you count the rare hoop-tailed Charger Daytona, built for the 1970 model year as a homologation special. Myriad options meant that the Charger could be tailored to customer requirements – some had quite mild 5.2-litre V-eight engines – but for the cognoscenti the 1968 R/T (Road and Track) model was the only one to have.

Under the bonnet was a 7.2-litre engine giving 375bhp and fairly throbbing with tyre-smoking torque: off

■ LEFT *Buttresses beside the rear window were probably inspired by Italian design, but the Charger has an all-American muscle-car look of its own.*

the line, the Charger could outpace most Italian exotica with a 0–60 (96) time of six seconds, steaming up to 100 (160) in 13 seconds with wheel spin in every gear; foot to the floor, it would eventually wind up to 150mph (241kph). By the simple expedient of bolting the heavy-duty suspension down rock hard and fitting scaffolding-sized anti-roll bars, Dodge actually made the Charger R/T handle. With the optional front discs you had half a chance of

DODGE CHARGER R/T (1967–70)	
Engine	V-eight
Capacity	7206cc
Power	375bhp
Transmission	3-speed auto 4-speed manual
Top speed	150mph (241kph)
No. built	96,100

■ FAR LEFT *Rear wheel drive and the massive power of the R/T version meant wild handling, especially on loose surfaces.*

■ NEAR LEFT *The fastest versions of the Charger could manage up to 150mph (241kph).*

■ OPPOSITE *By the mid-1960s, many American cars had got away from the chintzy look of earlier times: the Dodge Charger was one of best examples of this trend.*

■ BELOW *The 7.2-litre V-eight engine had a claimed 375bhp and was hitched up to manual or automatic transmission.*

■ BELOW *The Charger name was first used on a much less attractive coupe, first seen in 1964.*

stopping it, too. Like most American cars the Charger came as a 3-speed automatic, but for serious drivers there was a heavy-duty Hurst manual box.

The Charger model line continued until 1978, but its credibility as a performance car was progressively whittled away as the American automotive industry moved its emphasis away from performance towards luxury, safety and economy.

OTHER MAKES

■ DAF

Dafs first appeared in 1958, from a Dutch firm which had been making commercial trailers since 1928 and HGVs since 1950. A unique "easy driving" transmission was their main distinguishing feature. In the 1960s, this belt-drive transmission was adapted to both military and racing (Formula 3) uses. In 1975, a majority share in the car side of the firm was acquired by Volvo, which has ousted Daf models from its inventory.

■ DELAGE

Louis Delage was a real maverick of the French motor industry, a perfectionist who would build only the finest vehicles. He started modestly enough in 1905 with a conventional shaft-drive-single-cylinder 6.5hp car, and this was followed by equally conventional touring machines, early examples having De Dion engines. It was in racing that the firm made its mark, and after the First World War it made superb touring cars and several vastly expensive forays into Grand Prix racing and record-breaking. It was acquired by Delahaye

in 1935 and thereafter the cars evolved into derivatives of that make. Along with Delahaye, it died in the Hotchkiss merger.

■ DELAHAYE

This French firm is best known for its stunning sportscars built in the 1930s, but its history dates back to the dawn of motoring when Emile Delahaye branched out into car production in 1894. Before the First World War, the range was diverse, but this changed in the 1920s when the firm only offered lacklustre "cooking" vehicles. After 1935, it made conventional but soundly-executed sporting cars as well as venturing into Grand Prix racing. This was its heyday. After the Second World War, the French Government's penal taxation killed off luxury-car manufacture. The firm merged with Hotchkiss in 1953 and from shortly afterwards made only trucks and Jeeps.

■ DELLOW

A rugged British mud-lugging trials car, the Dellow originally used a Ford Ten engine in an Austin Seven chassis, with a tubular-framed alloy body. In production, the Seven chassis was replaced by one made of chrome-moly

rocket tubes. A part-time project, manufacture fell away by the early 50s and in 1955 a new company took over the enterprise. The uncompetitive MkVI followed and in 1959 Dellow Engineering was wound up.

■ DE TOMASO

The Italy-based Argentine Alejandro de Tomaso made racing cars, but in 1967 he entered passenger-car production in earnest with the mid-engined Mangusta supercar. His 1970s products include the Pantera, still made in small numbers today. In 1976 he acquired Maserati and in the 80s the De Tomaso marque faded away.

■ DKW

The German firm DKW initially made motorcycles, starting car manufacture in 1928. In 1931 it introduced the pioneering front-wheel-drive F1 model, retaining two-stroke power and a year later became part of the Auto Union combine. This was re-established in the then Federal Republic of Germany in 1949 and resumed building cars in 1950. The firm came under Daimler-Benz control in 1958 and was bought by Volkswagen in 1965.

EDSEL

■ EDSEL

The 1957 Edsel has become a byword for the marketing man's blunder.

Ford pitched their new car at the lower medium market sector, between the bigger Fords and the budget Mercury models. Sadly for Ford, by the time it was launched the market was in a slump: buyers were looking for smaller cars, and the Edsel, the wrong car at the wrong time, became an unfortunate victim of its own massive hype. Forecasting 200,000 sales in the first year, Ford claimed that the new car – named after the dead son of Henry Ford – had cost $250,000,000 to develop.

When only 62,000 buyers were tempted in the first season, the critics blamed the styling with its unusual vertical grille, described by one wag as an Oldsmobile sucking a lemon. In fact, the Edsel was reasonably restrained by the extreme standards of the period, with fins well clipped and with a clean profile.

Spanning 15 different models, the Edsel was actually a separate Ford division with saloon, convertible and station-wagon bodies on the same ultra-conventional basic floorpan. As usual, there were six-cylinder and V-eight engine options (ranging in output from 145 to 345bhp) with three-speed

■ ABOVE *The Edsel missed the mark by a mile and cost Ford millions.*

■ ABOVE *The car's unusual grille – one of its trade marks – was not liked by customers.*

■ ABOVE *Ford marketed the Edsel as a marque on its own in a range spanning 15* *different models. This is the top-of-the-line Citation of 1958.*

EDSEL (1957–59)	
Engine	Straight six and V-eight
Capacity	3655–6719cc
Power	147–350bhp
Transmission	3-speed manual 3-speed auto
Top speed	90–108mph (145–174kph)
No. built	110,847

■ RIGHT *The styling was toned down for 1959 but the controversial grille remained. The car came as an estate (Villager), a two- or four-door saloon or a convertible.*

■ RIGHT *Today the relatively rare Edsel is a coveted collectors' piece, particularly the early cars as shown here.*

■ BELOW *Ford claimed that the Edsel had cost $250,000,000 to develop and predicted sales of 200,000 in the first year.*

manual and automatic transmission options. There was a mild restyle for 1959, as Ford tried to arrest a dramatic fall in sales, and in 1959 a totally new shell appeared in a much-reduced line-up for the 1960 model year. In the event, the Edsel line was dead by the turn of the new decade, cancelled owing to lack of interest.

Today, ironically, the once-shunned Edsel is a prized collectors' piece, a prince among lemons.

OTHER MAKES

■ ELVA

The name of this British car is derived from the French for "she goes" ("*Elle va*"), and the original 1955 Frank Nichols design was a low-cost sports/racing car with various power units. The most successful model was the Courier road-going sportscar. Manufacture was taken over by Trojan Ltd in 1962 and the company later bought Elva. Production passed in 1964 to Ken Sheppard Customised Sports Cars Ltd, of Hertfordshire.

■ ABOVE *The interiors featured all the usual glitz expected of a mid-range American car.*

■ RIGHT *The Edsel came with six-cylinder or V-eight engines giving as much as 350bhp.*

FACEL VEGA

■ FACEL VEGA FACEL II

Rolls-Royce comforts; super sports-car urge; American reliability and driving ease. The Facel Vega Facel II offered a combination of qualities you couldn't buy anywhere else in the early 1960s, though there were plenty of imitators on the scene by the time Facel – Forges et Ateliers de Construction d'Eure et Loire, of Paris – closed its doors in 1964. This, perhaps, was at the core of the Facel Vega's unique appeal. To drive a Facel, unlike an Aston Martin or a Ferrari, you didn't need racing-driver skill or a mechanic in the boot.

You would, nevertheless, have to put uniquely French elegance at the top of its list of attributes. As a pure piece of automotive artistry in the Pininfarina mould, the Facel II might never make the Museum of Modern Art; but as a stylishly charismatic period piece, there is nothing to touch it. This was a car with glamour by the truckload, true gravitas of a calibre that no mere hybrid – for the big Facels were unashamed mongrels with their Chrysler V-eight engines – has since achieved. Celebrities lined up to buy them in the early 60s, while race-owners like

■ BELOW *The Facel marque died in 1964, when the firm was made bankrupt by warranty claims on its unreliable smaller car, the Facelia.*

■ LEFT *Facel Vega was easily France's most stylish and expensive marque in the 1950s and 60s, favoured by celebrities, royalty and racing drivers.*

■ BELOW *Top of the range was the four-door Excellence, built to compete with Rolls-Royce and Mercedes. Its structure was too flexible, giving problems with doors.*

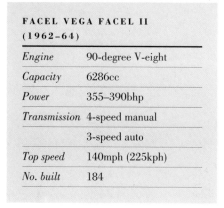

FACEL VEGA FACEL II (1962–64)	
Engine	90-degree V-eight
Capacity	6286cc
Power	355–390bhp
Transmission	4-speed manual
	3-speed auto
Top speed	140mph (225kph)
No. built	184

■ RIGHT *The HK500's styling was inspired by American models – hence the wrap-around screen – but had a brutish look all of its own.*

Stirling Moss and Rob Walker gave the marque the stamp of approval. As you would expect, it was an expensive car, costing the equivalent of two E-Type Jaguars and a Lotus Elan.

The shape suggested weight and strength. The bold, sculptured rear flanks – forming clipped, tense tail fins – looked hewn from solid rock; the squat, square roof was taut and spare. Cast in the mould of France's pre-Second World War *Grand Routiers*, the Facel II, like the HK500 before it, was as stormingly quick as these rocket ship looks promised. The automatic version could top 130mph (209kph). The rare manual was good for 140mph (225kph). This four-speed manual Pont a' Mousson box, with a twin-carburettor 390bhp V-eight from the Chrysler 300, was a no-cost option. With the Torqueflite came the slightly less powerful 355bhp (gross) single-carburettor version of the 6.3-litre Chrysler engine. The simplistic suspension was unchanged from the HK: coils and wishbones at the front – with anti-roll bar – and beefy half-elliptics on the live rear axle. To soften the car's thumpy ride, importers HWM would fit Armstrong selecta-ride rear dampers as an option. Dunlop discs were used all round. Power steering,

■ LEFT *The fastest of the HK500 and Facel II models could top 140mph (225kph) and came with manual or automatic transmission. The V-eight engines were American Chrysler units.*

leather seats and electric windows were standard.

Like the HK500, the Facel II did not escape the tyranny of excess weight. Even among contemporary big GTs it was a heavy car at 37-cwt (1880kg) dry, actually nearer two tons with four passengers and its 22-gallon (100-litre) fuel tank topped-up. A total 182 Facel IIs were built. The Facel Register shows the survival rate in Britain is good: 15 or 16 survive out of 23 right-hand-drive cars sold.

■ LEFT *The last of the V-eight cars was the Facel II, with cleaned-up styling but almost identical running gear.*

FERRARI

■ BELOW *The 275GTB is one of the most beautiful road-going Ferrari Berlinettas. This is the desirable long-nose four-cam.*

■ FERRARI 275 GTB

With the 275 GTB of 1964 the Ferrari road car really came of age. For the first time, here was a Ferrari with sophisticated suspension, answering demands for a car that could be driven quickly in comfort.

For good weight distribution and traction the five-speed transmission was separated from the engine, in unit with the final drive casing, connected on early cars by a slim prop shaft, later replaced by a torque tube for better rigidity. Double wishbone rear suspension replaced the usual solid axle with leaf spring found on the 250 GT Series, and there were obligatory four-wheel Dunlop-type disc brakes all round. Up front was Ferrari's famous all-alloy 3.3-litre 60-degree V-twelve engine, producing 280bhp in this single overhead-cam form. The 275 nomenclature was taken from the capacity, expressed in cubic centimetres, of each of the engine's cylinders.

Clothing all this was a two-seater coupé body, styled by Ferrari's favoured couturier Pininfarina, on a short 94.5-in

■ ABOVE *The nose styling was influenced by the 250GTO.*

■ ABOVE *For lightness and strength, Ferrari used Borrani alloy wheels with knock-on centre hubs.*

■ ABOVE *The exquisite cabin featured the traditional Nardi steering-wheel and open transmission gate.*

■ LEFT *The long-nose four-cam 275 GTB/4 did a claimed 165mph (265kph).*

■ BELOW *There was more than a hint of the 250 short wheelbase in the rear pillar.*

■ LEFT *The sensual and curvaceous 275 was as delicate as the Daytona that replaced it was brutal.*

(240-cm) wheelbase. The hunched and organically muscular steel body was built by Scaglietti, just up the road from Ferrari's Modena factory. The frame was of the traditional multi-tube type, and the car sat on handsome Campagnolo alloy wheels.

From 1965, there was a Series Two car with a longer nose and a smaller air intake and, from 1966, the four-cam 275 GTB/4 with six carburettors and dry-sump lubrication. Top speed soared from about 150mph (241kph) to 165 (265kph), with 0-60 (96) in under seven seconds.

As well as the 275 GTB there was the GTS, an open version developed specifically for the American market. It looked completely different from the GTB and its heavier body was actually

built in the Pininfarina factory. Much rarer were the nine NART Spider versions of the GTB and the 12 lightweight aluminium GTB/C cars built for competition drivers.

The 275 was replaced in 1968 by the 365 GTB/4 Daytona, which was faster but perhaps not as well balanced.

■ ABOVE *There was a lightweight GTC version of the 275 with all-aluminium bodywork.*

■ LEFT *With its rear-mounted transaxle, the 275 had superbly balanced handling.*

FERRARI 275 GTB AND GTB/4 (1964–68)	
Engine	V-twelve
Capacity	3286cc
Power	280-300bhp
Transmission	5 speed
Top speed	150-165mph (241-265kph)
No. built	200/280

■ RIGHT *For those addicted to open-topped motoring, Pininfarina also built the 275GTS.*

FERRARI

■ FERRARI DINO 206/246

Although the 206/246 Dino was never to wear a Ferrari badge (Enzo tried to market it as a separate marque) it was, in every respect other than the number of cylinders, a "proper" Ferrari. A 140mph (225kph) car with superb handling and a stunningly beautiful shape – one of Pininfarina's finest moments – it was for many the first step on the ladder of Ferrari ownership.

To understand the 206/246 Dino you have to understand the Fiat Dinos, the first fruit of Ferrari's liaison with Fiat and the first road car to bear the name of Enzo Ferrari's much-missed son and heir. A conventional front-engined, rear-wheel-drive monocoque design – made as a Pininfarina Spider and a low-key Bertone coupé – it had its genesis in the 1967 1.6-litre Formula 2 racing regulations. Ferrari's Dino V-six engine dating from the mid-1950s was ideal for the job, but the rules stipulated a 500-off, production-based block. Ferrari didn't have the capacity, whereas producing 500 cars was a mere sneeze

FERRARI DINO 206/246 GT (1968–73)	
Engine	V-six
Capacity	1987/2418cc
Power	180–190bhp
Transmission	5-speed manual
Top speed	140–148mph (225–238kph)
No. built	152 206GTs 2,487/1,274 GT/GTS

■ ABOVE *The Dino GTS was popular in sunny North American climes because of its removable "Targa" roof panel.*

■ ABOVE *From any angle, Pininfarina's Dino was stunningly beautiful.*

■ LEFT *Early Dino 206 models had more fragile two-litre engines, alloy bodywork and knock-on alloy wheels*

■ BELOW *The styling of the 206/246 Dino evolved gradually from a series of mid-60s Pininfarina dream cars. Mid engine location was inspired by racing practice.*

■ RIGHT *The Dino name is shared by a family of racers – this is the 246S of 1959. "Dino" correctly refers to the racing V-sixes and V-eights on which Ferrari's son Alfredino was working when he died in 1956.*

■ BELOW *The featured Alacantra covered dash, sports wheel and plastic seats.*

to Fiat. Enter the Fiat Dino, powered by a production version of Ferrari's quad-cam V-six, first as an all-alloy two-litre, later a 2.4-litre with an iron block. The ruse allowed Ferrari to qualify its engine for F2 racing, and for Fiat this was something of a prenuptial courtship before the eventual marriage of the two companies in 1969. The alloy-bodied two-litre Dino 206 arrived in 1968 with 180bhp and was powered by the same 65-degree V-six engine as in the Fiat Dino. The big difference was that this was turned through 90 degrees and mounted transversely behind the two-seat passenger cell, with five-speed gearbox and transaxle. Clothed in alloy by Pininfarina, it handled as well as it looked, but it soon became apparent that, in the face of faster opposition from Porsche, the 206 was underpowered. The 246 was Ferrari's answer, with 195bhp from a 2418cc iron-blocked version of the V-six with more torque produced lower down. Made as a fixed-head GT and GTS open targa (from 1971), it now had a steel body. Bolt-on alloys, rather than the more attractive centre-locking hubs found on the 206, were another recognition point. Just over 4,000 of the 206/246 were made between 1968 and 1973 before the introduction of the much less attractive two-plus-two Dino 308GT4.

■ LEFT *The 246 was replaced in 1974 by the uglier 308GT4, with a V-eight engine and two tiny extra rear seats.*

■ BELOW *The Ferrari badge on the rear of this car is an extra added by the owner: the 246 wore only Dino badges and was marketed at first as a separate marque.*

FERRARI

■ LEFT *The
ultimate Daytona
was the 365
lightweight
competition model
with alloy body
and Spartan trim.*

■ FERRARI DAYTONA

The Daytona 365GTB/4 was a proud,
last-gasp statement by Ferrari in the
superfast front-engined Grand Tourer
stakes. It was named Daytona in honour
of Ferrari's success in the American 24-
hour race of the same name; 365
denoted the capacity of each cylinder;
four stood for the number of camshafts.

It is odd to think that when this
sensational V-twelve supercar appeared,
replacing the 275GTB/4, it was greeted
with a sense of disappointment. The
world had been waiting for a mid-
engined Ferrari to challenge the
Lamborghini Miura, but what was
shown at the 1968 launch was a
conventional, front-engined Grand
Tourer clothed in a boldly elegant,
muscularly handsome coupé steel shell
– with a classic multitube chassis
frame – from the pen of Pininfarina.

Early cars had Plexiglas covered
lights, but most used retractable units
that gave the Daytona a menacing squint
from the front. At 3,530lb (1,601kg)

unladen it was a heavyweight, but it
packed a punch to match: against the
clock it would wind out to 174mph
(280kph), out of the reach of the more
radical Miura, soaring to 60 (96) in a
neck-straining 5.4 seconds. It would
even do 70mph (112kph) in reverse, if
you felt the need.

If the Daytona wasn't exactly cutting-
edge under the skin, neither was it
technically backward. The engine was a
magnificent 4.4-litre quad-cam V-twelve
producing 352bhp at 7500rpm. For good
weight distribution and traction, power
went through a rear-mounted five-speed
gearbox/transaxle unit while suspension
was by classic wishbones and coils all
round, stiffly set up to resist roll. Inside,

■ ABOVE *The
standard Daytona
had a well-
equipped cabin
with leather seats,
electric windows
and a superb Nardi
steering-wheel.*

■ LEFT *Most
sought-after of the
road-going models
is the Spider, of
which only 165
were produced.*

■ RIGHT *Only five competition specification Daytonas were built: with up to 450bhp it also made a sensational road car.*

FERRARI DAYTONA 365 GTB/4 (1968-73)

Engine	V-twelve
Capacity	4390cc
Power	352 @ 7500rpm
Transmission	5-speed manual
Top speed	174mph (280kph)
No. built	1,426

it was comfortably functional rather than luxurious, though electric windows and leather for the hip-hugging seats was standard. A few buyers wisely opted for air-conditioning too, because the cabin could get pretty stuffy when you were heaving away at the heavy unassisted steering around town. It was on the open road, of course, that the 365GTB/4 – often accused of being truck-like by its detractors – really sparkled: the steering shed its weight, the clunky suspension seemed to smooth out and the car simply flew. For many years it was the world's fastest road car. As word got around about the Daytona, buyers began to knock on Ferrari's door and, far from being a failure, the Daytona turned out to be one of the best-selling big Ferraris. When production ended in 1973, sales had reached 1,426, of which 165 were of the much-fancied Spider. Its replacement, the Boxer, never recaptured Daytona's muscular appeal.

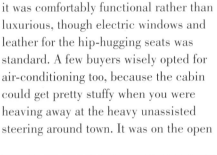

■ FAR LEFT *The production Daytona coupe was surprisingly successful, with 1,426 built in less than five years.*

■ NEAR LEFT *Early Daytonas had plexiglass headlight covers, but flip-up lights were a much more elegant solution.*

■ ABOVE *The dramatic profile of the Daytona-inspired Rover's 1976 SD1 saloon. It is now one of the most sought-after road Ferraris of all.*

■ RIGHT *The classic all-alloy Ferrari V-twelve had four overhead camshafts, 4.4 litres and 352bhp.*

FIAT

■ BELOW *Fiat built more than four million of the tiny 500s in a 20-year run, helping to put ordinary Italians on four wheels for the first time.*

■ FIAT 500

The tiny Fiat 500 is now something of a trendy cult car, its rounded egg-like body and diminutive size endearing it to millions. It was no joke when it was introduced in 1957: designed as utilitarian transportation for the masses, it put Italy on wheels during the 1960s and spawned several variants. More than four million were built in a 20-year production run.

A minimalist four-seater with kart-like handling, the original cars were powered by an aircooled 479cc flat-twin, mounted in the rear, later boosted

■ ABOVE *Early cars had rear-hinged "suicide" doors, but this is a post-1965 model with conventional arrangements.*

■ LEFT *The 500's tiny proportions still give it great appeal to modern drivers. All cars had sun-roofs.*

to 499cc that gave 18bhp. Hardly breath-taking – but the 500 could cruise at 55mph (88kph) and boasted Scrooge-like economy within over 52mpg with reach. Early, poorly built cars had rear-hinged "suicide" doors and a full-length sun-roof, post-1965 500F models had conventional front hinges, but the 500 kept its drum brakes and crude non-synchro "crash" gearbox to the end. The 1968 500L version gave buyers an alternative to the stark basic car, with reclining seats and carpets. The 500R was a last-of-the-line model using the engine and floorpan from the 126.

■ RIGHT *The Giardiniera was a useful estate version that outlived the standard saloon by two years.*

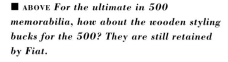

■ ABOVE *For the ultimate in 500 memorabilia, how about the wooden styling bucks for the 500? They are still retained by Fiat.*

From 1960, there was an estate version called the Giardiniera, with a surprisingly useful load area, and this model, latterly badged as an Autobianchi, outlived the standard model by a couple of years. Till the end, it retained rear-hinged doors. The pick of the crop, however, must be Carlo Abarth's SS models, which in 695 form were good for nearly 90mph (145kph).

You can recognize an Abarth by its flared arches, oil cooler and raised rear engine cover, which assist both cooling and stability.

■ BELOW *The Jolly was a special Vignale-built fun-car, now highly prized by collectors of 500s.*

■ ABOVE *The 500L of 1968 had plusher trim than the stark standard model, with carpets and reclining seats.*

FIAT 500 (1957–77)	
Engine	2-cylinder
Capacity	499cc
Power	18bhp
Transmission	4-speed manual
Top speed	60mph (96kph)
No. built	3,427,648 saloon 327,000 Giardiniera

FIAT

■ FIAT 850 COUPÉ

The sports versions of Fiat's bread-and-butter 850 arrived a year after the saloon version in 1965. Bertone styled a pretty two-seater spider variant while Fiat's own styling department produced a neat fastback four-seater coupé. The rear seats were near useless and the luggage space in the nose was modest, but this didn't stop people buying the little 850 in huge numbers.

■ ABOVE *With its sporty wooden steering-wheel and hooded instrument binnacle, the 850 had a real mini-Ferrari touch.*

■ ABOVE *The softer front-end treatment means this car is a Series 2 with the bigger 903cc engine.*

■ ABOVE *The 850 coupé was styled in-house by Fiat rather than by an outside designer.*

FIAT 850 COUPÉ	
Engine	4-cylinder
Capacity	843/903cc
Power	45-52bhp
Transmission	4-speed manual
Top speed	91mph (146kph)
No. built	380,000

With a little more power than the stock saloon, the coupé had a top speed of 90mph (145kph) and, despite the overhanging rear position of the willing little water-cooled pushrod engine, the handling was excellent, with light, positive steering, lots of grip and responsive brakes (discs at the front). 40mpg was another inducement.

The Geneva show of 1968 saw the introduction of a revised coupé with a bigger 903cc engine that pushed the top speed to about 95mph (152kph). There were minor styling revisions too, and the car carried on in this form until 1971, by which time the number of 850 coupés produced was 380,000. The Spider soldiered on until 1974 because of its popularity in America, although it was effectively replaced by the mid-engined X1/9.

■ NEAR RIGHT *The slats in the engine cover were the only give-away that the 850 was rear-engined.*

■ FAR RIGHT *Although 380,000 of the 850 coupes were built, rust has got the better of most.*

■ FIAT 124 SPIDER

With a production run of nearly 20 years, the Fiat 124 Spider must be the most successful Italian sportscar ever. It was deservedly successful and much more than just a pretty face. With a belt-drive twin-cam engine under the bonnet,

■ ABOVE *The 124 Spider in late form, with extra ride height and big Federal bumpers.*

■ FAR LEFT *The interiors had a high level of trim compared with rivals, as well as a superb hood that could be raised or lowered with one hand.*

■ NEAR LEFT *Abarth did a handful of specially tuned 124s to homologate the model for rallying.*

it was a spirited and sweet performer, while a well-located, coil-sprung rear suspension and four-wheel disc brakes gave it handling and refinement way beyond its British competitors. The handsome body was by none other than Pininfarina and had enduring appeal, even when ugly federal safety bumpers were hung on it in the mid-70s for North America, which was always the model's biggest market. Five gears were initially optional, later standard, and in later years there was even an automatic.

Engine size grew over the years, first to 1608cc in 1969, then to 1756cc in 1972, with a new 1592cc 1600 base model. A two-litre engine was standard across the board from 1979 as Fiat tried to counter progressively power-strangling emission regulations. Injection was introduced in 1980. The ultimate version was the supercharged VX, with a 135bhp engine.

Production ceased in 1985, later variants being marketed as Pininfarina rather than Fiat Spiders. There would be no proper Fiat-badged sportscar for another 10 years.

■ ABOVE *A specially tuned 124. Note the special alloys and hardtop.*

■ LEFT *The Spider Abarth was successful in international rallying. Its best results were second and third in the Monte Carlo Rally.*

FIAT 124 SPIDER (1966–85)	
Engine	In-line four
Capacity	1438/1608/1756/1995cc
Power	90–135bhp
Transmission	4/5-speed manual 3-speed auto
Top speed	102–120mph (164–193kph)
No. built	198,000

FIAT

■ FIAT 130 COUPÉ

Fiat's unloved, unlovely 130 saloon of the late 60s was always a much better car than people gave it credit for, with some fine engineering under its square-rigged body. Ironically, it spawned one of the best-looking cars of the 70s, the Pininfarina-styled 130 coupé of 1971. Perfectly proportioned and superbly elegant from any angle, it stood apart from many luxury coupés of its day in having ample room inside for four. Few coupés were as sumptuous either, with rich velour on the seats, veneer door cappings and high equipment levels:

■ LEFT *Simplicity and lack of fuss are the keys to the success of the shape. Few big cars look this good even today.*

■ BELOW *The original prototype wearing 130 saloon-style alloy wheels. Production lasted from 1971 to 1977.*

FIAT 130 COUPÉ (1971–77)	
Engine	V-six
Capacity	3235cc
Power	165bhp
Transmission	3-speed auto
	5-speed manual
Top speed	115–118mph
	(185–189kph)
No. built	4,491

electric windows, twin-tone "town and country" horns and an electric aerial were all standard.

Mechanically it was identical to the saloon, the smooth, free-revving V-six recently uprated from 2.8 to 3.2 litres to answer gripes about power performance. Power was a still modest 165bhp but torque went up dramatically, and these heavy 130s always felt quicker on the road than they were against the clock. Most were autos – by Borg Warner – though there was a five-speed manual option. These cars had the sophisticated independent suspension, shared at the rear with the Fiat Dino, and fine balance as well as a supple ride worthy of a

■ OPPOSITE *Pininfarina still rates the 130 coupé as one of the best designs it has ever put its name to.*

■ BELOW *More than anything, it was the unprestigious Fiat badge that led to the cars' poor sales.*

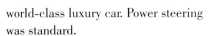

world-class luxury car. Power steering was standard.

In the end, it was the Fiat name that killed off the 130 coupé before its time: its prestige pulling power, in a class dominated by BMW and Mercedes, was always going to be limited. Production ceased in 1977, the coupé holding on a year longer than the saloon.

Today, rust has savaged many of the 130 coupés and good ones are highly sought-after.

■ ABOVE *The style of the 130 influenced the Lancia Gamma coupé and the Rolls-Royce Camargue.*

■ LEFT *The interior was sumptuous with velour seats, electric windows and plenty of room in the back.*

■ ABOVE *The 130 competed head-on with the likes of BMW's 3.0 CS coupé and the Citroen SM.*

■ RIGHT *The 130 was the biggest and most expensive car in Fiat's range. The company has not made anything like it since.*

FORD

■ FORD CONSUL/ ZEPHYR/ZODIAC MK I/II

The 1950 Consul was the first of the modern post-war cars from Dagenham, with a whole raft of new technology that brought the big Ford bang up to date.

Out went the separate chassis frame, in came unitary construction for the first time, making for a lighter, stiffer structure. Front suspension was by Macpherson struts – the old Pilot had to make do with a beam axle – while brakes were fully hydraulic at last. Overhead valves for the 1508cc four-cylinder engine meant more power, though it wasn't until 1951 that the big Ford got much-needed performance in the 2262cc six-cylinder Zephyr. There was a power-top convertible version by

■ ABOVE *A gathering of MkI and MKII Zephyrs and Zodiacs, the first post-war Fords.*

■ LEFT *The 90mph (145kph) Zephyr MkII, built by Carbodies, is one of the most sought-after models.*

FORD CONSUL/ZEPHYR/ZODIAC (1950–62)	
Engine	In-line 4 and 6-cylinder
Capacity	1508, 1703, 2262, 2553cc
Power	48–87bhp
Transmission	3/4-speed manual 3-speed auto
Top speed	75–90 mph (120–145kph)
No. built	406,792/682,400

■ FAR LEFT *The MkI Zephyr was the top-of-the-range six-cylinder car, here in typical two-tone livery with whitewall tyres.*

■ NEAR LEFT *Press advertisement for the new MkII models of 1956.*

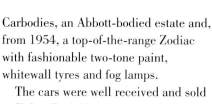

Carbodies, an Abbott-bodied estate and, from 1954, a top-of-the-range Zodiac with fashionable two-tone paint, whitewall tyres and fog lamps.

The cars were well received and sold well, but Ford did not rest on their laurels: the MkII Consul, Zephyr and Zodiac range arrived in 1956 with new, bigger styling and bigger four and six-cylinder engines of 1703 and 2553cc. The Zephyr/Zodiac could now top 90mph (145kph), the Consul about 80

(128). Again there was a Carbodies convertible – flash and now much sought-after – and a rare Abbott estate. From 1959, a sleeker MKII version had a lower roof line. Options included disc front brakes (from 1960), overdrive and Borg Warner automatic transmission.

Introduction of the MkIII in 1962 marked the end of the classic 50s-style Consuls, Zephyrs and Zodiacs. They had been among the best-loved British family saloons of their era.

■ ABOVE *The Zepyhr MkIII was made famous by the TV series Z Cars.*

■ RIGHT *All early Lotus Cortinas were finished in white with a green side flash.*

■ FORD LOTUS CORTINA

The 1963 Lotus Cortina was the product of a deal between Colin Chapman and Ford to produce a race and rally winner: Ford wanted to reflect a more sporting image on to its run-of-the-mill family saloon, while Lotus needed an entry into the mass production mainstream and another outlet for their twin-cam Ford-based engine. Ford supplied the basic two-door Cortina shell – with front suspension – to the Lotus factory at Cheshunt, Hertfordshire. Lotus installed their own 105bhp twin-cam engine, close-ratio four-speed gearbox and special rear suspension comprising coil springs, radius arms and an A bracket. Sitting lower on wider wheels and fitted with disc front brakes, all the MkI Lotus

Cortinas were painted cream, with a green flash on their flanks and featured split front bumpers and a matt black front grille. The light, powerful Lotus Cortina was an instant winner in saloon car racing and particularly memorable in the hands of Grand Prix ace Jim Clark. Its rallying prowess was initially held back by its unreliable A-frame rear suspension, but this reverted to semi-elliptics in 1966. Just 3,301 were built.

LOTUS CORTINA (1963–70)	
Engine	In-line four
Capacity	1558cc
Power	105–109bhp
Transmission	4-speed manual
Top speed	105–107mph (168–172kph)
No. built	3,301/4,032

■ RIGHT *The MkII version looked much more ordinary but had more power and was slightly quicker.*

■ FAR RIGHT *The MkII twin-cam engine gave 109bhp, pushing the car up to 107mph (171kph).*

■ RIGHT *MkII models were closer to stock production models inside and a bit plusher than the MkI.*

■ LEFT *The twin-cam engine was essentially as found in the Lotus Elan sportscar.*

The MkII of 1967 had all new bodywork but underpinnings basically similar to the MkI. Power rose to 109bhp. A limited slip diff and an oil cooler became options. The cream-green livery was no longer obligatory. The MkII was slightly quicker than the MkI but has not proved as sought-after. Connoisseurs see it perhaps as less authentic because it was built among ordinary Cortinas on Dagenham production lines. Ford removed the Lotus badges after seven months and called the car Cortina Twin Cam. Production ended in 1970.

FORD

■ FORD ESCORT RS

In Britain in the 1970s a young man's four-wheeled fantasy was a quick Escort, the hot-shot saloon based on the best-selling Ford family runabout.

Leaving the exotic Lotus and Twin-Cam cars on one side, the mass-market hot Escort generation really began with the Mexico (named in honour of Ford's victory in the London to Mexico Rally) and RS2000 models of 1970 and 1973. These were punchy, raucous cars with knockabout rear-wheel-drive handling

■ ABOVE *MkI and MKII Escorts were formidable rally contenders throughout the 1970s.*

■ ABOVE *RS Escorts got more instruments on the dashboard, special bucket seats and a sports wheel.*

■ ABOVE *Many RS Escort owners removed the bumpers to make their cars look even more aggressive.*

■ ABOVE *A shovel-nosed RS2000 MkII lines up with a MkI RS model and a Mexico.*

and distinctive trim, including laddish quarter bumpers and broad body striping. They were capable of more than 100mph (160kph) in their day, and their enormous appeal was bolstered by Ford's endless rallying success with the model.

Technically the cars were straightforward and they performed all the better for it, with MacPherson strut suspension and disc brakes at the front and a live rear axle suspended on leaf springs at the rear. The steel shell was a monocoque which was stiffened on some

FORD ESCORT RS (1968–80)	
Engine	In-line four
Capacity	1993cc
Power	86–110bhp
Transmission	4-speed manual
Top speed	103–112mph (165–180kph)
No. built	N/A

versions to take the extra power.

The MkII Escort-based RS2000 of 1975 took the concept a stage further, its shovel-nosed styling (the "droopsnoot" was a tacked-on piece of polyurethane

■ ABOVE *Relatively light bodywork, lots of power and agile rear drive handling gave the Escort its competition prowess.*

said to reduce drag by 16 per cent) and up-market interior setting it apart from both the lesser family car Escorts and the enthusiast types who bought the original MkI RS cars.

Not that the Escort had gone soft: with 100bhp the RS2000 was quicker than ever and just as much fun to drive on a twisty road. Order books were soon

■ ABOVE *The RS 1800 in action. This model was a low volume homologation special with a twin-cam engine and four wheel disc brakes: many were rallied by their owners.*

■ LEFT *The rounded MkI shell with its dog-bone shaped grille has more appeal for collectors...*

■ BELOW *...than the squared-up MKII which appeared in 1975. This is an RS1600 MkII.*

bulging, its profile undoubtedly raised by regular rubber-burning television appearances in a British TV show called *The Professionals*.

Ford boosted its profit margins even more with X-Pack options for boy racers who wanted to go that bit faster.

The MkII Escorts were replaced by front-wheel-drive cars in 1980, the sporty flagship role taken over by the XR3. Totally different in style and engineering it might have been, but in many ways the appeal – purebred boy-racer – was identical.

FORD

■ FORD MUSTANG

The Ford Mustang is one of the great American success stories, a sporty compact with youthful appeal that captured the spirit of the times perfectly when it was launched in 1964 and entered the history books as one of the fastest-selling cars of all time: 418,000 in the first year, over a million by 1966.

Such was the hype surrounding the Mustang when it appeared at the New York World Fair in 1964 that the first cars were auctioned off to the highest bidders: one buyer slept in his car overnight while the cheque cleared, to ensure he wasn't out bid. Brainchild of young hotshot Ford executive Lee Iacocca, the Mustang was based on the floorpan of the Budget Falcon range, with coil-spring and wishbone suspension at the front and a beam axle on leaf springs at the rear. Its crisp, pseudo-European styling came in notchback, fastback and convertible

FORD MUSTANG (1964–73)	
Engine	Straight six and V-eight
Capacity	2788–6997cc
Power	101–390bhp
Transmission	3/4-speed manual 3-speed auto
Top speed	90–130mph (145–209kph)
No. built	2,204,038

MUSTANG BOSS 302

■ ABOVE LEFT *From the late 1960s onwards, Mustangs started to get bigger and uglier, though top-of-the- range models like this Boss 351 were certainly rapid.*

■ ABOVE RIGHT *Worst of the bunch was the flabby Grande model with its ugly vinyl roof, an attempt to take the Mustang up-market.*

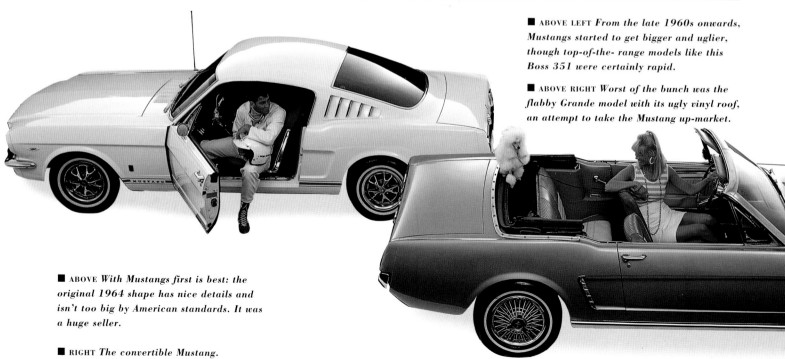

■ ABOVE *With Mustangs first is best: the original 1964 shape has nice details and isn't too big by American standards. It was a huge seller.*

■ RIGHT *The convertible Mustang.*

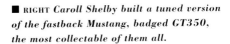

■ ABOVE *Sport models tried to emulate European sportscars with a dashboard packed with dials. This is a rare manual.*

■ RIGHT *Caroll Shelby built a tuned version of the fastback Mustang, badged GT350, the most collectable of them all.*

form and could be ordered with a vast range of options that allowed buyers to tailor the car to their own requirements: poseurs could opt for the weakling straight six, enthusiasts for a whole raft of V-eights escalating in power from 195 to 390bhp. There were lazy automatics, urgent "stick-shift" manuals, sports handling packages, disc front brakes (to counter fade on the more powerful models) and innumerable trim options.

For the ultimate in Mustang muscle, Carroll Shelby offered an officially sanctioned road racer based on the

fastback called the GT350 that has passed into legend, a muscle car par excellence with up to 425bhp in later seven-litre GT500 form. In the film *Bullitt* (1968), it was a GT390 that Steve McQueen used to pursue the Dodge Charger.

The basic, pretty shape continued fairly unmolested into 1968 as rivals began to hurriedly prepare their own "Pony" cars.

Then longer, paunchier 1969 Mustangs marked the start of the rot (particularly the awful vinyl-roofed Grande) and by

1971 the once lithe 'stang had become a tubby nag, though high-performance models such as the Mach 1 and the Boss were at least still quick.

The Mustang reached its nadir with the 1973 model Mustang II, a meek and mild little economy car launched in the wake of the oil crisis that was intended to recapture a little of the spirit of the original.

Nobody was fooled but it sold well, notching up more than a million sales. Unlike the 1964 car, however, it will never be a classic.

■ LEFT *The fastback is the best-looking of the Mustangs. A GT350 like this one could top 130mph (209kph), while the meekest of the six-cylinder shopping models could hardly manage 90 (145).*

FORD

■ BELOW *The Thunderbird was Ford's answer to the Chevrolet Corvette: it was faster in a straight line, but no sportscar.*

■ FORD THUNDERBIRD

Designed as a retort to the Chevrolet Corvette, the original 1955 Ford Thunderbird was a styling high-water mark in 1950s America. Standing aside from the hordes of wallowing barges that ruled the American roads, Ford created a two-seater sporty "personal car" with simple, elegant lines (modest fins, restrained bumpers) and minimal brightwork but with a classic long nose and sweeping rear deck proportions around a snug-two seater cockpit.

It wasn't a sportscar in the true European sense, more of a brisk luxury tourer, but the image was right and the car scored over the contemporary

■ LEFT *From 1957, the previously clean shape gained bigger fins. The "Continental" spare wheel kit was optional.*

■ BELOW *The dashboard was typical 1950s fare, with fussy details and poor ergonomics. Power steering and automatic transmission were standard.*

Corvette – which it outsold handsomely – in having a V-eight engine under the bonnet. With 200bhp from a Mercury-sourced 4.8-litre V-eight, the Thunderbird would steam up to 114mph (183kph) and whisk you up to 60 (96) in under 10 seconds: rather quicker, in other words, than an Aston Martin of the

day. Bigger 5.1-litre engines saw a power hike to 212bhp in 1957. Around corners it was a different story with its soft springs and low-geared steering, though compared to the average Detroit barge it was reasonably nimble.

There was an automatic model and a three-speed manual with optional

overdrive transmission available. There was a power soft-top and an optional hardtop (with that whimsical porthole in the pillar for 1956), while the 1956 Thunderbirds also had the "Continental" spare wheel.

It wasn't to last. The grille and fins grew more gawky for 1957, and for 1958

■ TOP *In America, the early Thunderbirds have a loyal following.*

■ ABOVE *The cigar-shaped styling of 1960s Thunderbirds was clean, but the cars had grown much bigger.*

■ ABOVE *Fins were restrained on the first cars, which were strictly two-seaters.*

■ LEFT *Although the Thunderbird was no sportscar, it was at least fast, capable of 120mph (193kph) with the biggest 212bhp 5.1-litre V-eight engine.*

■ BELOW *By the 1970s, the Thunderbird had become just another big American car, based closely on contemporary saloon models.*

FORD THUNDERBIRD (1955–57)	
Engine	V-eight
Capacity	4785–5113cc
Power	193–212bhp
Transmission	3-speed manual 3-speed auto
Top speed	110–120mph (177–193kph)
No. built	53,166

Ford introduced a completely new Thunderbird, a bigger, flabbier device with ugly squared-up styling and a grille like a mouth organ. In the early 60s the "Bird" regained some of its youthful good looks, if not its sports-car pretensions. The 1955–57 cars, almost a legend, are highly collectable.

FORD

■ FORD CAPRI

The Ford Capri of 1969 was the European version of the hugely successful Mustang, a basic four-seater GT sold in endless combinations of engine and trim. Built in Britain and West Germany, the range started with a humble 1.3-litre in-line four as found in the Escort. In Britain there were 1.6 and 2.0-litre V-four models going right up to the three-litre V-six. In Germany there were additional 1.7 and 2.3-litre models. There were enough trim options to send your head reeling: the L was the poverty model, the XL the mid-ranger, with the GT and luxury GXL models at the top of the range. The basic shell and struts with beam rear axle were the same throughout. There were various types of four-speed manual gearbox and, on the bigger-engined versions, an automatic option. All cars had front disc brakes, with drums at the rear, and rack-and-pinion steering power assisted on some of the 3 litre models.

Everything from the 1.6 GT up could

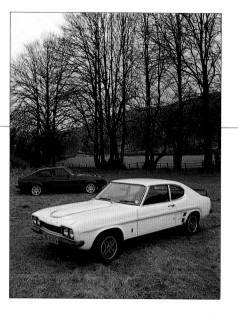

■ LEFT *MkI and MkIII Capris compared: the MkIII had a rear hatchback and cleaner lines, but most of the mechanics and general proportions were identical.*

do over 100mph (160kph), with 117mph (189kph) on offer from the fastest 3.0-litre model, quite a hairy car in its day. Easily the most desirable of the MkI Capris were the RS2600 and 3100 cars: the German-built RS2600 with its Harry Weslake-improved, fuel-injected V-six was a hot homologation special with 150bhp. The 3100 followed it in 1973,

FORD CAPRI (1969–86)

Engine	In-line four, V-four, V-six
Capacity	1297–2994cc
Power	61–160bhp
Transmission	4/5-speed manual 3-speed auto
Top speed	86–130mph (138–209kph)
No. built	1,172,900 MkI/403,612 MkII/ 324,045 MkIII

■ LEFT *The RS2600 and 3100 models were homologation specials with more power, produced in small numbers.*

■ ABOVE *The MkII Capri of 1974, here in mid-range XL trim. Mechanically the cars shared much with the Escort.*

■ RIGHT *Early MkI Capris like this are now rare. This is the top-of-the-range 3.0 GT.*

■ LEFT *The Capri made an ideal tin-top racer. Here a pair of MkIII models fight it out at Silverstone.*

■ RIGHT *Perhaps the best of all the Capris was the 280 Brooklands, a special last-of-the-line model with leather seats and special green paintwork.*

OTHER MAKES

■ FAIRTHORPE

The initial attempts by Air Vice-Marshal Donal "Pathfinder" Bennett to produce a British "people's car" (the bubble-like Atom) gave way to the manufacture of sportscars. The cars – the Electron, the Electrina, the Zeta and latterly the TX-S/TX-SS – were always on the fringes and in the late 70s the firm closed its doors.

■ FALCON

Falcon Shells was formed in Britain in 1957 to produce glassfibre shells for Ford-based specials. About 2,000 were made. The closest the company got to making a complete car was the 515, a pretty coupé with, as usual, a Ford engine on a tubular chassis. Only 25 were built.

■ LEFT *The 2.8 Injection could manage 130mph (209kph) and had improved suspension and a five-speed gearbox.*

■ FRAZER NASH

Frazer Nash Cars built in the 1920s and early 1930s were stark, chain-driven and fast, but after 1936 virtually the only cars coming through the Isleworth showrooms, Middlesex, were BMWs with Frazer Nash badging. After 1945, Frazer Nash sportscars were modern and well-engineered and used the Bristol engine and gearbox – the result of an ultimately aborted collaboration between the two British companies. Its most famous post-war car was the Le Mans, with Bristol power: just 34 were built.

again built to homologate Ford's race Capri of the day with its 400bhp quad-cam V-six. The British-built road car made do with a Weber carburettor and an over-bored version of the stock V-six, giving a still respectable 148bhp. These rare and highly desirable Capris are not difficult to spot with their fat alloy wheels, sporty quarter bumpers and – on the 3100 – duck-tail spoiler.

The MkII Capri of 1974 updated the model with a three-door hatchback body on the same floorpan. The MkIII Capri four years later smartened up the look with four-shot lights and detail improvements. It lived until 1986 when the final 280 Brooklands Limited edition rolled off the German production lines.

Today, early Capris are rare and all of the more interesting high-performance versions are much sought-after.

GORDON KEEBLE

■ GORDON KEEBLE

The Gordon Keeble sounded like and should have been an ideal recipe for commercial success: cheap American V-eight muscle combined with Italian styling and British chassis know-how.

First seen in 1960 as the prototype Gordon GT (and inspired by the Corvette-powered Peerless created by Jim Keeble and John Gordon), the Gordon Keeble didn't go into faltering production until 1964, renamed GK1. With a 300bhp engine from the Chevrolet Corvette, the Gordon Keeble, with its glassfibre body – the prototype

GORDON KEEBLE (1964–66)	
Engine	V-eight
Capacity	5395cc
Power	300bhp
Transmission	4-speed manual
Top speed	135mph (217kph)
No. built	99

■ BELOW *The original steel-bodied prototype at its Motorshow debut in 1960. It was nicknamed "The Growler".*

■ ABOVE *Styled by Bertone, the Gordon Keeble was produced at Eastleigh near Southampton. It was one of the fastest four-seaters of its day.*

■ BELOW *Gordon Keeble boss George Wansborough hands over a new GK to a happy customer. By this time the company was already in trouble.*

■ ABOVE *The dashboard looked like something from a jet flight-deck, with toggle switches for everything.*

■ LEFT *Just 99 Gordon Keebles were built, but because the glassfibre body does not suffer from rust, the survival rate is high. The styling had echoes of Bertone's Alfa 2600 Sprint of the same period.*

was steel bodied – was devastatingly quick, good for 70mph (112kph) in first and nearly 140 (225) in top. In fact, so lusty was the torque, the gearbox was nearly superfluous. Handling was good too, with a DeDion axle at the rear and a complex space-frame chassis of square section providing grip, balance and a good ride although the unassisted steering suffered from too much kickback. The simple, restrained four-seater coupé shape with its elegantly slanted twin lamps was the work of a 21-year-old Giugiaro, then chief stylist at Bertone, who later to moved on to Ghia before finally setting up his own studio in the late 60s.

By 1965 only 80 cars had been built as the fledgling company battled with component supply problems and under-capitalization. Had the factory – based at Eastleigh, Southampton, on the site of the local airport – been able to build the cars quickly enough, there was no doubt the Gordon Keeble would have been a success, if only because it was under-priced. A further 19 were built under new management in 1966, but to no avail, and the company closed its doors that year. Today, 90 Gordon Keebles are still on the road.

OTHER MAKES

■ GILBERN

The only car manufacturer based in Wales, Gilbern was started in 1959 by Giles Smith and Bernard Driese, and they marketed some fine sporting products until 1973. The firm successfully made the transition from kit cars to genuine complete cars. These included the Genie and the last-of-the-line Invader with Ford V-six power. Genie and Invader were also sold in component form to beat purchase tax.

■ GINETTA

Four enthusiastic British brothers, Bob, Ivor, Trevor and Douglas Walklett made their first production vehicle, the G2, in 1958. Before 1968, the cars were remarkably successful in club racing, and thereafter the firm's staple product was the G15 coupé, with the Hillman Imp power unit, until the imposition of VAT in 1973 killed the fiscal attraction of component cars.

■ GLAS

Hans Glas GmbH was an old-established German manufacturer of agricultural machinery when it started making the Goggo scooter in 1951, following up with the production of the Goggomobil in 1955. By 1965 the firm was offering a full range of cars, including a pretty 1700GT and a 2600 V-eight coupé, both with styling by Frua of Italy. In 1966 BMW acquired Glas, and the marque name disappeared in 1968, the last GT coupés using BMW engines. The Glas 1700 saloon stayed in production in South Africa for some years.

■ GSM

A successful club racer in its day, the GSM Delta was another Ford-based British sportscar. Its origins were in Capetown, where in 1958–59 Bob van Niekirk built the Ford-based Dart, styled out-of-hours in England by a Rootes stylist. A subsidiary venture saw the car also being made in Kent, in England. Undercapitalization led to collapse in 1961, just a year after the car came to England.

HONDA

■ HONDA S800

After the Second World War, Honda made its fortune building motorcycles. Only in 1962 did it make its first car, the tiny S500 sportscar. Available in convertible and coupé, it was heavily influenced by motorcycle design, its double overhead camshaft (DOHC), hemi-head 531cc engine having a roller-bearing crank and four carburettors. Maximum power –

■ BELOW *The Honda started life as the S500 but wasn't exported until it had become the S800 in 1965.*

■ ABOVE *The interior was cozy but well-equipped by small sportscar standards.*

HONDA S800 (1965–79)	
Engine	In-line four
Capacity	791cc
Power	70bhp
Transmission	4-speed manual
Top speed	95mph (152kph)
No. built	11,400

44bhp – came at a screaming 8000rpm, almost unheard-of in a road car you could buy in a showroom. Interestingly, the car had chain drive to independently-sprung rear wheels, redolent of motorcycle practice. Discs on front wheels hinted at the S500's cost-no-object specification, although the separate chassis was backward even in the mid-1960s. In 1964 the S500 became the 606cc S600, and finally in 1965 the S800, the best-known variant.

When the S800 became available in Britain in 1967 it had conventional drive to the rear wheels and an ordinary live axle located by trailing arms and a Panhard rod. It was good value, undercutting the Mini Cooper and Triumph Spitfire, and was praised for slick gearchange, excellent 30mpg economy and remarkable acceleration for engine size. Handling was predictable, ride firm.

■ LEFT *The coupé version was offered alongside the convertible. With an amazing 70bhp from just 800cc, the S800 could do 95mph (152kph).*

■ OPPOSITE *The S800 was Honda's answer to small British sportscars like the Triumph Spitfire and Austin Healey Sprite, although it tended to be more expensive.*

■ BELOW LEFT *The last S800s were built in 1970 and have since gained a dedicated following among sportscar enthusiasts.*

■ BELOW RIGHT *The tiny powerhouse of the S800. With its roller-bearing crankshaft – inspired by Honda's motorcycle experience – it would rev to 10,000rpm.*

OTHER MAKES

■ HEINKEL

This aircraft-manufacturing firm from Stuttgart was a robust player in the bubblecar boom of the mid-1950s, with its 174cc Cabin Cruiser models. With one wheel to the rear and two at the front, the cars featured entry through the front – the whole nose of the car was a hinged door. In 1958, the last year of German production, the design was sold to Dundalk Engineering in the Irish Republic, and from 1961 the machine was manufactured in England by Trojan. Approximately 2,000 were also made in Argentina.

■ HERON

Heron Plastics of Greenwich, London, manufactured its first Europa coupé in 1960, having earlier made special bodies for cars such as the Austin Seven. The car finally made limited production in 1962, and Peter Monteverdi used it as a basis for his two-off MBM coupé. Unfortunately, after only 12 cars had been sold, Heron was wound up.

■ HILLMAN

Hillmans were always fairly conventional British cars, a trend continued after the Second World War with the mainstay Minx model. One highlight was the rear-engined Imp, but the manufacturing facility at Linwood, near Glasgow, in Scotland, was to prove disastrous. In 1964 the Chrysler Corporation acquired a substantial stake in Rootes, leading to a full take-over in 1967. The Hillman name disappeared in 1976, before the company's purchase by Peugeot in 1979.

■ HOTCHKISS

Hotchkiss began making cars in France in 1903. Early products were medium-to-large tourers. In 1937 Hotchkiss acquired Amilcar but this did not much help the company, nor did its post-war manufacture of the front-wheel-drive Hotchkiss-Grégoire, though its post-war cars maintained a reputation for good performance and quality. In 1950 Peugeot bought controlling interest. Three years later amalgamation with Delahaye saw the end of car manufacture.

■ HRG

HRG of Tolworth, Surrey, was founded in 1936 by Ron Godfrey, Guy Robbins and EA Halford. After the Second World War the firm's 1100 and 1500 models were intended to carry on the Frazer Nash tradition and looked much the same as they had done pre-war, although the 1500 Aerodynamic was a brief experiment with a modern low-drag closed-body design. After 1956 the firm concentrated on general engineering. Either Meadows or Singer engines were employed and the drive was by propshaft.

■ HUMBER

Sister marque to Hillman, Humber was always at the upper end of the British market. Like many Midlands car firms in Britain, the classic Humber, the Super Snipe, came in the late 1940s and typified a range of luxurious saloons used as official cars and as chauffeur-driven bank managers' carriages, which continued until the late 60s. From 1967, when Rootes was taken over by Chrysler, the only Humber produced was an up-market version of the Hillman Hunter.

Iso

■ ISO GRIFO

Iso of Italy began its car manufacturing career in the mid-1950s producing the Isetta bubblecars (also built under licence by BMW), but in 1962 they decided to enter the high-class GT car market with the Rivolta. In many ways this cleanly styled four-seater coupé was an Italian Gordon Keeble featuring a similar box-section frame with Dedion rear suspension and a Bertone-built steel body. Like the Keeble, it had a Corvette V-eight engine under the bonnet, so performance was impressive:

■ ABOVE *The ISO Grifo of 1963 had styling by Bertone, with the panels pressed out in steel. The engine was not their own unit, but a Corvette V-eight.*

■ LEFT *In profile, the Grifo looked as exciting as any Ferrari and had better roadholding than many of its supercar contemporaries.*

■ BELOW *The four-seater Rivolta was the first ISO and used many of the same mechanicals as the Grifo in a more sober coupé body, also styled by Bertone.*

it had a top speed of 140mph (225kph) with the manual gearbox. Comfortable and agile, the Rivolta was well received – and enjoyed much more success than its Gordon Keeble alter ego. It was only with the début of the Grifo a year later, however, that the fledgling supercar builder really made its mark. By shortening the Rivolta chassis (schemed by the celebrated ex-Ferrari engineer Bizzarrini) and clothing it in a sensational coupé body – again by Bertone – Iso now had a car to challenge Ferrari, even if purists would always turn their noses up at the American V-eight engine.

The original 5.4-litre V-eight came in two states of tune – 300 and 365bhp –

■ RIGHT *The Grifo came first as a 5.4-litre, then as a 7-litre – each with a unit borrowed from the Chevrolet Corvette range. A few late cars had Ford engines.*

with a top speed of up to 160mph (257kph) in its most potent form. Buyers could opt for four- or five-speed gearboxes or even an automatic, a fitment unheard-of on the Grifo's pure-bred rivals. Naturally, four-wheel disc brakes were deemed necessary for a car of such weight and power and in the right hands these elegant, well-engineered cars were as quick as anything on the road. The ultimate version was the 390bhp seven-litre, manufactured from 1968 to challenge the Ferrari Daytona and Maserati Ghibli.

■ LEFT *From any angle the Grifo had stunning good looks.*

ISO GRIFO (1963-74)

Engine	V-eight
Capacity	5359-6998cc
Power	300-390bhp
Transmission	4/5-speed manual 3 speed auto
Top speed	150-170 mph (241-273kph)
No. built	504

Iso claimed 170mph (273kph) for this flagship coupé and, although this figure was never confirmed independently, there was no doubting its formidable acceleration: 70 (112) was attainable in the first gear alone. A bonnet hump distinguished the seven-litre car from lesser Grifos.

Later Grifos had a redesigned, chisel-edged nose with pop-up lights and for the last two years of production employed Ford "Cleveland" V-eights rather than Corvette engines. By then Iso were on the rocks financially, and the company died in the midst of the fuel crisis in 1974.

OTHER MAKES

■ **INVICTA**

The British marque Invicta lasted only four years after the Second World War. By 1950, AFN Ltd had taken over its assets after the failure of the mythical Black Prince model with its twin-cam straight six, semi-auto gearbox and built-in hydraulic jacks. Before the war, the firm, founded by Noel Macklin and Oliver Lyle (of Tate & Lyle) in 1925, had made some very fine cars with Henry Meadows and Blackburne power units, but they were always extremely expensive.

■ ABOVE *Just 504 Grifos were built in a production run lasting ten years. Later cars* had a restyled nose with retractable headlights.

JAGUAR

■ JAGUAR XK 120/140/150

In a Britain battered by war and starved of motoring excitement, it is perhaps little wonder that the Jaguar XK120, launched at the Earls Court Motor Show in 1948, was such a sensation. Conceived as a low-volume dream car rather than a serious production machine, it was destined to become a great dollar-earner for Britain (most XKs went to America) and one of the most celebrated classics of all.

The package was unbeatable. Jaguar boss William Lyons shaped a flowing two-seater roadster body that was a model of elegant purity, taking for inspiration the pre-war BMW 328 roadster. On looks alone it would have sold handsomely, but there was more: under the long, tapering bonnet was a brand-new twin-cam straight-six engine, the classic 3.4-litre XK unit that was to survive well into the 90s and power everything from Le Mans winners to tanks and fire engines. Pumping out a smooth 160bhp on twin SU carburettors, it made sure the '120' tag was no idle boast: in fact the 120mph (193kph) XK was for a time the world's fastest

■ ABOVE *The XK in-line six in its original form. It made the 120 the world's fastest production car.*

■ ABOVE *The drophead coupé version of the XK140.*

standard production car. Later SE (Special Equipment) versions with high-lift cams and twin exhausts would hike power to 180bhp. Few sportscars were as civilized as the XK with its supple suspension, though the brakes (drums, of course, but poorly cooled because of the modern all-enveloping bodywork) were never much to write home about.

Jaguar were unprepared for the demand, and XK production remained tiny in 1949 as the company tooled-up for the big-volume steel-body version that came on stream in 1950.

From then on, there was no looking back. An elegant fixed-head version was announced in 1951 and a roomier drophead coupé in 1953. The XK140 of

■ ABOVE *NUB 120, the famous Alpine Rally-winning XK120.*

■ RIGHT *The interior of the XK120 coupé was more luxurious than that of the roadster, with wood veneer on the dash.*

■ OPPOSITE *The XK120 in coupé form, its bulbous roof-line inspired by Bugatti coupés of the 1930s.*

■ RIGHT *The XK140 – here in coupe form – had new bumpers and a different grille as well as improved steering.*

JAGUAR XK 120/140/150 (1948-61)	
Engine	Straight six
Capacity	3442-3781cc
Power	160-265bhp
Transmission	4-speed manual 3-speed auto
Top speed	120-135 mph (193-217kph)
No. built	12,055/9,051/9,398

■ BELOW LEFT *Last of the XK line was the 150 of 1957, now with disc brakes all round and an optional 3.8-litre engine.*

■ BELOW RIGHT *In S form with the triple-carb 3.8-litre engine, the XK150 was good for 130mph (209kph).*

1954 gained more power (190bhp as standard, 210 with SE pack), bigger bumpers and – best of all – rack-and-pinion steering while retaining all three body options. If the coupé's roof line didn't improve its looks, then at least it offered rear seats for the first time.

Last of the XK line was the 1957 150, basically on the same chassis but with all new body panels: there was a voguish wrap-around front screen, a higher scuttle and more width as Jaguar tried to string out the model's appeal until the E-Type arrived in 1961. The braking problem was met with four-wheel Dunlop discs, and in the car's triple-carburettor 3.8-litre 'S' form (from 1959) power soared to 265bhp with a top speed of 135mph (217kph). There were 210bhp and 250bhp 3.4 cars, twin-carburettor 3.8s, and the odd automatic, highlighting demands for more luxury, particularly from Americans. Like all XKs, the 150 was great value, half the price of the contemporary Aston DB4 and Mercedes 300SL. It was getting old, though, and Jaguar had something more exciting in the wings – the E-Type.

■ ABOVE *The 150 came as roadster, drophead or coupé and with a choice of manual or automatic transmission.*

JAGUAR

■ JAGUAR MKII

The sight of a Jaguar MkII inspires a misty-eyed emotional response like no other 60s saloon. For a decade from 1959, the year of Britain's first motorway, the compact Jaguar was the bread and butter of Browns Lane, Coventry. It was the last proper sports saloon the company ever made.

The MkII was nothing if not versatile. It was favoured not just by the criminal fraternity (it was no accident that the James Fox character drove a white MkII in Donald Cammell's superb 1970 film *Performance*, or Michael Caine's pursuers a red one in the classic *Get Carter* of 1971) but also by the law itself because it was so wickedly fast. At the same time the MkII was also a very respectable car: a quiet, comfortable and classy businessman's express for the stockbroker belt. It made a fine name for itself on the track as a saloon-car racer, and industry personalities such as

■ ABOVE *The classic lines of the Jaguar MkII, first seen in 1959, were derived from the MkI 2.4, announced in 1955.*

■ BELOW *The MkII featured leather seat trim and up-market wood veneer for the dash and door cappings.*

■ LEFT *Jaguar gave the MkII a bigger rear window and different semi-open wheel spats to help brake cooling.*

■ LEFT *With the 3.8 engine the MkII could reach 125mph (201kph).*

■ BELOW *This 1966 MkII is one of the last to have big bumpers: slimline bumpers were announced for the 240/340 models of 1967.*

Graham Hill and Colin Chapman gave the MkII the stamp of approval by using them off-duty too.

Technically the MkII wasn't vintage Jaguar (though the unitary shell had broken new ground for the company on its 2.4 'MkI' progenitor of 1955), but its beautifully-balanced shape had the classic William Lyons touch, as did the interior with its leather seats and wooden dash and door cappings, the facia packed with dials and switches like a wartime bomber's flight deck. The MkII owner could do a legal 125mph (201kph) if he owned the full-house 3.8

manual overdrive car – it was the fastest saloon on the road for a time in the early 60s – or 120 (193) in the 3.4. The leisurely 2.4, on the other hand, couldn't even manage 100 (160) – which was why Jaguar's press department never allowed one out to be tested.

More than 80,000 MkIIs were sold, and the model inspired a whole raft of more expensive variations on the same theme: the S-Type, the 420 and even a Daimler with its own special V-eight engine. It is the pure original MkII, however, that has won the hearts of the public.

JAGUAR MKII (1959-69)	
Engine	Straight six
Capacity	2483/3442/3781cc
Power	120-220bhp
Transmission	4-speed manual 3-speed auto
Top speed	(3.8) 125mph (201kph)
No. built	83,980

■ BELOW *The 3.8-litre engine gave a claimed 220bhp, making the MkII one of the fastest saloons on the road.*

■ ABOVE *The famous leaping Jaguar designed by motoring artist Gordon Crosby. Safety legislation outlawed its use on later Jaguars.*

■ RIGHT *The XK engine was a tight fit in the MkII, with not much room for maintenance.*

JAGUAR

■ JAGUAR E-TYPE

The Jaguar E-Type was an instant classic, an exercise in cool aerodynamic theory and unashamed showmanship producing probably the most beautiful sportscar of the 60s. It had the ability to live up to the looks, too. The 150mph

■ ABOVE *On the open road the E-Type was good for over 140mph (225kph). The car nearest the camera is an early Series 1 3.8 roadster, behind is a Series 2 coupe.*

■ RIGHT *From the outside the 3.8 and 4.2 Series 1 E-Types are hard to tell apart, but the bucket seats are a giveaway: this is a 3.8.*

(241kph) that Jaguar claimed for the E-Type was devastatingly quick in 1961 (in reality only the tweaked-up press cars could achieve it, and 140 [225] was nearer the truth), making the new Jaguar Britain's fastest production car. Better still, it was probably Britain's greatest bargain pricewise, undercutting its nearest rival, the Aston Martin DB4, by a third.

That curvy shell, inspired by the Le Mans-winning D-Type racer, was immensely stiff – all the better to take advantage of its new wishbone and coil-spring independent rear suspension. Combining near-limousine ride comfort with vice-like grip, even on the slender cross-ply tyres that looked like something off a bike to modern eyes, the new Jaguar handled superbly. Providing the power was the 3.8-litre XK engine, already 13 years old but still well worthy of the new chassis. The same couldn't be said of the elderly, slow-shifting Moss gearbox, a feature of all Jaguars since the 1930s or the disc brakes that were spoilt by an uncertain-feeling pedal.

■ LEFT *Series 1 and Series 2 compared. The later car has open headlights to comply with American safety regulations.*

JAGUAR E-TYPE (1961-75)	
Engine	Straight six/V-twelve
Capacity	3781/4235/5343cc
Power	265bhp
Transmission	4-speed manual 3-speed auto
Top speed	Up to 150mph (241kph)
No. built	All models: 72,507

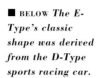

■ LEFT *In 1971 the E-Type became a Series 3 with a brand new V-twelve engine. Performance was back up to levels achieved with the Series 1 cars. Note the bigger grille and flared arches.*

■ BELOW *The E-Type's classic shape was derived from the D-Type sports racing car.*

■ ABOVE *Early E-Types had rather shallow footwells, restricting legroom. These "flat-floor" models are now few and far between.*

Pop stars, racing drivers and royalty jostled for position in an ever-lengthening waiting list for the car. Lew Grade wanted to borrow one for his new British TV series, *The Saint*, but Jaguar turned him down – they could sell every car they could make.

Despite the demand, development continued. The bigger 4.2 engine from 1964 was torquier and came with a much better gearbox and brakes. Seats and trim improved, as did the electrics,

making the 4.2 Series 1Es the best of the bunch. Appeals for a roomier car were answered by a two-plus-two version in 1966 and there was even an automatic as Jaguar tried to reconcile the E's performance image with a need to increase sales in America.

The rot was beginning to set in, however, and from the launch of Series 2 in 1968, middle age seemed to creep up on the E unawares. North American safety demands tarnished the purity of its styling with fussy open lights and strangled its power with emission controls, so that by the turn of the decade the car was a shadow of its youthfully vigorous former self. The final V-twelve Series 3 cars completed the sanitation process. Smooth and fast but somehow less soulful, the sylphlike shape was ruined on the longer, fatter V-twelve by fashionable fat arches and a cheap chrome grille. The once legendary sex symbol was a flabby spent force, living on old glories, not to mention borrowed time. It is amazing to think that Jaguar, gearing up for the E's

■ ABOVE *The shape everyone recognizes. The bonnet hump was needed to make room for the tall XK power unit.*

successor, the XJS, had trouble getting rid of the last few in 1975.

The E-type's design found a place in the Museum of Modern Art and is sensual rather than sexy, for the car was designed from the heart and the world has been in love with it from the start.

JAGUAR

■ JAGUAR XJ6

When Jaguar launched the XJ6 in 1968 they brought together in one design the standards of ride comfort, quietness, handling and roadholding – qualities previously thought incompatible in a luxury car – that eclipsed the best in Europe and set the pace for the succeeding 20 years.

In one stroke, Jaguar's boss Sir William Lyons rewrote the luxury-car rule book, not with radical new concepts – the XJ was a conventional front-engine, rear-wheel-drive coil-sprung saloon – but by fine-tuning existing components. On its plump tyres,

■ LEFT *To get around European tax laws regarding engine capacity, Jaguar offered the XJ6 with a short-stroke 2.8-litre engine. The only outward difference was the badge on the back.*

JAGUAR XJ6 (1968–87)

Engine	6-cylinder
Capacity	2791/4235/3442cc
Power	180-245bhp
Transmission	4/5-speed manual 3-speed auto
Top speed	(4.2) 124mph (199kph)
No. built	(Series 1) 79,000

specially designed for it by Dunlop, this new British world-beater would out-corner Jaguar's own E-Type but had a ride that was softer and quieter than a Rolls-Royce. This was the world's most beautiful saloon too, a car with a feline aggression and organic muscularity that proved amazingly enduring: the last XJ saloons, the V-twelves, were built in 1991 and looked embarrassingly more attractive than the new XJ40.

Initially using the well-proven six-

■ LEFT *By 1979 the XJ had become the Series 3, with new styling touches by Pininfarina.*

■ BELOW *There was a Daimler version from 1970. This is the V-twelve engined double-six Vanden Plas in rare Series 1 form.*

■ RIGHT *The two-door coupé was a short-lived variant with pillarless side windows and a vinyl roof.*

■ RIGHT *The Series 3 XJ suffered build quality problems in its early career but went on to break all sales records in the 1980s.*

■ BELOW *Panther built a few up-rated XJ Series 3s in the 1980s.*

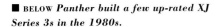

cylinder XK engine – the V-twelve didn't arrive until 1972 – most XJs were automatics, all had power steering and Jaguar built a few with a short-stroke 2.8-litre engine to beat European tax laws. That proved unreliable and is rare today. Like all Jaguars before it, the XJ was a bargain, often undercutting the nearest comparable Mercedes by more than half. As production got up to speed during the early 70s, the four-door XJ began to spawn other variants: the

inevitable badge-engineered Daimler, the short-lived XJC coupé (complete with vinyl roof), long-wheelbase and V-twelve cars.

The XJ wasn't perfect, of course. Quality, never top-drawer stuff, was looking very shaky on the first of the face-lifted Series 3 models at a time when the future seemed bleak for the still publicly-owned, strike-torn Jaguar. Buyers lost confidence and sales began to nose-dive. Enter, in March 1980, John

Egan, the man given the job of making or breaking British-flagship Leyland's problem child. The rest, as they say, is history: as his drive to improve quality at Browns Lane began to take hold, the flagging sales were arrested. Jaguar went public with spectacular success in 1984 and in North America the Jaguar range, spearheaded by the now 15-year-old XJ6, was breaking all sales records and creating the profits that allowed Jaguar to develop and build its successor.

JAGUAR

■ JAGUAR MK X

Broad in the beam, sumptuously curvaceous, the MkX/420G still holds the title of widest British production saloon, with 6ft 4in (1.93m) across its bulbous hips. It had and still has a chunky, slick elegance all of its own. A huge advance on its separate-chassis forefathers, this all-independently suspended and power-steered saloon was, half the price of its nearest true competitors in the tycoon luxury class of 1961.

British buyers were always resistant to the sheer bulk of the car – 5½in longer than the big MkIX it replaced, and a squat 8½in lower – yet if the scale of the MkX was very Detroit, the line was unmistakably Lyons.

The MkX was originally equipped with the triple-carburettor 3.8-litre XK engine from the E-Type. The 4.2-litre unit of 1964 brought more torque

■ ABOVE *With its E-Type three-carb engine, the MkX had excellent performance for its size.*

■ ABOVE *Handling was good too, thanks to its independent rear suspension derived from the E-Type.*

(283lb/ft – 384.9 N m – at 4000rpm) but an identical power curve (peaking at 265bhp at 3000rpm), enough to push the 4300lb (1950kg) saloon along at 120mph (193kph) even in automatic transmission form. In fact, through the gears, the automatic car was consistently faster than the manual, beating 10 seconds to 60mph (96kph); a hard-

driven MkX wouldn't have been far behind the tearaway MkII 3.8 and is quicker than a 4.2 XJ all the way up to 100mph (160kph). All this from a truly lavish five-seater saloon with a boot you could rent out as a bijou flatlet.

Yet buyers never took to this gentle giant of a car in the way they had to the Mks VII, VIII and IX before it. Interest

■ LEFT *The MkX, still Britain's widest ever saloon, featured monocoque construction, all-independent suspension and power steering as standard. Early cars had 3.8-litre engines, later models – from 1964 – 4.2-litre.*

■ RIGHT *The MkX competed head-on with large Mercedes models and even the Bentley S3, but was much cheaper.*

NEW 4·2 LITRE MARK TEN SALOON

■ ABOVE *The 4.2-litre MkX had more torque for better acceleration. There was a manual option, but most MkXs had automatic transmission.*

■ BELOW *In 1966 the MkX became the 420G, with detail improvements.*

■ ABOVE *This shot shows the sheer width of the MkX – 6ft 4in. It was common to see MkXs with scratched doors and wings.*

had fallen away dramatically even by the time the 4.2 was announced, and it took a mid-term name change to rejuvenate sales in its final years. Thus, at Earls Court in 1966, MkX became 420G, causing instant confusion with its slimmer sibling, the new S-Type-based 420, that continues to this day.

Nobody really knows what the G stood for – there was no official line – but the general consensus seems to be "Grand". The shape remained unchanged but an instant recognition point was a new bright metal beading which broke up the car's massive flanks. The front grille was

changed too – with a thick central strip – as were the wheel trims with their new black centre badges. Inside the G, the skull-threatening timber dash rail was now padded (and equipped with a transistorized clock), while its seats were reshaped slightly to give more lateral support – something that road testers had consistently griped about. The last 420Gs were built in 1970 as the standard-setting XJ got into its stride, but the model lived on, in a sense, as the big DS420 Daimler Limousine which used a stretched version of the same floorpan.

JAGUAR MK X/420G (1961-70)	
Engine	Straight six
Capacity	3781/4235cc
Power	265bhp @ 5400rpm
Transmission	4-speed manual 3-speed auto
Top speed	120mph (193kph)
No. built	10,870

J ENSEN

■ JENSEN INTERCEPTOR & FF

Of all the cars Jensen of West Bromwich ever made, the interceptor and FF were easily the most outstanding. Beautiful and fast, the Interceptor was based on the previous glassfibre-bodied CV8, but featured a new Touring-style body.

FF stood for Ferguson Formula, the four-wheel-drive system developed by Harry Ferguson that, not unlike systems found on off-road vehicles, split the torque unequally between the front and rear wheels – 67 per cent to the rear, 37 per cent to the front – to give the car unreal handling qualities for a big GT car of the mid-60s. This, combined with Dunlop Maxaret anti-lock braking – another first – is what led the pundits to call the FF the world's safest car. Not until the Audi Quattro appeared 15 years later was four-wheel drive again offered on a performance road car.

■ ABOVE *The Interceptor convertible was designed to appeal more to American buyers. Frank Sinatra owned one.*

■ BELOW *This is a late 7.2-litre SIII Interceptor on alloy wheels.*

■ LEFT *The Interceptor as it appeared in 1966. The styling was by Touring and early cars were built in Italy, sharing some bits with contemporary Maserati models.*

JENSEN FF (1966-71)	
Engine	V-eight
Capacity	6276cc
Power	330bhp
Transmission	3-speed auto
Top speed	130mph (209kph)
No. built	320

At first glance the FF, with its distinctive Vignale shape, looked identical to the much more conventional Interceptor, and indeed they had much in common. Under the bonnet was a 6.3-litre 325bhp V-eight engine driving through a three-speed Torqueflite automatic transmission to a live rear axle. A closer look revealed a 4-in (10cm) longer wheelbase and a slightly different nose, while the most obvious recognition point was the extra vent on either front wing. Underneath, the tubular chassis – welded to the steel body – was almost totally different, with the prop shaft passing along the left of the engine and box and, at the front, a chassis mounted differential taking the drive to the front wheels. Extra weight slightly blunted the performance of the car compared with the two-wheel-drive Interceptor, but not much: the FF was still good for 130mph (209kph) with 0-60 (96) in eight seconds.

Although the car was widely acclaimed, it suffered by comparison with the near identical-looking Interceptor, which was nowhere near as accomplished but a third less costly. A Series II version was introduced in 1969 with a tidied-up interior and front-end styling.

Sales were slow compared with the two-wheel-drive car. The FF was discontinued in 1971, the Interceptor in 1976.

■ OPPOSITE *With four-wheel drive and anti-lock brakes the Jensen FF was an outstanding road car. Extra vents in the wings distinguish the FF from the Interceptor.*

■ LEFT *The 541 had a low-drag aerodynamic shape for its day, designed by Jensen's own stylist Eric Neale.*

■ JENSEN 541R

When *Autocar* magazine's testers drove the 125mph (201kph) Jensen 541R in 1958 it was the fastest four-seater car they had ever tested. Its low-revving six-cylinder four-litre engine (from the Austin Sheerline) made light work of this high-quality, streamlined glass-fibre coupé. Low revs and ultra-long gearing gave the car a uniquely relaxed character.

Elegantly styled by Eric Neale, the 541's full-bodied, sweeping roof line blended into a clean, rounded tail. It was a low-drag shape, too: Jensen recorded a lowest-ever 0.39 candela (cd) at the Longbridge wind tunnel.

Work on the original 541 began in early-1953 and the car appeared at that year's Earls Court show. The show prototype was aluminium but production 541s were built in the newfangled glassfibre which was light and ideal for the new car's rounded form and subtle detail. It covered a new chassis consisting of 5-in (12.7-cm) tubes, braced by a blend of steel pressings and cross-members to make a platform. Suspension was modified Austin A70 with a live axle spring on half-elliptic at the back. For the steering a cam-and-roller system was used. There were big drum brakes all round.

■ BELOW *The 541R was for a time the fastest four-seater car you could buy, with a top speed of 120mph (193kph).*

JENSEN 541R (1957-60)	
Engine	OHV 6-cylinder
Capacity	3993cc
Power	150bhp @ 4100rpm
Transmission	4-speed with overdrive
Top speed	125mph (201kph)
No. built	193

The 541R of 1957 had the fittest DS7 version of the Sheerline four-litre engine, with twin carburettors on the right and a reworked cylinder-head In conjunction with higher 7.6:1 compression and a "long dwell" the power rose to 150bhp at 4100rpm with 210lb/ft (285.6 N m) of torque at 2500rpm.

Only 53 cars had the DS7 engine. Last of the 541 line was the S of 1961. This had a longer, wider body and standard Rolls-Royce automatic transmission. Styling never recaptured the earlier elegance and performance was down. Just 108 were built.

OTHER MAKES

■ JOWETT

Based in Bradford, Yorkshire, Jowett had its most exciting period after 1945. Both the Javelin and the Jupiter were technologically advanced flat-four engines, all torsion-bar springing and with a top speed of over 80mph (128kph). The R4 sports model was shown at Earls Court in 1953, but by then the firm was already in terminal financial trouble. It died the following year.

■ KIEFT

Cyril Kieft started making Formula 3 cars in 1950, progressing to produce a number of special sports-racing cars. These were succeeded by a pretty Climax-engined model in 1954, which was offered as a road car. In 1955 Kieft moved back into the steel industry from which he had come, selling out to Berwyn Baxter. He eventually sold the assets to Burman's, who showed a Formula Junior car in 1960.

■ RIGHT *The Jensen used many parts from the Austin range, including its big four-litre engine and some suspension components.*

LAGONDA

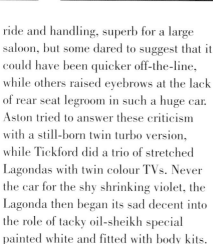

■ LAGONDA

A heroic last minute effort by freelance stylist William Towns, the Lagonda saloon that stole the 1976 Earls Court show looked as if it could have been beamed down from another planet: low and razor edged it was a show-stopper – and just the publicity – that back-from-the-dead Aston Martin needed.

170 deposits were taken at that show but prospective buyers weren't to know that their cars wouldn't be ready until 1979 because of problem with the high-tech electronics.

Towns' ambitious ideas for the interior with its digital dashboard and touch sensitive controls was somewhat in advance of the available technology as applied to motorcars, and in the interests of reliability, his concepts had to be watered down for production. Somewhere along the line the price had gone up by £10,000 – to £32,0000 – by the 1979 launch date but buyers willingly coughed-up. First to take delivery were Lord and Lady Tavistock.

Mechanically the Lagonda was well proven, essentially a stretched Aston Martin V-eight with meaty four-camshaft 5.3 litre V-eight engine. Suspension was same-again, too, but with the geometry and spring rates adjusted to cope with the extra weight, as well as self-levelling

■ ABOVE LEFT *The 1976 Lagonda, with its out of this world styling was the show stopper of the 1976 Earls Court show.*

■ ABOVE RIGHT *The engine was the familiar Aston 5.3-litre V-eight.*

LAGONDA (1976–90)	
Engine	V-eight
Capacity	5340cc
Power	340bhp
Transmission	3-speed auto
Top speed	140mph (225kph)
No. built	645

for the De Dion rear suspension. Scaling almost two tons, this was the biggest, heaviest and most opulently luxurious Lagonda since the war, nothing was left to chance in the labour-saving department, with air conditioning and electric seats all included in the price.

Pundits had nothing but praise for its ride and handling, superb for a large saloon, but some dared to suggest that it could have been quicker off-the-line, while others raised eyebrows at the lack of rear seat legroom in such a huge car. Aston tried to answer these criticism with a still-born twin turbo version, while Tickford did a trio of stretched Lagondas with twin colour TVs. Never the car for the shy shrinking violet, the Lagonda then began its sad decent into the role of tacky oil-sheikh special painted white and fitted with body kits.

Towns tried to redeem his rapidly aging super saloon with a more rounded offering in 1987, but Aston messed-up his specifications and the car looked, if anything, worse.

It was too late. The dream car made flesh that had raised so many pulses back in 1976 died quietly in 1990 with 645 cars sold. There is talk of a successor but new owners Ford may decide that Aston should stick to what they do best – building Aston Martins.

■ FAR LEFT *Englishman William Towns styled the car.*

■ NEAR LEFT *Razor-edged design aged rather quickly.*

L A M B O R G H I N I

■ BELOW *The 350GT was styled by Touring, though the basic proportions were inspired by the original prototype 350GTV.*

■ LAMBORGHINI 350GT

Launched in March 1964, the 350GT was the first Lamborghini production car.

Its Touring body was all new and prettier than the earlier 350GTV prototype, its alloy panels stretched over a steel frame on the usual Superleggera principle. At its heart was a four-cam 60-degree V-twelve engine, its crank machined from a solid billet. Detuned to 270bhp for the 350GT, the production engine had side-draught carburettors for a low bonnet line. Suspending the meaty round-tube chassis was a pukka coil spring and tubular wishbone suspension, with assisted Girling discs from the UK.

■ ABOVE *The classic 4-cam Lamborghini V-twelve engine which gave 280bhp.*

LAMBORGHINI 350GT (1964–68)	
Engine	V-twelve
Capacity	3464cc
Power	280bhp @ 6500rpm
Transmission	5-speed manual
Top speed	152mph (244kph)
No. built	143

■ ABOVE *The interiors were functional but luxurious. The five-speed gearbox was of Lamborghini's own manufacture and had synchromesh on reverse.*

ZF supplied the steering box and the five-speed transmission, and at the rear was a Salisbury differential. This advanced specification was schemed by rising star engineers Giampaolo Dallara and Giotto Bizzarini, laying the ground for the Lamborghinis yet to come.

Shatteringly fast, superbly smooth and very flexible, all this fine-handling 160mph (257kph) car lacked was matinée idol looks. Eschewing the classic, sinewy muscle tone of Pininfarina, Touring of Milan sketched a dramatic coupé for Lamborghini – memorably rounded, obviously fast,

■ ABOVE *For the rich family man there was always the 400GT two-plus-two with two small extra seats in the back. Note the quad lamps.*

definitely pleasing from some angles but, somehow, not quite right.

The initial alloy-bodied 350GT was the lightest and fastest of these early front-engined cars. Later 400GT and GT two-plus-twos were steel-bodied (the bootlid and bonnet were still alloy), with more torque and bhp in order to counteract the added weight, now a corpulent 2862lb (1298kg).

A four-litre engine became optional in 1965, but only 23 were built before the introduction of the steel-bodied 400GT two-plus-two in 1967.

LAMBORGHINI

■ LAMBORGHINI MIURA

Was there ever a more dramatic road car than the Lamborghini Miura? Pioneering the mid-engined configuration on a road car, it lifted this still-young company from promising newcomer to serious contender, eclipsing Ferrari in some people's eyes as a maker of advanced supercars: it would be a further seven years before Enzo produced a 12-cylinder mid-engined road car, the Boxer.

LAMBORGHINI MIURA (1966-72)	
Engine	V-twelve
Capacity	3929cc
Power	350-385bhp
Transmission	5-speed manual
Top speed	170mph (273kph)
No. built	762

■ LEFT *The Miura's beautiful shape was by the young Marcello Gandini of Bertone.*

■ ABOVE *It is hard to believe that this design came out in 1966: orders came flooding in when Lamborghini showed the prototype – and that was only a chassis.*

Though Ferruccio Lamborghini wouldn't let his young design team build a racer, he was happy to give the go-ahead for a super-sportscar, borrowing mid-engined principles from the latest crop of Formula 1 cars and sports racers, the 250LM and GT40. When the Miura was finished, Ferruccio thought it was too wild to sell to the public, seeing it more as an image-boosting show car that would help to sell his more conventional front-engined machines. The Miura – named after a Spanish fighting bull – turned out to be one of the company's best-selling and most profitable models.

Taking a sideways glance at the Ford GT40 chassis, designer Giampaolo Dallara schemed a unitary steel hull, but, unlike the Ford, comfortably big enough for two very rich occupants. To keep the length down, the four-litre, 350bhp V-twelve engine was mounted transversely behind the cockpit. To get the drive to the rear wheels, Lamborghini designed a special transaxle, mounted at the rear of the engine in unit with the light alloy crankcase, in a concept not unlike the BMC Mini but revolutionary on a car with such high performance. Suspending the whole chassis on coil

■ ABOVE *The interior was as futuristic as the body but could get very hot and noisy when the car was being driven hard.*

■ LEFT *With the nose and tail sections raised, the monocoque central hull is clearly evident.*

170mph (273kph) top speed. Sheer performance was only half the story: the balance, traction and cornering power conferred by the mid-engined location put the Miura in another dimension. For advanced students with the requisite buying power it was dream come true, and anyone who complained about the glorious noise, heavy gear change, and the misery of driving it in traffic could go out and buy a more compromised automotive trinket.

Not that Lamborghini didn't fine-tune the somewhat raw original P400. The S of 1969 had a stiffer shell, wider tyres, improved suspension, vented disc brakes and a bit more power, plus little luxury touches like power windows and the option of air-conditioning. Best of the breed was the 1971 SV, with 385 bhp and completely redesigned front and rear suspension to eliminate aerodynamic lift which some owners had complained they suffered from at high speeds. A new sump cured engine-damaging oil surge during sustained hard cornering. The SV lasted just a year, bowing out in late 1972 as the LP400 Countach came on stream.

■ ABOVE *Eyelashes around the pop-up headlights were a Miura trade mark.*

springs and wishbones, he displayed the ensemble, still without a body, at the 1965 Turin show. Orders soon started rolling in and with a stack of deposits Ferruccio felt able to commission Bertone to clothe the naked car.

Nuccio Bertone put his best man on the job – Marcello Gandini. Just 25 at the time, he designed a bold, sensual car that, 30 years on, has lost none of its head-turning appeal. 'Eyelashes' around the flip-up lights and louvered engine cover were memorable styling signatures for what was easily the best-looking Lamborghini made. It was a year after its 1966 Geneva show introduction that the car, designated P400, went into full production, beset by assembly-line hiccups. It was worth the wait, however, for the car hit the headlines with a

■ ABOVE *The Miura S of 1969 had a stiffer shell, wider tyres, vented disc brakes and improved suspension.*

■ RIGHT *The SV was the best of the lot, producing 385bhp and with the tendency towards high-speed lift finally cured.*

LAMBORGHINI

■ LAMBORGHINI ESPADA

While some lesser Italian supercars pretended to be four-seaters, only Lamborghini's Espada offered genuine comfort and space for its rear occupants.

Thus unique as a V-twelve express, this dramatically-styled car was certainly the fastest four-seater in the world when it was introduced in 1968. Top speed was an impressive 150mph (241kph), rising to 155 (249) on later versions; power crept from 325 to 350bhp on the 1970 Series 2, then 365bhp for the 1972 Series 3.

Inspired by the Marzal show car, Bertone designed a big waist-high coupé with a sweeping window line and a sharply cut-off tail. The glazed rear panel above the tail lights was unique

■ ABOVE *The first of the Espadas was seen in 1968. It was the world's fastest four-seater at 150mph, Lamborghini's answer to the Rolls-Royce.*

■ LEFT *You either love or hate Bertone's unmistakable shape, but you can't ignore it. It is blade-like and aggressive – and very big.*

■ BELOW *The original dashboard is bold and stylish. There really is room inside the Espada for four adults.*

■ ABOVE *Rear shot shows glazed rear panel to aid reversing. This early car has knock-on alloy wheels with spinners.*

and improved rear vision.

Up front under a huge alloy bonnet with NACA ducts was Lamborghini's classic quad-cam four-litre V-twelve, driving through a purpose-built five-speed gearbox. Wishbone suspension all round gave the big four-seater a superbly supple ride, but not at the expense of its handling, whose stability and lack of roll was in a different league to most big four-seaters. Early cars did without power steering, while on later versions there was the option of an automatic gearbox, not much fancied today.

The Espada ran from 1968 to 1978 and remains one of the best-selling Lambos ever. It is something of a supercar bargain today.

■ ABOVE *With the five-speed manual box and the most powerful 365bhp model, produced from 1973, top speed crept up to 155mph (248kph).*

■ BELOW *The wide track, fat tyres and suspension made for powerful cornering. Power steering and automatic transmission were available on later versions.*

LAMBORGHINI ESPADA (1968-78)	
Engine	V-twelve
Capacity	3929cc
Power	325-365bhp
Transmission	5-speed manual 3-speed auto
Top speed	150-155mph (241-249kph)
No. built	1,217

LANCIA

■ LANCIA AURELIA B20 GT

Honed through six series of careful
development, with little thought to cost
or compromise, the Lancia Aurelia B20
was a classic from birth. Discerning
drivers respected its pace and handling
– Formula 1 aces Fangio and Hawthorn
both loved their B20s – while styling
connoisseurs fêted Pininfarina's trend-
setting coupé envelope for its elegant
simplicity. Even in 1958, at the end of
its eight-year cycle, a B20 was still one
of the quickest, and most stylish,
methods of arriving at your destination.

Schemed by Vittorio Jano, the Aurelia
B10 saloon was at the frontier of
motorcar design in 1950, and even when
the final 6th series B20 coupés were
rolling out of the Pininfarina works in
1958, few, if any, cars had caught up
with it.

Early two-litre Aurelia coupés (1st
and 2nd Series) are much coveted by
the cognoscenti, while the 5th and 6th
Series B20 coupés have a softer, more
touring character than the earlier cars.
You can spot a 6th Series coupé by its
front-opening quarter-lights in the doors
and chrome gutter and bonnet strips.
The monocoque shell was assembled
from hand-beaten steel panels, welded
together, Lancia supplying a rolling
platform to Pininfarina.

At the B20's heart was a V-six engine,

the first in series production, its
capacity increased to 2451cc for the 3rd
Series coupé of 1953. By the time the
6th Series cars were announced in 1957,
it was producing a modest 112bhp: 5th
and 6th Series Aurelias were actually
detuned for increased torque by way of a
softer cam. Its alloy block was short and
stiff and well mounted on rubber to
absorb some of the unavoidable
roughness – inherent – in some parts of
the rev range in a V-six design. It made
do with a single camshaft in the valley of
the V, operating light alloy pushrods. In-
line valves worked in a modern

hemispherical combustion chamber. A
double-choke Weber 40 sat in the centre
of the V.

All Aurelias used a new rear-
mounted, alloy-cased gearbox housing
clutch, gears, final drive and the
mountings for the inboard drum brakes.
It even had its own oil pump and used
massive aluminium pot joints mounted
outside the wheel hub to reduce angular
movement and wear. The 5th and 6th
Series cars had a strengthened first gear
and clutch but retained the fashionable
column gear change: a Nardi floor-shift
was a contemporary conversion. The 6th

■ RIGHT *Vignale built this coupé on the platform chassis supplied to coachbuilders.*

■ BELOW *The Aurelia was just as beautiful from the back, with its smooth, sweeping roof line.*

■ BELOW *Vignale was one of many coachbuilders who tried to improve on the Pininfarina design. None could match the elegance of the original.*

Series pulled 22mph (35kph) per 100rpm in its non-overdriven top ratio. From the 4th Series onwards, the Lancia semi-trailing arm suspension was discarded for a DeDion system that gave slightly more predictable wet-weather handling. Classic sliding pillar suspension remained at the front, its "I" beam axle strengthened on these later cars in an attempt to banish brake judder and steering shimmy.

Such was the popularity of the B20 that production carried on into the Flaminia era, the last 6th Series being built in the summer of 1958.

LANCIA AURELIA B20 GT 6 SERIES (1950-58)	
Engine	V-six
Capacity	2451cc
Power	112bhp
Transmission	4-speed manual
Top speed	112mph (180kph)
No. built	All models: 3,871

LANCIA

■ LANCIA FULVIA 1.6 HF

Shrouded in mystique and mythology, the 1.6 HF was a prince among Lancia Fulvias. It had a magnificent rally pedigree (with two world championship wins), 115mph (184kph) ability and an exotic and muscular specification.

Under the bonnet was a gem of a narrow-angle 1585cc V-four only used on early HFs. Carburettors were twin Weber 42s which made a throaty 115bhp, peaking at 6200rpm, though a handful of specially-tuned factory cars had 132bhp. The bespoke "piggy-back" five-speed gearbox – using the four-speed casing extended to house an extra set of gears – drove the front wheels, and like all Fulvias the HF had excellent handling. It did without a servo for its Dunlop disc brakes.

Outwardly the wheel arches probably gave it away first; black glassfibre fillets covered wider tyres on deep-rimmed Campagnolo alloys. The back sat quite high, the nose low, sniffing the road, and from the front there was a definite touch

■ LEFT *The 3rd Series Fulvia in its UK market version with higher-mounted headlamps.*

■ ABOVE *The 2nd Series 1.6 HF with flared arches, alloy wheels and high-backed seats.*

■ LEFT *The Zagato was a rare, special-bodied version with good aerodynamics. This is the desirable 1600 version.*

■ ABOVE *The Fulvia as it first appeared in 1965, with steel disc hubcaps and big lights.*

of grip-enhancing negative camber. Other HF giveaways were the lack of bright trim around the windscreen rubber, the subtle badges, alloy opening panels and, most significantly, massive 7-in (17.8-cm) driving lamps. HF points inside are more numerous. Seats are lightweight skeletal buckets, with a skimpy padded bench behind, rather than the standard coupé's proper moulded affair. Later *"lusso"* 1600HFs were softer, more luxurious cars, still fast but much less specialized.

Just 1280 1.6 HF Fulvias were built in 1968 and 1969 to homologate the car for international rallying. A batch of 30 came to the UK in right-hand-drive form with more trim for British customers who didn't want Plexiglas and vulnerable bumperless bodywork.

The HF was the spiritual progenitor of today's pocket-rocket homologation specials such as the M3 and Integrale "Evo".

When the final chapter on the motorcar in the 20th century is written, the jewel-like 1.6 Fulvia will probably go down as one of the great driving machines.

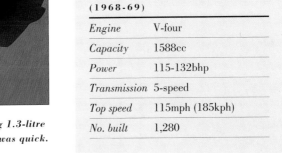

■ BELOW *With its very free-revving 1.3-litre engine, even the standard Fulvia was quick. It was practical, too.*

LANCIA FULVIA 1.6 HF (1968-69)	
Engine	V-four
Capacity	1588cc
Power	115-132bhp
Transmission	5-speed
Top speed	115mph (185kph)
No. built	1,280

■ LEFT *The V-four engine was a jewel which – in its most powerful guise – sent up to 132bhp to the front wheels through a four- or five-speed gearbox.*

■ RIGHT *The unmistakable tail-end of the Fulvia. You can see simple but effective beam-axle and leaf springs underneath.*

LANCIA

■ LEFT *The road-going Stratos was good for 142mph (227kph) with the Ferrari Dino engine.*

■ LANCIA STRATOS

The sensational wedge-shaped Lancia Stratos was conceived because Lancia needed a new rally weapon for the 1970s. The Fulvia HF, by the late 60s/early 70s, was looking and feeling old and couldn't put enough power through its front wheels for predictable handling. The 170bhp Renault Alpines – despite delicate gearboxes – were embarrassing the once-proud Lancia coupé. What Lancia's competitions boss Cesare Fiorio knew he needed was a specially tailored rally car homologated for Group 4: powerful, light, mid-engined and strong enough to compete on rough events like the Safari with suspension that could be adjusted to suite the conditions.

He saw his salvation in an unlikely place: the Bertone stand of the 1970 Turin motor show. Here sat an incredibly low wedge of a car called Stratos (short for stratosphere). It was designed by the young Marcello Gandini, best known

■ BELOW LEFT *The engine sat behind the passengers' heads, the lights were flip-up, and the short wheelbase meant hair-trigger handling.*

LANCIA STRATOS (1973-75)	
Engine	DOHC V-six
Capacity	2418cc
Power	190bhp @ 7000rpm
Transmission	5-speed
Top speed	142mph (228kph)
No. built	492

■ LEFT *Nothing looked quite like the Stratos, designed by Marcello Gandini of Bertone. It has inspired at least one kit-car replica.*

■ BELOW RIGHT *The Stratos was conceived as a rally car. The road car was incidental, existing only to homologate the car for competition.*

then for his Lamborghini Miura. Mid-engined and light, it used a Lancia engine, the V-four 1600HF from the Fulvia: Fiorio saw at once that the screen-cum-door layout and the extremely laid-back driving position could never be practical on a rally car,

but the car ran under its own power and *concept* was there.

With the blessing of Lancia's new managing director Ugo Gobbato, Bertone – and Gandini – were commissioned in 1971 to build a more conventional device, still mid-engined

and sitting on the same wheelbase but built around a new drive train, the Ferrari Dino 2.4 V-six and its five-speed transaxle. There was talk of a cheaper alternative Fiat 132 drive train, and Lancia even threatened to use the Maserati Bora 4.7-litre V-eight when the

■ LEFT *Although Stratos production finished in 1975, new cars were still available in 1980.*

■ BELOW *Some say 1,000 Stratos road cars were built, but 500 seems more likely. All were Dino-powered, although a cheaper Fiat-engined car had been proposed.*

request for 500 Dino engines met with some political resistance within Maranello. In fact – apart from a single four-cylinder prototype – the Stratos only ever used this four-cam iron block unit, mounted on a beefy box section with beams welded to the firewall of the steel driving compartment/monocoque. Front suspension was coils, wishbones and an anti-roll bar, while at the rear a stronger system of Beta-style struts with lower wishbones replaced a double wishbone and coil-spring set-up that had proved fallible during testing.

A prototype, looking more or less like the eventual production car, was shown at Turin in 1971 on the Bertone stand: testing continued in 1972 and 1973 until production finally began tentatively late in 1973. They needed to build 400 cars to homologate the Stratos for Group 4 international rallying. Some say Bertone built 1,000 cars, others say under 500, and the latter figure seems to be the most widely accepted. The car was finally passed for homologation on 1 October 1974.

Bertone built the monocoque and glassfibre nose/tail sections in Turin with final assembly (trimming, painting, testing etc.) at Lancia's Chivasso factory. Production was pushed quickly during the summer to get the car homologated and officially ended in 1975.

■ LEFT *The Stratos in the famous works livery with Alitalia sponsorship.*

■ BELOW *The Stratos was the ultimate expression of the wedge. Its wheelbase was no longer than a Mini's.*

LINCOLN

■ LINCOLN CONTINENTAL

Collectors now recognize the 1961
Lincoln Continental – the "clap door" –
as one of America's most influential
motorcars. At a time when fins and
chrome were still popular on most
domestic cars, Lincoln – an up-market
division of Ford – launched a car with
clean, unadorned lines, very much
American in scale but almost European
in feel. The rear-hinged rear door gave it
the clap-door nickname and chrome was
applied sparingly to its crisp-edged
flanks. It became the "in" car with the
rich and famous in America and was
even the White House vehicle of choice:
it was in a stretched, Presidential clap-
door that President John F Kennedy was

LINCOLN CONTINENTAL (1961-79)	
Engine	V-eight
Capacity	7045/7565cc
Power	300-365bhp
Transmission	3-speed auto
Top speed	125mph (201kph)
No. built	342,781

■ ABOVE *The
Continental of the
mid-1950s was the
most luxurious car
in the American
industry: Lincoln
lost money on
every one they
built.*

■ ABOVE *The
original
Continental was an
instant classic,
inspired by Henry
Ford's son Edsel.*

■ RIGHT *The
presidential
stretched Lincoln
Continental, with
bullet-proof
windows and
metal-work.*

■ BELOW *The MKII Continental was virtually hand built and featured every extra you could think of.*

■ RIGHT *The MKII Continental of 1956 had very clean lines for the period and was colossally expensive.*

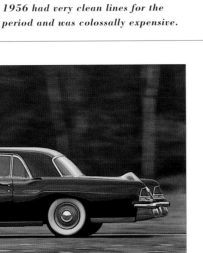

■ ABOVE *The 1961 Continental won much praise for its styling.*

assassinated in Dallas, Texas in 1963.

Lincoln knew they were on to a winner and changed the Continental only subtly in a long nine-year production run: some new chrome here, a new grille there (and almost every year a longer wheelbase) but essentially the same clean shape all the way through. There was a power-top four-door convertible version alongside the saloon from the start and a hardtop coupé from 1966. The Continental always had the biggest V-eight engine – 7.0-litre at first, 7.5-litre later – automatic transmission and every conceivable labour-saving device as befitted a car comparable with the most luxurious in the world: power seats, air conditioning,

power steering, electric windows and much more. Packing up to 365bhp, the 5215lb (2366kg) Continental was a fast car, capable of up to 125mph (201kph) but like all large American saloons was an unruly handful on anything but a straight, smooth road. Not that such things mattered to the middle-aged Americans who bought the Continental: it had a boot big enough for the golf clubs, lots of snob appeal and it never broke down.

It was the last good-looking Lincoln for a long time. The MkIII Continental – a two-door personal luxury car with a strong whiff of the pimp-mobile about it – ushered in a new era of chintzy styling. But it was nice while it lasted.

■ NEAR RIGHT
Lincoln emphasized the elegance and good taste of their flagship, not to mention its White House connections.

■ FAR RIGHT *The Continental had cleaner styling and smaller fins – though the car remained huge.*

LOTUS

■ LOTUS 7

Although the first production Lotus was the Six of 1953, sold as a kit and intended for use in club racing, it was the now-legendary Seven of 1957 that put the fledgling company on the road to success. A skimpy and extremely basic two-seater, the new car had a cleverly designed multitubular space-frame chassis with a stressed aluminium body making no concessions to access for the driver and passenger: there were no doors, just cutaway sides, and if the hood was up it was nearly impossible to

■ ABOVE *The Seven was a Spartan sportscar ideal for club racing. It was light and fast.*

■ BELOW *A super-Seven like this is stunningly quick owing to its excellent power-to-weight ratio. The style has changed little over the years.*

■ ABOVE *This is a very early Seven and could be had with a Ford side-valve or Coventry Climax engine. The body was made from stressed aluminium.*

■ RIGHT *Only 15 Sevens were fitted with the desirable Lotus twin-cam engine, as used in the Elan.*

get in. Minimal mud-guards covered the front wheels and the headlights were free-standing.

There was coil-sprung independent front suspension and a well-located live rear axle with radius arms and coil spring/damper units, which produced superb handling. Straight-line performance depended on the engine fitted by the owner: most went the Ford route with a side-valve 100E unit; a few used the Coventry Climax FWA engine and some late S1s had the BMC A Series unit. The space frame was

■ RIGHT *The early car again, with its wire wheels and polished aluminium body. The Seven was Colin Chapman's first true production model.*

■ BELOW *The S4 of the 1970s was an attempt to cash in on the Midget/Spitfire market.*

LOTUS SEVEN AND SUPER SEVEN (1957-70)	
Engine	4-cylinder
Capacity	997-1599cc
Power	37-115bhp
Transmission	4-speed
Top speed	80-108mph (128-173kph)
No. built	242/1,350/350

■ BELOW *The dashboard had the bare minimum of instruments, and the hood was functional rather than attractive.*

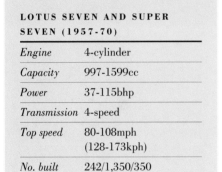

simplified on the S2 of 1962, which could also be recognized by its flared clam-shell wings.

The Super Seven, available from 1961, came with a series of progressively more powerful engines: a Cosworth-tuned 1340cc Ford Classic unit and, later, a bigger 1498 Cortina GT or Cosworth 1599cc engine. Disc brakes appeared on the front for the first time. The S3 car used a 1600 Cortina engine, although 15 had a Lotus twin-cam engine of the type fitted to the Elan. Attempting to bring the concept up to date – and take some of the

Midget/Spitfire market – the Seven S4 of 1970 had a chunkier-looking glassfibre body bonded on to a modified chassis with Europa Type front suspension and a Watts linkage at the rear.

It was softer and more civilized than the earlier cars and hard-bitten Seven enthusiasts didn't take to it, yet it sold respectably – more than 900 cars in three years.

With the arrival of value added tax (VAT) in 1973, Lotus decided to bail out of the kit-car market altogether and sold the design rights to Catherham Cars who build the car in S3 form to this day.

■ LEFT *As with most Lotus parts, the instruments and switch gear could be found on lesser production saloons.*

■ ABOVE *The cycle wings offered minimal protection from road spray. Doors were detachable to give more elbow room.*

LOTUS

■ BELOW *With its pure, elegant shape, the Elite is rated as probably the most beautiful Lotus. It was designed by the relatively unknown Peter Kirwan Taylor.*

■ LOTUS ELITE

If the Seven was a spartan club racer, then the Elite was the first proper Lotus road car, a sophisticated little GT blessed with superb handling and memorable looks. Launched in 1959 (prototypes had been seen as early as 1957), it was the first car to have a glassfibre monocoque made up of floor, body and a structural centre section with the outer opening panels bolted into place afterwards. Power for this lightweight structure came from an

LOTUS ELITE (1959-63)	
Engine	4-cylinder
Capacity	1216cc
Power	71-105bhp
Transmission	4/5-speed
Top speed	110-130mph (177-209kph)
No. built	998

■ LEFT *Thanks to lightweight construction and clever suspension, the Elite had superb handling: few cars could out-corner it.*

overhead-cam 1216cc Coventry Climax engine, first with 71bhp in single-carburettor form, later with 83bhp and twin carbs giving 118mph (189kph) potential. The high top speed was attributable to the low drag shape by stylist Peter Kirwan Taylor, with its amazing 0.29(cd). A creditable 35mpg was well within reach.

What made the Elite really special was its nimble handling. With coil-spring damper units at the front and modified MacPherson struts (Chapman struts) at the rear, it cornered like a go-kart, yet not at the expense of ride

■ LEFT *The Elite was launched in 1959, but the first prototypes had been seen as early as 1957. The body is a glassfibre monocoque – there is no separate chassis.*

■ RIGHT *From the rear you can see how the Elite inspired the Elan, its much more successful younger sister. Because of the shape of the door glasses the windows wouldn't wind down very far.*

comfort. It had rack-and-pinion steering and high-specification disc brakes on all four wheels.

The model was much praised but had its problems. The monocoque shell promoted lots of drumming and vibration, and the cabin was very poorly ventilated – the profile of the door glass meant it was impossible to wind the windows down! Quality was never top-drawer stuff and the price was high – more than a Jaguar XK150. From 1960

there was revised rear suspension and improved interior trim.

The SE model had 85bhp and a close-ratio five-speed ZF gearbox rather than the standard BMC-derived unit. The 95, 100 and 105bhp versions were offered

before Lotus eventually pulled the plug on their prodigy in 1963.

By then Lotus needed all the production capacity they had for the Elan, which was much easier to produce and equally talented.

■ LEFT *Because of its low-drag shape the Elite had a high top speed – up to 130mph (209kph) with the most powerful engine option.*

■ ABOVE *The simple dashboard echoes the profile of the car. Interior comfort wasn't a strength of the Elite.*

■ RIGHT *Superb handling and a good power-to-weight ratio made the Elite a popular racing car.*

LOTUS

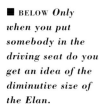

■ **LEFT** *The Elan took over from the troublesome Elite in 1962. This is the big valve sprint of the early 70s.*

■ LOTUS ELAN

First seen in 1962, the Elan put Lotus of Hethel, Norfolk on the map as a make of world-class road cars. Central to design was a steel back-bone chassis, fork-shaped with wishbones and coils at the front, Chapman struts and lower wishbones at the back with centre-lock steel wheels. All gave the car tremendous agility and excellent ride. The steering rack came from Triumph. Girling disc brakes were used all round.

The Elan's 105bhp engine had twin chain-driven cams. The block and bottom end came straight from Ford, pre-Heron head iron lump bored out to 1558cc. The four-speed gearbox was from Ford, too.

This powerful, light car, innately balanced and voraciously quick, set the standard for the perfect B-roads dicer. Current for 10 years, it spawned a coupé and a bigger two-plus-two sister. Quality and reliability improved all the while.

The 1971 Sprint was the final flowering of the 1962 Elan with a Tony Rudd-developed big-valve engine giving 25 per cent more power – 126bhp at 6500rpm. Acceleration, always rapid, was now explosive: to put things in perspective, the big-valve Sprint could

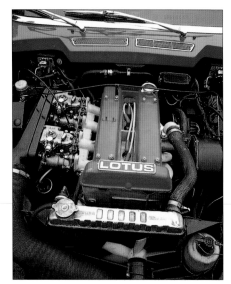

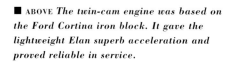

■ **ABOVE** *The twin-cam engine was based on the Ford Cortina iron block. It gave the lightweight Elan superb acceleration and proved reliable in service.*

■ **BELOW** *Only when you put somebody in the driving seat do you get an idea of the diminutive size of the Elan.*

LOTUS ELAN (1962-73)	
Engine	In-line four
Capacity	1588cc
Power	105-126bhp
Transmission	4/5-speed manual
Top speed	115-118mph (185-189kph)
No. built	12, 220

■ **FAR LEFT** *The Elan coupé proved a popular option from the mid-60s onwards.*

■ **LEFT** *Like all Lotuses, the Elan had a glassfibre body. It wouldn't rust but was subject to crazing and cracking.*

■ RIGHT *Three ages of Elan: early car, SE and Sprint. Note knock-on wheels with spinners and rude exposed door handles. Bonnets come away completely for good engine access.*

get to 60 as quickly as a Lamborghini Islero and, in top gear, had the edge on the likes of the 246 Dino and Porsche 911E at up to 80mph (128kph). It was a more oil-tight and quieter engine, claimed Lotus, with a less raucous exhaust note than earlier cars. Big-valve Sprints reverted to Weber carbs, and a few had the five-speed Austin Maxi-derived gearbox from the Plus 2.

Elan production ended in 1973 as Lotus tried to move away from its kit-car image – the car had been available in weekend do-it-yourself form from the start – and moved towards more up-market machines like the Elite and the Esprit. Today the spirit of the Elan has been revived in the Elise.

OTHER MAKES

■ LAGONDA

Bought by David Brown in 1947 and now part of Aston Martin, Lagonda was founded in 1906 by an American, Wilbur Gunn, at Staines, Middlesex (from 1974 Surrey). The firm made both light cars and more powerful tourers before 1939, the late 30s models being honed by WO Bentley, notably the V-twelve. The David Brown takeover enabled Bentley's last design to enter production, as the 2.6-litre. Lagondas were made – with one break – until 1965 (the DB4/5-based Rapide), then there was another gap until 1974–75. Latterly, the most famous Lagonda-badged car has been the wedge-shaped V-eight, first seen in 1976, but there have been no Lagondas since 1990.

■ LANCHESTER

The Lanchester of 1895 was remarkable in that it was designed as a motor car from the ground up rather than as a horseless carriage. The Lanchester brothers' innovatory spirit can be seen in all their pre-1930 products. A pioneer British motoring concern, Lanchester faded after acquisition by BSA in 1931 – the armaments and motorcycle firm also controlled Daimler. By 1956, the make had been quietly phased out of production as fellow-marque Daimler teetered towards extinction.

■ LEA-FRANCIS

In the late-1920s the British firm Lea-Francis made fine small sporting cars, but in 1935 the cash ran out and reorganization was needed before another sporting range emerged in 1938. Updated versions of the pre-war cars were made after the Second World War but were always expensive, with limited appeal, and by 1952 the firm was in trouble. They made their last car, the Lynx, in 1960.

■ LLOYD

Production of the Lloyd car, brainchild of British motor trader Roland Lloyd, started in Grimsby, Lincolnshire (Humberside) in 1936 with the rear-engined 350 model. The car which followed, the 650, built from 1946, was far more advanced and lasted until 1950. Sales were poor because of price.

■ LMB

Leslie Bellamy made his name as the creator of the LMB split-beam ifs conversion. Associated with Nordec in the 1950s, he became a key figure in providing tuning gear for Britain's "perpendicular" Fords. The short-lived LMB Debonair was the logical conclusion to these endeavours, intended for assembly by both LMB and EB.

MASERATI

■ MASERATI GHIBLI

Maserati conceived the 1967 Ghibli as its ultimate late 60s road car. It might not have been as technically advanced as its rivals from Ferrari (the 275 GTB/4) and Lamborghini (the 350GT) but it was at least as beautiful, with a lean, low shape by the talented young designer Giorgetto Giugiaro, then working for Ghia. Even today it is one of the designs of which he is most proud, and some say it is a better-looking car than the Daytona.

The performance left nothing to be desired, even though Maserati made no attempt to keep weight down with this luxurious, steel-bodied car. With the earlier type of 4.7 V-eight engine – a four-cam design closely related to a type that originated in a 300S racer in the 1950s – the Ghibli was a 150mph (241kph) car.

With the later 4.9-litre SS engine. the

■ ABOVE *The Ghibli was Maserati's answer to the Ferrari 275 GTB and Lamborghini 350GT. It was more beautiful than either, if not quite as sophisticated.*

■ LEFT *The blade-like lines were penned by Guigario, then working for Ghia. A Spider version was also available.*

■ LEFT *The Maserati V-eight engine started life in the beautiful 450S racer of 1957 and was still in production in the 90s.*

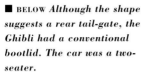

■ RIGHT *Unlike some rivals, the Ghibli's body was constructed in steel, so the car was no lightweight. Top speed was in the region of 165mph (265kph) with the biggest engine and manual box.*

■ BELOW *Installed in the Ghibli, the V-eight gave 330-335bhp with enormous torque.*

■ BELOW *Although the shape suggests a rear tail-gate, the Ghibli had a conventional bootlid. The car was a two-seater.*

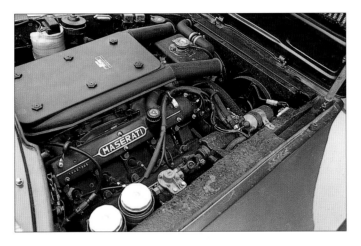

■ RIGHT *The rare Ghibli Spider, built to compete with the Daytona Spider on the American market. It is the most valuable Ghibli model today.*

MASERATI GHIBLI (1967-73)	
Engine	V-eight
Capacity	4719/4930cc
Power	330-335bhp
Transmission	5-speed manual 3-speed auto
Top speed	165mph (265kph)
No. built	1274

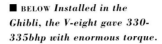

top speed went up to 165 (265), though it only produced 5bhp more. Smooth and tractable, these engines majored on torque rather than ultimate power, with a fairly modest rev limit. The auto box option obviously cut performance considerably, but most Ghiblis had the five-speed ZF manual.

Maserati made the traditional suspension work beautifully. Cornering was flat, heavy steering precise,

lightening nicely at speed. The leaf-sprung live rear axle gave the game away, however, with a jiggly ride. The brakes, big four-wheel discs, were well up to the job of stopping the portly Ghibli.

To increase its appeal – especially on the American market – a Spider version of the Ghibli was launched in 1969 and is now one of the most collectable post-war Maserati road cars.

Those who required four seats could

buy the Indy from 1969, a car technically almost identical to the Ghibli but with a less pleasing body by Vignale.

Ghibli production faded away in 1973 as the Citroën-influenced Bora and Khamsin began to come on stream as Maserati's flagship supercars. By the standards of low-volume supercars, the Ghibli was successful, with 1,149 cars built plus a further 125 Spiders.

MASERATI

■ MASERATI KHAMSIN

The Maserati Khamsin was a front-engined supercar dating from the 1972 Paris show, although production didn't begin until 1974. Named after an Egyptian wind, it was crafted in steel by Bertone and angular and dart-like in

■ BELOW *The car's low build made retractable headlights obligatory.*

■ ABOVE *The top speed of the Khamsin was 153mph (245kph) with the manual gearbox.*

■ ABOVE *The interior was as well-stocked with dials as an airliner's flight-deck.*

MASERATI KHAMSIN	
Engine	V-eight
Capacity	4930cc
Power	320bhp at 5500rpm
Transmission	5-speed manual 3-speed auto
Top speed	153mph (246kph)
No. built	421

shape, with a swoopy wedge profile and an abruptly sawn-off tail. A feature was its glazed rear panel, with the tail-lights held in suspension by the glass.

Inside, the chunky dash, with its awful nylon-covered top, lacked both the symmetry and restraint of more tasteful 60s Maseratis, but air conditioning was standard and there was an adjustable steering column and hydraulic up-down seat movement.

All Khamsins came with the classic Maserati four-cam V-eight engine, mounted well back against the bulkhead so that, with the 20-gallon (91-litre) fuel tank filled, weight distribution was an ideal 50/50. The pedigree of this all-alloy powerhouse was impeccable. It was launched in the 450s in 1956 and its first road car application was in the flagship 5000GT in 1959. Thereafter, Maserati juggled with bore and stroke ratios depending on the application. There were 4.2 and 4.7 V-eights but the Khamsin came only as a dry-sumped

4.9, red-lined at 5500rpm to make a full-bodied 320bhp. Torque, though, was its forte: a colossal 354lb/ft (481.4Nm) at 4000rpm. Needless to say, the Khamsin had massive low-speed lugging ability, so thickly spread is this torque across the 800-5500rpm power band.

Conceived as a successor to the Indy and Ghibli, the Khamsin differed from its 60s front-engined predecessors in having proper double-wishbone rear suspension rather than an outdated, if well located, live axle. Further, it used Citroën hydraulics for steering, brakes, clutch and the pop-up headlights and driver's seat adjustment. It was the last Maserati to feel the technical influence of French control: by the time Khamsin production was getting into its stride in 1975, Citroën had pulled out.

As the last great, front-engined car to carry the Trident – a proper supercar rather than a jumped-up executive saloon – the Khamsin holds a special place in the history of the marque.

■ MASERATI BORA AND MERAK

With Lamborghini setting the technical pace with the mid-engined Miura, critics knew it was only a matter of time before Ferrari and Maserati would have their own mid-engined flagship supercars. In fact it wasn't until 1973 that Ferrari's Berlinetta Boxer became commercially available, just beaten by the Maserati Bora of 1971.

As on the Ghibli, the styling was by Giugiaro, who by this time had left Ghia and was running his own studio, Ital Design. His shape, first mooted in 1969, was elegant and clean-limbed but lacking perhaps the sheer animal beauty

of the Ghibli and the Lamborghini Miura. That the Bora was fast almost goes without saying: the 12-year-old 4.7-litre V-eight engine, punching out 310bhp, could push the slippery Bora up to 175mph (281kph) with 80 (128) coming up in second gear. What's more, the Bora was a refined car: audible conversation with a passenger was possible up to 150mph (241kph), then

MASERATI BORA (1971-80)	
Engine	V-eight
Capacity	4719/49430
Power	310-320bhp
Transmission	5-speed manual
Top speed	160mph (257kph)
No. built	571

■ ABOVE *The Bora's cabin was civilized and remarkably quiet at speed.*

■ RIGHT *From the front the Bora and Merak were almost impossible to tell apart, but the smaller-engined Merak had extra rear seats and different three-quarter treatment.*

■ ABOVE *The Maserati badge dates back to the birth of the company in 1926.*

■ LEFT *The Bora was capable of 160mph (257kph) but was never as popular as contemporary Ferraris.*

unheard-of in a mid-engined. With Citroën now at the helm, it came as no surprise that a few complex hydraulics entered with super-sharp brakes and powered adjustment for the pedals, seats and steering-column rake. Handling was the last word in stability, a major advance on the front-engined Ghibli.

The Bora was joined in 1972 by a little brother, the Merak. At first glance, this new entry-level Maserati looked identical to the Bora, with the same front end panels, but from the B pillar back used awkward single-buttress sections sweeping down from the roof. The engine was the three-litre V-six from the Citroën SM. It was much shorter than the V-eight and allowed two rear seats to be incorporated. It handled well but lacked ultimate punch, a criticism answered by the 1975 SS version in which power was increased from 190 to 220bhp. For Italy there was a two-litre tax-break special Merak.

The Bora changed little in its nine-year history, gaining only the larger 4.9-litre engine in 1976 before bowing out in 1980. The Merak followed in 1981.

MAZDA

■ MAZDA COSMO

With the futuristic-looking 1967 Cosmo 110S, Mazda just pipped NSU to the post as a producer of twin-rotary wankel-powered production cars. Like the Ro80, it was designed from the ground up for the new engine, taking advantage of its compact dimensions and good power-to-weight ratio. Capacity was equivalent to about two

MAZDA COSMO (1966-72)	
Engine	Twin-rotary wankel
Capacity	2000cc (nominal)
Power	110-128bhp
Transmission	4/5-speed manual
Top speed	116-125mph (186-201kph)
No. built	1,176

litres with an output of 110bhp at 7000rpm. Rather than using peripheral ports for maximum power, Mazda had its inlet ports in the casing in the name of increased low-down torque, idling

smoothness and fuel consumption at low speeds.

In most other respects, the 110S was a conventional, stylish luxury sports coupé pitched against the likes of the

■ **FAR LEFT** *Rear lights split by bumpers were among Cosmo's styling features.*

■ **ABOVE LEFT** *The Cosmo was Mazda's first foray into the world of exciting, high-performance cars.*

■ **BELOW LEFT** *The Cosmo name lives on today on top-line cars but is almost unknown outside Japan.*

■ **LEFT** *With the Cosmo, Mazda just pipped NSU to the post as makers of the first rotary-powered production car. Even so it was something of a test-bed and only 1176 were built.*

■ BELOW *The rotary engine built under licence to Dr Felix Wankel. It had fewer teething troubles than the NSU unit.*

Porsche 911 and the Jaguar E-Type. Top speed was 116mph (186kph) with 0-60 (96) in about 10 seconds, revving to 7000rpm in the usual smooth, vibration-free wankel fashion. With a DeDion axle at the rear and wishbones at the front, it had excellent handling with a rather hard ride and a good brake set-up with discs at the front and drums at the back. The Cosmo changed little in its six years of production, gaining a

closer-ratio five-speed gearbox, a longer wheelbase and a little more power – 128bhp – on the 1968 "B" model.

The Cosmo name lived on in a series of rather more conventional-looking saloon-based coupés and survives to this day on Mazda's high-tech luxury flagship. Mazda is the only company that still markets rotary engines in production cars most famously in its best-selling RX7 sportscar.

■ ABOVE *The Cosmo was designed to compete with the Porsche 911 and Jaguar E-Type and featured a Dedion rear axle. More powerful later models could reach 125mph (201kph).*

OTHER MAKES

■ **MARAUDER**
The 100mph (160kph) Marauder was the brainchild of Rover engineers George Mackie, Peter Wilks and Spen King, who set up their own firm to produce it. Bodies were made by Richard Mead and Abbey Panels. Just 15 of the P4-based cars were produced before rising costs sidelined the project.

■ **MARCOS**
Marcos has been making cars in Britain since 1959, when Jem Marsh and Frank Costin used a composite chassis and a lower body made of marine ply for their first car. The classic Dennis Adams-designed 1800 made the company's reputation, but the four-seater Mantis model of 1970 was badly timed and the company ceased production the following year. Manufacture restarted in the 1980s.

■ ABOVE *Today's Cosmo is a very high-tech luxury flagship packed with sophisticated electronics.*

■ RIGHT *By the mid-1980s, the Cosmo had begun to look very ordinary, as the coupe version of 1975 shows.*

MERCEDES-BENZ

■ BELOW *The 300SL roadster was announced in 1957 and had better handling than the gullwing.*

■ MERCEDES-BENZ 300SL

The Mercedes-Benz 300SL was one of the most sensational sports cars of the 1950s. It was easily one of the fastest, with a top speed of 130-155mph (209-249kph), depending on axle ratio. Only a handful of Ferrari and Maserati road cars could approach this performance at the time – and, strictly speaking, they were not fully fledged production cars like the SL ("super light").

The original Gullwing coupé, with its unique roof-hinged doors, was launched in February 1954, though the Le Mans-winning prototypes had already been given a sneak preview in 1952. The body, built in steel with alloy panels, was supported by a complex space frame of tubes not seen before or since on a road car, the deep sills necessitating the use of Gullwing doors. With its blistered wheel arches and smoothly-curved rump, it was one of the most instantly recognizable shapes on the road.

Under the bonnet was an advanced, fuel-injected overhead-cam three-litre engine canted over to keep the bonnet

■ LEFT *The convertible model was designed to appeal to the Americans and was easier to service.*

■ ABOVE *The cutaway shows canted-over straight-six engine and coil-spring suspension.*

■ RIGHT *Mr and Mrs Tony Hancock with their new 300SL convertible. These cars were popular with celebrities.*

■ RIGHT *The 280SL was the last of the Pagoda-roofed cars and probably the best. Many were automatic yet performance was still strong – over 120mph (193kph).*

the doors, bonnet, bootlid and hood stowage panel, made of aluminium.

The first 230SLs – with removable "Pagoda" steel roof panel – were built in March 1963. They featured a 150bhp four-bearing straight-six engine (with Bosch injection pioneered by Mercedes on its W196 Grand Prix cars of 1954 and 1955), front disc brakes and optional power steering. Sales neared

■ FAR LEFT *The SL for the 1970s was the V-eight engined 350SL, hugely popular during a near 20-year life span.*

■ NEAR LEFT *Its wide track and fat tyres gave the SL impressive grip and handling.*

■ ABOVE *All these SLs had a fuel-injected straight-six engine renowned for its reliability.*

20,000 in 1967 when the 230 made way for the 250SL. Power stayed at 150bhp but the engine was sweeter and had more torque, while the 250 had discs all round and power steering as standard. Best of the bunch was the 280SL, built from November 1967 to March 1971. With a 170bhp seven-bearing engine

this version goes well with automatic transmissions, though there were four-speed manual options and a rare five-speeder. The only external recognition point was one-piece wheel trims. Some later cars had optional alloy wheels. Production totalled 23,885, making the 280SL the most popular model.

■ LEFT *The 230SL was launched in 1963. Its styling hardly changed in nearly a decade of production.*

MERCEDES-BENZ

■ MERCEDES-BENZ 280SE 3.5 COUPÉ

Elegant Mercedes-Benz W111 coupés and convertibles were based on new mid-range W111 saloons, though styling – by Paul Braqc who later penned the 230SL – was bereft of the saloon's clumsy fins. He drew a tight, handsome, Detroit-influenced pillarless hardtop for the coupé, with fashionable wraparound front and rear screens, squared-off rear haunches and stacked lights at the front, glass-bubble covers echoing the design of the top-of-the-range Fintail saloons. Doors were long and heavy. The rounded profile of the flanks – with a crease to break up the flat expanse of steel – suggested weight and solidity.

For 1962, the 220 was joined by the air-suspended, fully disc-braked power-steered 300SE coupé using the big alloy 160bhp three-litre straight six first seen in the Fintail saloons a year earlier. It was all change again for 1965 when the 250 replaced the 220 range. From this point, the two-door cars took technical lead from the new W108 S-Class saloons that replaced the upper-range Fintails that year. With higher final drive gearing and bigger, 14-in (35.6-cm), wheels, the 250 coupé was almost as quick as the 300. It shared the bigger car's disc

■ RIGHT *From the front you can tell a 3.5-litre convertible by its stacked headlights. The bodyshape dates from the early 60s.*

■ ABOVE *This is an earlier six-cylinder convertible 220 with single vertical lights each side.*

■ ABOVE *The handsome coupé had distinctive American-influenced pillarless styling and vestigial tail fins. The 3.5 badge on the back lets you know it's a V-eight.*

brakes. Thus, it seemed perfectly rational to Benz-watchers when Stuttgart rationalized the coupé range with a single 280SE model in 1967, the smooth, flexible 2778cc unit pumping 160 real horsepower in fuel-injected form.

The final and best W111 coupé derivative was the 1969 V-eight, confusingly badged 280SE 3.5. Conceived to appease American buyers

weaned on lazy, high-torque V-eights, this single-cam per bank electronically-injected engine gave a full-blooded 200bhp at 5800rpm in "dirty" European tune, good for 125mph (201kph) with 60 (96) in under 10 seconds.

Still top of the Mercedes range – if you discount the 600 Limousine – the W111 two-door stayed in production until 1971, when it was replaced by the 350SLC.

MERCEDES-BENZ 280 SE 3.5 COUPÉ (1969–71)	
Engine	SOHC injected 90-degree V-eight
Capacity	3499cc
Power	200bhp @ 5400rpm
Transmission	5-speed manual 4-speed auto
Top speed	125mph (201kph)
No. built	4,502

■ LEFT *Apart from the 600, the 3.5 coupé and convertible were the flagships of the Mercedes range – and very expensive.*

■ RIGHT *The 600 was designed to take on the best cars in the world. Apart from its width it looks, at a glance, very similar to other models.*

■ BELOW *The stretched six-door model was much loved by tycoons and pop stars: this one belonged to John Lennon.*

■ MERCEDES-BENZ 600

With the 1961 600, Mercedes set out to build the world's ultimate saloon – a Rolls-Royce beater – with no regard to cost or compromise. Millionaires could choose the standard 126in (320cm) wheelbase, 18ft (5.5m) four-door 600. Heads of state had the Pullman, its wheelbase stretched to 153in (389cm) and available with an optional six doors,

MERCEDES-BENZ 600 (1963–81)	
Engine	V-eight
Capacity	6332cc
Power	250bhp
Transmission	4-speed auto
Top speed	123mph (197kph)
No. built	2,190 saloon/487

■ LEFT *The 600 in its normal wheelbase form was the ultimate in saloon car luxury with its V-eight engine, air suspension and electric adjustment for everything.*

extra occasional seats and a glass division between front and rear compartments. Both used a 6.3-litre fuel-injected V-eight engine producing 300bhp, driving through an obligatory four-speed automatic transmission. Independent suspension used air bags on all four wheels, powered by an under-bonnet pump, for a firm, comfortable ride. Seat adjustment, steering assistance and door locks were linked to

a central hydraulic system.

Despite its enormous weight – 5000lb (2268kg) for the saloon, 5850lb (2654kg) for the eight-seat Pullman – the 600 was no sluggardly barge: it would top 120mph (193kph), storming to 60 (96) in not much more than 10 seconds – though the penalty was fuel consumption in low teens. Handling, too, was surprisingly nimble, with good power steering, plenty of grip and

brakes – big four-wheel discs – that were beyond reproach. There were plenty of sports cars, never mind luxury saloons, that couldn't live with a well-driven Mercedes 600. Hugely expensive and hand built in tiny numbers, the 600 stayed on the Mercedes price lists until 1981 and had no effective replacement. The technology found its way on to lesser Mercedes, most famously the 300SEL 6.3 saloon of 1968.

■ RIGHT *The massive six-door car had extra occasional seats and a glass division. It would do 120mph (193kph).*

MG

■ MG TC/TD/TF

To get back into production quickly after the Second World War, MG of Abingdon, Oxfordshire had no option but to warm up its pre-war model, the TB. Thus the TC of 1945 had the same big 19in (48cm) wheels, fold-flat screen, crude semi-elliptic suspension and slab-tank body with ash framing. The body was wider now to give more elbow room for its passengers, while synchromesh on second, third and top gear made it more pleasant to drive. Hydraulic brakes were

■ ABOVE *The TD of 1949 was the first MG sportscar to have the independent suspension system from the YA saloon.*

MG TC/TD/TF (1945-55)	
Engine	In-line four
Capacity	1250/1466cc
Power	54-63bhp
Transmission	4-speed manual
Top speed	78-86mph (125-138kph)
No. built	10,000 TC/ 29,664 TD/9,800 TF

another welcome improvement.

Traditionalists loved it: it was nippy – 78mph (125kph) flat-out – and fun to drive. Nobody seemed to mind the heavy steering and rock-hard suspension. US servicemen stationed in the UK loved them so much they took them home and gave Americans a taste they never lost for European sports cars. Soon the TC was spearheading an export drive to the USA – and that's where most of the 10,000-car production run ended-up.

Charming as it was, the outdated TC couldn't go on for ever, so for 1949 MG introduced the TD: same chassis, same 1250cc four-cylinder engine but with

■ ABOVE *The TC has been a successful club racer. The normal screen is replaced by aero screens on this car; the roll-bar is a modern addition.*

■ RIGHT *A standard TC had a 1250cc engine and differed from the pre-war TC in its use of a wider body, synchromesh gearbox and hydraulic brakes.*

■ RIGHT *The TF was announced in 1953 with a more modern, sloping grille, and fuel tank. Inside there was a restyled dashboard and better seats.*

■ BELOW *The trade mark MG grille looked much as it did before the war.*

■ ABOVE *MkII TDs had a higher compression engine; 29,664 of them were built.*

■ LEFT *The TF was a holding operation until the MGA appeared. Later cars had a 1500cc engine.*

the new independent front suspension and the rack-and-pinion steering of the YA. Bumpers front and rear and smaller-disc wheel didn't do much for the looks, but the TD was roomier and slightly faster, especially in higher compression MkII form from 1952. The TD was a big seller, racking up 29,664 units in its four-year production run.

The final flowering of the traditional MG was the TF of 1953. By moulding the headlamps into the front wings, which sloped the grille and fuel tank,

Abingdon had gently modernized the shape. Inside, there were individual front seats and a restyled dashboard. Early cars had the 1250cc engine, but from 1954 a 1500cc unit giving 63bhp restored some of the performance.

The TF looked what it was – warmed-up leftovers – and was really a holding operation while Abingdon prepared its first modern post-war model, the MGA of 1955. Ironically, the TF is the most sought-after of the three "square-rigger" post-war MGs.

OTHER MAKES

■ **MESSERSCHMITT**
This West German aircraft manufacturer took over production of this design in 1953, continuing until 1962 before selling the project back to Fritz Fend, the maker of invalid carriages who had originally designed the car. The TG500 (Tiger) model was the most interesting, with a top speed of 75mph (120kph) on 20bhp and four wheels.

■ **METROPOLITAN**
Made by BMC and variously known as an Austin, Nash or Hudson, the little Pininfarina-designed coupé and convertible Metropolitan was conceived by Nash president Bill Mason as a small car for the American market. It was never a huge success, but at one time was the best-selling US import after the Volkswagen Beetle.

M G

■ MGA

The A was the first modern post-war MG. As the first new MG produced after the merger of Nuffield and Austin, it was also the first to use the corporate mechanical parts: much of the drive train was derived from the Austin A50 saloon. Its pretty pinched-waist body was derived from a special TD raced at Le Mans and was based on an enormously strong box-section chassis. Some said it was too strong and unnecessarily heavy, but it was certainly rigid.

There was nothing groundbreaking about the suspension, with its front wishbones and leaf-spring rear beam axle, yet the handling of the A was more than a match for its contemporary Triumph and Austin Healey rivals. Bolt-on steel wheels were the standard offering, with centre-lock wires as an option. On 1489cc and 72bhp from its B Series engine, it wasn't wildly quick, but 95mph (152kph) was respectable, as was the potential 30mpg.

It was joined by a handsome coupé version in 1956 and in 1958 by the exciting twin-cam with its Harry Weslake-designed twin overhead-camshaft 1588cc engine. With 108bhp, top speed went up to 110mph (177kph). It was a highly desirable property but the engine – based on a modified B series block – had a poor reliability record,

■ LEFT *The A was the first modern MG in years. It had very pretty styling and a stiff box-section chassis, the last used on an MG.*

MGA (1955-62)	
Engine	In-line four
Capacity	1489/1588/1622cc
Power	72-108bhp
Transmission	4-speed
Top speed	95-110mph (152-177kph)
No. built	101,081

■ LEFT *The MGA twin-cam was an exotic development using a new double overhead camshaft version of the B Series engine. It was powerful but troublesome. Dunlop centre-lock disc wheels are a twin-cam signature.*

■ RIGHT *The 1600 MGA had front disc brakes and could do a genuine 100mph (160kph). With its recessed front grille, this is a MkII.*

■ BELOW *The coupé version had well-balanced styling but was not as popular.*

■ BELOW *The simple dash featured basic instrumentation and a large steering-wheel.*

with a reputation for burning pistons. It was available in coupé and roadster form and could be recognized by its handsome Dunlop centre-lock lightweight steel wheels. Dunlop disc brakes on all wheels were standard. High prices and its dodgy reputation kept sales low. BMC killed this most exotic of MGs in 1960.

By that time the standard MGA had become the 1600, with 80bhp, disc front brakes and genuine 100mph (160kph) ability. The only outward difference, aside from badging, was the separate rear indicators. Optional was the DeLuxe, with the standard pushrod engine but the disc brakes and centre-lock wheels of the slow-selling twin-cam.

The final MkII 1600 of 1961 had a slightly bigger bore 1622cc engine, pushing the power output to 86bhp. You can identify a MkII by its recessed front grille and horizontal rear lights. Production finished in 1962, giving way to the unitary MGB, certainly a more modern MG than the A but not such a pretty one.

■ LEFT *To use up the remaining twin-cam parts, MG built the 1600 deluxe with the same disc brakes and centre-lock wheels.*

■ ABOVE *The B Series was an uninspiring engine but was reliable, cheap to build and simple to work on.*

■ LEFT *Today, enthusiasts have the twin-cam's engine problems licked.*

M G

■ LEFT *From the rear in particular, the B lacked the character of the more curvaceous MGA.*

■ MGB

The MGB is still one of the most numerically successful sports cars ever built, with more than half a million made between 1962 and its demise in 1980. At the height of its popularity Abingdon was making more than 50,000 a year.

The main difference between the MGB and its forebear the A was in construction: gone was the rugged and heavy separate chassis, replaced by a

■ BELOW LEFT *From 1962 to 1967, the MGB roadster looked like this with a chrome grille.*

■ BELOW RIGHT *The interiors were traditional but comfortable. Early cars had a large, sprung wheel.*

lighter unit construction shell. The car appeared originally as an open roadster with a three-bearing version of the venerable B Series 1798 four-cylinder engine. Torque was its main strong point – 110lb/ft (149.6Nm) at 3000rpm – but on twin SU carburettors its 95bhp at 5400rpm was creditable, if unsensational. Suspension, steering and rear axle came straight from the BMC parts bin to keep costs down, so there were few technical highlights, but the B was a genuine 100mph (160kph) car with safe, if uninspired, handling.

It was joined in 1965 by the Pininfarina-inspired BGT with its tailgate rear doors and occasional rear seat – strictly for children. It was 160lb (72.7kg) heavier than the roadster but

had the five-bearing engine and quieter rear axle from the start. MkII models from 1967 had the improved rear axle across the board as well as an all-synchromesh gearbox and the option of automatic transmission. Fashion dictated some minor styling tweeks in 1969 in the form of a recessed matt black grille and trendy Rostyle wheels. The interior suffered some minor styling tweeks around this time too, with more modern seats and steering wheel. For the American market this was when, in terms of power output, the rot began to set in, with lower compression ratios to satisfy local emission regulations.

There was much worse to come, however: in 1974, MG announced the black bumper cars with grotesque plastic

bumpers and increased ride height to keep the aging model legal in North America, where most production still went. Performance was in decline – the GT wouldn't even manage 100mph (160kph) – and the handling was ruined by its new, taller stance, but the car

MGB (1962-80)	
Engine	4-cylinder
Capacity	1798cc
Power	95bhp
Transmission	4-speed with overdrive
Top speed	106mph (170kph)
No. built	387,259 125,621 GTs

■ RIGHT *The hood folded well out of sight but was difficult to erect compared with foreign convertibles like the Fiat and Alfa Spider.*

■ BELOW *The B would do around 100mph (160kph) and could be had with overdrive or – later on – an automatic option.*

continued to sell because it was one of few open cars available. The B survived until 1980 with few changes, and it seemed likely that it would be the last proper MG sports car when British Leyland announced its decision to abandon the Abingdon factory.

There were two rather more exciting versions of this evergreen sports car. The MGC of 1967 was a three-litre version of the B designed to take the place of the "Big" Healey 3000 models. Bigger 15-in (38-cm) wheels and a bonnet bulge differentiated the C from the B and, underneath, there was torsion-bar front suspension rather than wishbones. With a 145bhp six-cylinder engine, the C was certainly fast, but nose-heavy weight distribution spoiled the handling. Just

under 9000 roadsters and GTs were sold in less than two years.

Four years later, British Leyland answered calls for a more powerful version of the car with the GT V-eight. With its smooth, quiet and very torquey Rover 3.5 V-eight this was a much better prospect, but yet again success eluded this 125mph (201kph) machine. It didn't look different enough from the stock four-cylinder car, and the critics panned its lack of suspension refinement, the wind noise and its relatively high price. Few wanted the V-eight in its day – only 2,591 were sold between 1973 and 1976 – but today it is a sought-after and entertaining classic, easily the best B of the lot.

■ ABOVE *The MGC was a six-cylinder version of the B. Its three-litre engine gave it 120mph (193kph) capability, but too much weight over the front wheels spoiled the handling.*

■ BELOW *An early three-bearing MGB on rare disc wheels. The styling was influenced by Pininfarina.*

MINI

■ LEFT *The Mini Cooper was the precursor to today's hot hatchbacks.*

■ MINI

The BMC Mini, launched in 1959, is Britain's most influential car ever. It defined a new genre. Other cars used front-wheel drive and transverse engines before but none in such a small space. Packaging was its greatest strength – interior space was staggering. Every square inch was used: there were big door-bins, tiny 10-in (25-cm) wheels that didn't intrude on passenger space and a bootlid you could fold down to use as a luggage platform.

Designer Alec Issigonis sketched his ideas on the back of envelopes, envisaging the most compact possible "cube" in which four passengers would sit, headed by a space-saving front-wheel-drive system. The gearbox was mounted *under* the engine instead of behind it, saving more inches. Another major innovation was a new rubber-cone suspension system designed by Dr Alex Moulton. Inspired by the Suez Crisis of 1956, the Mini amazingly took BMC just two years to develop and put into production. Launch was set for 26 August 1959.

There were four initial versions: the Austin Mini Seven and Morris Mini-

■ ABOVE *You can spot an early Mini by its outside door hinges, but the shape remains basically unchanged to this day.*

■ ABOVE *One of the famous works rally Minis still in action today.*

Minor, both available in basic or de luxe trim. Costs were pared down by fitting sliding windows, cable-pull door releases and those trademark externally welded body seams.

On the road, it handled better than any rival (and most sports cars) and

boasted "penny-a-mile" running costs. Nippy, easy to park, it quickly became fashionable to own and the word Mini passed into everyday English language. Subframes allowed a huge variety of Mini derivatives: van, pick-up, estate, long-boot Riley Elf and Wolsley Hornet,

■ ABOVE *Initially the cars were sold as the Austin Seven and the Morris Mini-Minor but in the late 1960s the Mini became a marque.*

■ RIGHT *The quaint Countryman version used non-structural timbers, in contrast to the Morris Minor.*

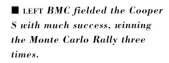

■ LEFT *BMC fielded the Cooper S with much success, winning the Monte Carlo Rally three times.*

■ LEFT *Today Rover has reinvented the Cooper as a trendy town car, but the original went out of production in 1971, in favour of the 1275GT.*

the Mini Moke workhorse-turned-leisure-vehicle and, recently, the Mini Cabriolet.

What sealed the Mini's reputation among enthusiasts, however, was the legendary Mini-Cooper, launched in 1961. Grand Prix-winning constructor John Cooper persuaded BMC to extract the most out of the Mini's innate handling prowess by stroking the 848cc Mini engine up to 997cc (later 998cc) and increasing power from 34bhp to 55bhp. Now 87mph (139kph) was possible, fast enough to justify fitting tiny front disc brakes. Later, there was an "S"

■ LEFT *An unmistakable shape, the superbly packaged Mini was voted "car of the century" by motoring pundits.*

MINI (1959–)	
Engine	4-cylinder
Capacity	848-1275cc
Power	33-76bhp
Transmission	4-speed manual 4-speed auto
Top speed	74-96mph (119-154kph)
No. built	More than 5,300,000

model with 70bhp on tap (later 1275cc versions were boosted to 76), capable of almost 100mph (160kph). BMC fielded works Mini-Coopers with incredible success. "Normal" Coopers won the Tulip Rally in 1962-63. The "S" was all-conquering in British saloon car racing and the Monte Carlo Rally, which it won in 1964, 1965 and 1967. Sadly, the Cooper was dropped in 1971 in British Leyland's rationalization.

The Mini has seen many technical changes: hydrolastic liquid suspension

from 1964; winding windows from 1969; the option of square-nosed Clubman and 1275 GT versions from 1969; bigger 12-in (30.5-cm) wheels from 1984 and standard 1275cc engines from 1992. Nearly 40 years on, the Mini has as passionate a following as ever and was recently voted "Car of the Century" by motoring pundits. It provides cheap transport and is a technical triumph, a dominant rally car, a packaging masterpiece and, as Britain's best-selling car ever, a runaway sales success.

■ ABOVE *Radford and Wood and Pickett offered luxury Minis trimmed to Rolls-Royce standards in the 1960s and 70s. Peter Sellers owned a Radford Mini.*

MORGAN

■ MORGAN 4/4

Morgan made its name with three-wheeled tricycles. It didn't make its first four-wheeled sports car until 1936. That, the original 4/4, disappeared in favour of the more powerful Vanguard-engined Plus Four in 1950. However, by the mid-50s Morgan perceived a need for a more basic car priced below the Plus Four. Thus the Series II 4/4 was reborn after five years.

Like all Morgans, it used a simple ladder-frame chassis, sliding-pillar front suspension and ash framing for the traditional-looking steel or light alloy bodies with the new-style cowled waterfall grille seen on the Plus Four from 1954. Up to 1960, power came from the Ford side-valve Anglia 100E engines. From 1960, in SIII form, there were 997cc overhead-valve engines from the 105E Anglia and four speeds at last.

Series IV cars from 1961 to 1963

were given a bigger 1340cc engine, pushing the top speed above 70mph (112kph) and now there were front disc brakes for the first time. In 1963, it was given the latest Cortina engines in

standard 1498cc and GT form. In 1968, it had the crossflow Kent engine, usually in 95bhp competition form, which was standardized anyway from 1971. From 1969, a four-seater body – with an ugly

■ ABOVE *The shape of the Morgan has hardly changed since the early 1950s. Only the disc wheels date this car.*

■ ABOVE *The car that started it all, the Morgan three-wheeler.*

■ LEFT *The body is aluminium fashioned over a traditional ash frame.*

■ ABOVE *Today Morgans are still built slowly by hand in the Malvern factory. There is a long waiting list.*

■ ABOVE *The period styling of the Morgan is its main attraction, but it also drives like a car from the 1930s, with a hard ride and very few creature comforts – but that's how the buyers like it.*

pram-like hood – was offered.

Since the early 80s, various power plants have been available, including the Fiat 1600 twin-cam and 1600 CVH Ford Escort engine. A five-speed gearbox was offered from 1982. The car continues to this day with the Rover twin-cam engine.

With its rock-hard ride, flexing body and anachronistic looks, the Morgan 4/4 has a unique post-vintage thoroughbred appeal. Hand built very slowly in Morgan's Malvern factory in Hereford and Worcester County, the 4/4 is still hugely popular – if you want one, you'll have to join a five-year waiting list.

MORGAN 4/4 (1955–)	
Engine	4-cylinder
Capacity	1172-1599cc (Ford engines)
Power	36-96bhp
Transmission	3/4/5-speed
Top speed (120–177kph)	75-110mph
No. built	6,803 up to 1991

■ LEFT *Minimal instruments and a big, sprung steering-wheel give the Morgan a traditional feel inside, too.*

OTHER MAKES

■ MINIJEM
Closely derived from the 1964 DART prototype of Dizzy Addicott, the Jem was thus a sister-car to the Mini-Marcos, which was also spawned by the DART. It was made at four locations over the years, its principal homes being Penn, in Buckinghamshire, and Cricklade, in Wiltshire.

■ MONTEVERDI
These Swiss-built, American-engined supercars were designed by Peter Monteverdi, who built his first car in 1951 at the age of 17. In 1956 he took over his father's repair shop in Basle (Basel), and orientated it towards specialist sports cars, becoming the world's youngest Ferrari importer. The first of the big V-eight cars was the "High Speed" of 1967. Vehicle manufacture continued until 1982. It included luxury saloons and off-roaders based on Mercedes saloons and American models.

MORGAN

■ MORGAN PLUS 8

When supplies of the 2138cc Triumph four-cylinder engine dried up in the late 60s, Morgan were left without a high-performance engine for their flagship Plus 4 model. Help was on the horizon, however, in the form of Rover's all-alloy 3.5-litre V-eight derived from a discarded Buick design of the early 60s and recently introduced in the big P5B saloon and coupé. Light, compact and powerful (165bhp), it was ideal for the job and transformed the Morgan into a real road-burner: top speed leapt to more than 120mph (193kph) with stunning rapid acceleration matched by very few road cars. Renamed the Plus 8, it looked at first glance identical to its predecessor but in fact had a slightly longer wheelbase and wheel track and subtly different body contours. The most obvious change was the light alloy wheels but, underneath, the sliding pillar front suspension and leaf-sprung live rear axle remained – along with the rock-hard vintage-style ride.

It was an immediate success, with more than 4,000 built to date, though

■ ABOVE *You can spot a Plus 8 by its light alloy wheels, though the wheelbase was longer and the track wider than the 4/4.*

■ LEFT *The Rover V-eight engine gave the Plus 8 electrifying performance.*

■ ABOVE *The body of the Plus 8, like all Morgans, was fashioned in alloy over a timber frame.*

■ RIGHT *Announced in 1968, the Plus 8 is still in production today.*

■ BELOW *The four-seater Plus 4 Morgan was practical but suffered from an unattractive hood.*

■ RIGHT *The body of the Plus 8 was wider than lesser Morgans. By the late 70s there was a five-speed gearbox from the Rover SD1 saloons.*

never at a rate of more than 15 per week. Steel bodywork was standard – with ash framing, of course – but there was an optional sports lightweight version from 1975. Early cars used the noisy, old-fashioned Moss gearbox familiar on Jaguar saloons, but from 1972 the Rover four-speed transmission was used. The five-speed unit from the SD1 Rover saloon was used from 1977. Fuel injection was introduced in 1984 and rack-and-pinion steering in 1986. The latest cars have a 3.0-litre version of the Rover engine, giving 190bhp.

As with the 4/4, demand for this anachronistic car remains healthy, with a waiting list of several years.

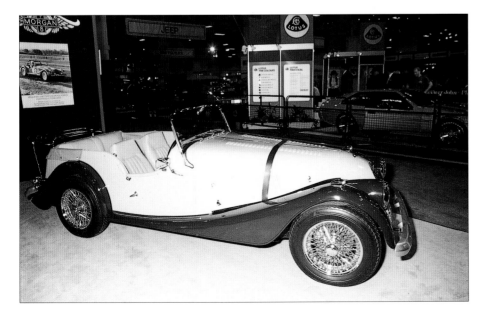

■ ABOVE *More than 4,000 Plus 8s have been built since production started in 1968.*

■ LEFT *Production of the four-cylinder models continues alongside the Plus 8.*

MORGAN PLUS 8 (1968-)	
Engine	V-eight
Capacity	3528cc
Power	160-190bhp
Transmission	4-5 speed
Top speed	125mph (201kph)
No. built	4,000 plus

MORRIS

■ BELOW *The 1950 Minors retained the split screen and side-valve engine, but the headlights were moved to the tops of the wings.*

■ MORRIS MINOR

The much-loved Morris Minor was the outstanding economy car of its day and became one of the best-selling and longest lived too – production ran from 1948 to 1971.

Its rack-and-pinion steering and torsion-bar independent suspension gave superb handling. Modern unitary construction and smooth styling made the Minor seem ultramodern after the warmed-up pre-war cars British motorists were used to. Designer Alec Issigonis had wanted a flat-four engine for the car but had to make do with the existing Series E flat-head in-line unit,

■ ABOVE *The early Minors had a split two-piece front screen.*

MORRIS MINOR (1948-71)	
Engine	In-line four
Capacity	918/803/943/1098cc
Power	27-48bhp
Transmission	4-speed manual
Top speed	60-78mph (96-125kph)
No. built	1,583,619

smooth but under-powered. These, known as the MM Series cars, had low-mounted headlights until 1950. The two-door and open tourer were joined by the four-door at about the same time, but the most important change came in 1952 when the overhead-valve Austin engine was fitted, first fruit of the BMC merger. The classic half-timbered Traveller was announced in 1953.

■ RIGHT *A later Minor 1000 tourer. By 1959, production of the Minor had turned a million cars. The last cars had a bigger 1098cc engine.*

■ ABOVE *The classic Minor convertible, or tourer, was announced alongside the saloon in 1948. It is now the most sought-after of them all.*

■ ABOVE *Overhead-valve A Series engines from the Austin A35 much improved the Minor's performance. The last cars could achieve 70mph (112kph).*

■ ABOVE *The four-door Minor 1000. All Minors had excellent handling thanks to rack-and-pinion steering and well thought-out suspension.*

The next landmark was the introduction of the 948cc engine in 1956 when the cars were badged Minor 1000. Combined with the higher final drive, this put the top speed up to a respectable 70mph (112kph). You could recognize the Minor 1000 by its larger rear window (on the saloons) and one-piece front screen. There were wider opening doors from 1959. Flashing indicators replaced semaphores in 1961. When production turned 1 million in 1959, BMC produced 350 commemorative Minor 1,000,000s with lilac paint and white seats. The last major update was introduction of the 48bhp 1098cc engine in 1962. The open tourers and four-door saloons died out in the late 60s, but the two-door – and the Traveller – continued until 1971. Simple, enjoyable and easy to drive, Minors survive in large numbers and remain one of the most affordable true classics you can buy.

OTHER MAKES

■ MORRIS

William Morris introduced his "Bullnose" Morris Oxford in 1913. His aggressive price-cutting enabled the Morris car to be made in such quantity and at such a price that by the end of the 1920s the company held 51 per cent of the market. The best-selling Eight was the mainstay of the 30s, replaced in 1948 by the Minor. In 1952 came the merger with Austin to the British Motor Corporation (BMC). From then, the marque began to lose its identity, culminating in the demise of the name in 1983.

■ MOSKVICH

Moskvich – "Son of Moscow" – was at first a pre-war Opel Kadett, built from 1947 with appropriated German tooling. Home-grown products took over in 1956. The model most sold in Britain was the 412 Series, universally panned for its handling and terrible brakes, although its performance was good for the low price.

■ LEFT *The Traveller with its half-timbered rear end was a much-loved variant. Along with the two-door, it was the last Minor to be dropped in 1971.*

NSU

■ NSU Ro80

The German company NSU established its reputation in the post-Second World War years building well-engineered rear-engined economy cars. The Ro80, its first and only big luxury car, startled the motoring world. Here was the world's first purpose-built twin-rotor wankel-engined saloon. Not only was the Ro80 fast – top speed 112mph (180kph) – and supersmooth, but it was beautiful, too, with a futuristic and slippery five-seater body that pointed the way to styling in the 1980s.

Front-wheel drive, superb power

■ LEFT *The Ro80 looked amazingly futuristic in 1967 with its rising waistline, high tail and big glass area. Many considered it the world's finest saloon.*

■ ABOVE *NSU's gamble with the Ro80 didn't pay off, and VW ended up buying the company in 1969.*

■ ABOVE *The shape was highly aerodynamic, making for relaxed and quiet high-speed cruising.*

■ ABOVE *In their advertising, NSU tried to convince buyers that they had the car's problems licked.*

steering and four-wheel disc brakes gave it excellent handling; long-travel strut suspension gave it a comfortable, absorbent ride. To mask the wankel's poor low-down torque and over-run snatch, NSU specified a three-speed

NSU Ro80 (1967-77)	
Engine	2-rotor wankel
Capacity	1990cc (nominal)
Power	113bhp
Transmission	3-speed semi-automatic
Top speed	112mph (180kph)
No. built	37,204

■ LEFT *An early Ro80 on steel wheels. With its three-speed semi-automatic transmission, the car could achieve 112mph (179kph), but fuel consumption was heavy.*

■ OPPOSITE *The shape of today's Audis and VWs owes much to the bold originality of the Ro80.*

■ LEFT *Later cars like this had revised tail lights. Otherwise the style changed hardly at all in the 10-year production run.*

■ BELOW *The engine was a two-rotor unit giving 113bhp: it was nominally rated at just under two litres.*

semi-automatic transmission: there was no clutch pedal but an electric switch in the gearknob that operated a vacuum system when a gear was selected. NSU called them "performance ranges", with second gear taking the car from a standstill to 80mph (128kph).

The car, a minor masterpiece, had a fatal flaw: its engine. Inadequately developed, it suffered from acute wear of its rotor-tip seals, and after 15,000 miles (24,150km) (or less) owners

noticed lack of power and higher fuel use. Engines became difficult to start and smoked like chimneys. NSU were generous with warranty claims. Many cars had as many as nine new engines! Owners, legend has it, didn't wave when they saw another Ro80 but displayed fingers to denote how many new engines they had had.

The costs sent NSU into the arms of Volkswagen in 1969. As word spread about the wankel engine's problems,

sales plummeted. Production, at a lower level, lasted until 1977 when the NSU name died along with this beautiful, innovative saloon. Values of second-hand cars also plummeted in the 70s and 80s, and many owners fitted Ford V-four engines to keep the cars going. Twenty years after the Ro80's demise, collectors are rediscovering it now that engine problems are solved (many have fitted the Mazda RX7 unit). For the brave, a good one is still a superb car.

OTHER MAKES

■ NOBEL

This was a licence-built version of the fellow-German Fuldamobil, which was also manufactured (apparently) in South Africa, Chile, the Netherlands, Greece, Sweden and India. In Britain, it was assembled by Ulster shipbuilders Harland & Wolfe, with a chassis made by aviation firm Shorts and a group body by the Bristol Aircraft Company; it was briefly marketed by the fading Lea-Francis concern.

OLDSMOBILE

■ OLDSMOBILE TORONADO

The Oldsmobile Toronado of 1965 brought front-wheel-drive (FWD) technology to the mass American market for the first time, not in a compact runabout but a huge, stylish supercoupé. In Europe, the likes of Issigonis said big engines and front drive would never mix, but Oldsmobile didn't listen: the Toronado was always going to be a big one.

Under the flamboyant sheet metal, the Toronado was a clever concoction of conventional Detroit practice – drum brakes all round, beefy perimeter-frame chassis – but plenty of trick stuff, at

least by American standards. The seven-litre "Rocket" engine was mounted in-line with the torque converter on the back but, cunningly, the usual three-speed Hydra-Matic gearbox (running the opposite way to normal) was nestling under the left-hand cylinder bank. They were connected by a multiple-link Morse chain – lots of work went into making this quiet – and the power fed into a spiral bevel diff.

The resultant power-pack was mounted on a rubber-insulated sub-frame which allowed a complete

■ ABOVE LEFT *Headlights live under electrically operated flaps. The style is commendably fuss-free.*

■ ABOVE *The Toronado's shape was free of excessive glitz, although the dimensions were very Detroit.*

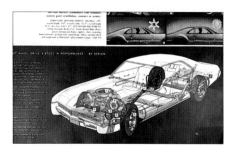

■ ABOVE *The cutaway shows the perimeter frame chassis and front-drive power-pack. But the brakes were not up to the job.*

OLDSMOBILE TORONADO (1965-70)	
Engine	V-eight
Capacity	7446cc
Power	385 @ 4600rpm
Transmission	3-speed auto
Top speed	130mph (209kph)
No. built	143,134

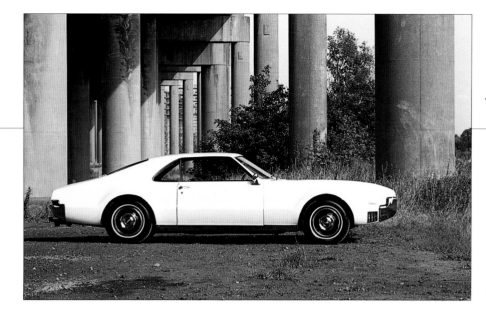

■ RIGHT *The two-tone Toronado could do 135mph (217kph) and had better handling than the average American car – but few buyers noticed the difference.*

flat-floor. Torsion-bar suspension was used up front, attached to the subframe, while a dead axle, single-leaf springs and twin vertical and horizontal dampers were used at the rear to limit hop under hard braking. Firestone developed special tyres for the Toronado with stiffer sidewall construction and more grip to take advantage of the front-wheel drive, although in service they gained a reputation for savage wear rates. Wheels were slotted to cool the finned brake drums.

After being exhaustively tested – General Motors didn't want any reliability problems prejudicing buyers against FWD – the Toronado was finally launched in the autumn of 1965 to rave reviews. Not only did its bold styling set it apart from the big-coupé herd; its handling really was more capable on the road: 60 per cent of the weight overhanging the front driving wheels meant lots of traction and fine stability yet less of the plough-on than you'd find in the comparable Buick Riviera. The Toronado could pull you out of trouble, not push you into it. Only the too-small drum brakes were criticized in this

two-ton (2032kg), 135mph (217kph) car.

American buyers had a year-long honeymoon period with the Toronado (buying 40,000 in 1966) but from 1967 they tended to prefer the Riviera, which looked – and was – more conventional, as well as being cheaper. The purity of the original car was lost on most Americans, who couldn't tell if it was front driven or not – and didn't care. It was given a completely new and awful bodyshell from 1971 and from then on looked like every other slobwagon on the freeway.

Today, a good example of the original Toronado would make an entertaining and intriguing addition to any collection of milestone cars – if you have the room.

OTHER MAKES

■ OGLE

David Ogle's first design in 1959 was based on a Riley 1.5, with the neat SX1000 coupé following in 1963. However, Ogle's death in an SX1000 and the British firm's loss-making production saw car manufacture cease the following year. The firm did make some one-off designs afterwards and is most famous for its Reliant Scimitar.

■ OPEL

Opel produced its first car in 1898 and by 1928 was the largest car maker in Germany. In the late 1920s, the firm was reorganized as a joint-stock company, with majority shareholding going to General Motors. During the 1930s, Opel ranked first among European car producers. After the Second World War its products tended to be very Americanized, but by the mid-60s it was producing clean European designs like the Rekord, the Commodore and the little 1900GT. Opel is today the driving force behind GM's potent presence in Europe.

■ LEFT *Inevitably, the stylist began to fiddle with the clean shape. From the late 1960s, the shape got progressively boring.*

PANHARD

■ PANHARD 24CT

Founded in 1889, the French firm of Panhard was one of the pioneers of motoring, but by the 1950s its star had begun to fade as sales went into decline in the face of more conventional opposition from Peugeot, Citroën and Renault. This is not to say, however, that the company didn't make some impressive machines: the Dyna was one of the best and fastest economy cars of its era, giving 75mph (120kph) on two cylinders and 745cc, while the PL17 that followed was a futuristic family six-seater, still with a mere 845 air-cooled flat-twin engine yet capable of 90mph (145kph) in Tigre form.

■ ABOVE *The PL17 was one of the best, and fastest, economy cars of its era.*

■ RIGHT *In Tigre form the PL17 could achieve 90mph (145kph) on a mere 845cc.*

■ ABOVE *The last Panhard was the stylish 24 Series coupé, still with the small 650cc air-cooled flat-twin engine.*

PANHARD 24 CT (1963-67)	
Engine	Flat-twin
Capacity	845cc
Power	60bhp
Transmission	4-speed manual
Top speed	100mph (160kph)
No. built	23,245 all models

Even more desirable was the glamorous little 24 Series, introduced in 1963 and the last Panhard of all. Here was a modern-looking two-plus-two coupé with a stylish, slippery shape distinguished by large window areas and cowled-in lights behind glass. It used the same drive train as the PL17 with front-wheel drive, four speeds and two engine options, the most powerful being the Tigre unit giving 60bhp with a twin-choke carb (24CT). Top speed, even with just 845cc, was an amazing 100mph (160kph), still with potential if

■ LEFT *The original post-war Panhard was the Dyna, its design attributable to Gregoire.*

driven normally. The flat twin, related to the original Grégoire design of the 1940s, couldn't disguise its poor, low-speed torque and roughness, but it smoothed out beautifully at higher speeds where the CT excelled. The 24CT had the lower-powered 50bhp unit. The range was broadened by the 24B, BT and BA with a longer wheelbase and full four-seater body. All cars had a four-speed floor gear-change and, from 1965, four-wheel disc brakes.

By then, Citroën had taken over the ailing Panhard and were struggling to make the expensive-to-build 24 Series profitable. Sales were slow. and Citroën gave up the unequal struggle in 1967, killing the marque and using the Paris factory to increase their own production capacity.

■ ABOVE *The 24 Series handled well but would lift a wheel, as here, if pressed hard.*

■ LEFT *The Dyna was the French equivalent of the Morris Minor, but rather more advanced with its front-wheel-drive chassis.*

■ BELOW *Front-wheel drive made them competitive rally cars too. This is a PL17 on the 1956 Monte Carlo Rally.*

■ ABOVE *With special lightweight bodywork, the Panhards were successful in* *their class in competition. This is a Monopole Panhard at Montlhery.*

PEGASO

■ PEGASO Z102 AND Z103

The Spanish company Pegaso's main commercial concern has always been trucks and motor coaches, but for a brief period in the 50s it was also noted for its cars, perhaps the most glamorous and certainly among the fastest of their day. They combined racing-car design and engineering with exotic Italian styling, but only 100 cars were produced – some say only 84.

■ LEFT *Touring did many of the bodies on the Pegaso sportscars, in shape not unlike the Ferraris of the day.*

■ BELOW *Apart from the bodywork, everything for the Pegaso was produced in-house at the Barcelona factory.*

■ LEFT *The original Z102 prototype, had slightly dumpy styling and in steel, rather than aluminium.*

First of the line was the Z102 of 1951. Cast in the mould of the Aston DB2 and Lancia Aurelia, here was a super sports car with a specification that was pure copybook stuff: four-cam V-eight engine, dry-sump lubrication, five-speed gearbox mounted in unit with diff, all mounted in a state-of-the-art pressed platform chassis. Everything was produced in house at the Barcelona factory, including the rather dumpy – and overweight – coupé and convertible prototype steel bodies. Production Z102s had 2.8-litre

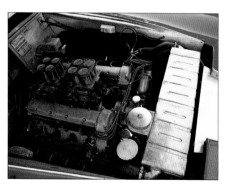

■ ABOVE *The four-cam engine had dry-sump lubrication and produced 175-360bhp.*

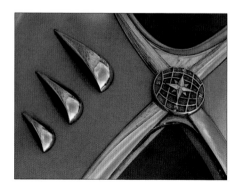

■ ABOVE *The four points of the compass badge showed ambitions for worldwide sales – in fact only eight were exported.*

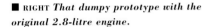

■ LEFT *The fastest of the Pegasos were good for 160mph (257kph). Surprisingly, they had little success in racing.*

■ ABOVE *The best-looking of the bodies used on the Pegasos was the Touring Spider, but only one was built.*

■ RIGHT *That dumpy prototype with the original 2.8-litre engine.*

■ ABOVE *The Pegaso badge: the company was better known for its trucks and motor coaches.*

engines and a much lighter and more elegant Touring body, crafted in alloy. This would become the definitive Pegaso style, although there was one beautiful Touring Spider. The French company Saoutchik also did a few coupés, without much success.

Pegaso constantly meddled with the specification of the car: the 2.8-litre engine came with single and multi-choke carburettors (giving between 175 and 190bhp), and later there was a 3.2-litre option with twin four-barrel carbs and 230bhp. A supercharged version of the 2.8 gave up to 280bhp, and there was even a 3.2-litre version with 360bhp.

The performance was fantastic, with up to 160mph (257kph) in its most powerful form and an amazing noise generated by its gear-driven camshafts. They were heavy, brutish cars to drive, and despite their good handling and power they never found much competition success.

The cars were always built on a cost-no-object basis, and the Z103 was a last-ditch effort to make them more commercially successful, using simpler single overhead-camshaft V-eight engines with 3.9, 4.5 and 4.9-litre capacities.

Pegaso built its last sports cars in 1958. They never made any money for

the company but at least they proved they could do it and compete with the best in the world.

PEGASO Z102 AND Z103 (1951-58)	
Engine	V-eight
Capacity	2816/3178/3988/4450cc
Power	175-360bhp
Transmission	5-speed manual
Top speed	120-160mph (193-257kph)
No. built	About 100

■ FAR LEFT *The gearbox was mounted in unit with the diff at the back for good handling.*

■ LEFT *This is the Pegaso racer, in Spanish racing colours.*

PORSCHE

■ PORSCHE 356

Ferdinand Porsche set up his design consultancy in 1931 but the first car to bear his name – the 356 – was not built until 1946. A dumpy-looking little rear-engined sports car, the 356 was closely related to the VW Beetle – another famous Porsche design – with an air-cooled flat-four pushrod engine and the same kind of trailing-link front suspension with high-pivot swing axles at the rear. There were coupé, cabriolet and shallow-screened sportster versions, the latter now much sought-after (and replicated by kit-car builders).

Early cars, built in Austria up to 1950, had split windscreens and 1100cc versions of the aircooled flat four producing just 40bhp. There were further 1287, 1290 and 1488cc versions producing up to 70bhp. The original

■ LEFT *The 356A was an improved version of the original 1946 car, announced in 1955.*

■ LEFT *An air-cooled flat-four engine was the trademark of the 356, mounted in the rear.*

PORSCHE 356 (1949-65)	
Engine	Flat four
Capacity	1086-1966cc
Power	40-155bhp
Transmission	4-speed
Top speed	87-130mph (139-209kph)
No. built	82,363

rounded roly-poly styling was changed on the 1955 356A to a crisper shape with a curved one-piece screen, improved front suspension and steering and a bigger 1600 engine.

From here on the story gets complex: the 356B of 1959 had a higher nose and came in two new styles – the speedster-based Roadsters and a notchback coupé by Karmann. Top of the standard range was the 110mph (177kph) Super 90, but even the standard 60bhp car could

achieve 100mph (160kph). The last-of-the-line, the 356C, had ZF steering and four-wheel disc brakes. The names were changed, too: the Super became the 1600C, the Super 75 the 1600S and the Super 90 the 1600SC, with an extra 5bhp.

For advanced students there were the Carrera versions of the 356 from 1955. Engines were still flat fours but totally different in detail: the crank was a roller bearing type and instead of pushrods

■ ABOVE *The interiors of all models were stark and functional but entirely comfortable.*

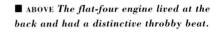

■ BELOW *Cabriolet versions, much sought-after today, could be had with a factory hardtop.*

■ RIGHT *Versions with a special four-cam with dry-sump lubrication and up to 125mph in two-litre form were also available.*

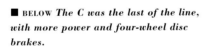

there were four overhead camshafts with twin-plug per-cylinder ignition. With lighter bodywork, the first 100bhp cars were good for 120mph (193kph) and 1.6-litre models from 1958 an amazing 130mph (209kph). The Carrera 2, based on the B/C series, appeared in spring 1960 with a new two-litre version of the complex four-cam flat four which produced up to 155bhp in GT form.

The 356 improved dramatically over the years, growing more and more specialized and increasingly distant from its VW Beetle roots. Compact, beautifully built and in some cases very fast, it was the car with which Porsche built its reputation in the 50s, and its passing was much mourned when the 911 Series took over completely in 1965.

This left a gap in the range for a cheaper Porsche, filled by the 912 which used the pushrod 356 engine in a 911 shell.

■ BELOW *The C was the last of the line, with more power and four-wheel disc brakes.*

■ ABOVE *The flat-four engine lived at the back and had a distinctive throbby beat.*

PORSCHE

■ PORSCHE 911

A triumph of development over design, the Porsche 911, launched in 1964, is still going strong. There have been countless variations, but first-generation pre-1974 cars are seen as the most classic. Built before impact bumpers, they have cleaner looks and are purer in conception. Conceived by "Ferry" Porsche (son of the company's founder) and styled by Butzi Porsche, the 911 has been honed year-by-year to iron out detail weaknesses and to conquer handling deficiencies inherent in having its air-cooled flat-six engine located behind the rear wheels. Fast and agile, the 911 is one of the most practical supercars, with rear seats and a formidable reputation for reliability.

All models had four-wheel disc brakes and five-speed gearboxes on manual cars. Front suspension was by wishbones and torsion bars, the rear tied down by trailing arms and torsion bars. Superbly communicative steering and faithful, pin-sharp handling endeared the car to many, though it has never shaken off the suspicion of unruly lift-off oversteer in extreme situations, promoted by the high inertia of the rear engine position.

The first cars used a 1991cc version of the SOHC flat-six engine producing 130bhp. The Targa with removable roof panel was announced in September

■ ABOVE *The first Porsche cars were built in Austria, but the 911s have always been built in Stuttgart, Germany.*

■ ABOVE *The ultimate early type 911 is the 2.7RS Carrera with its lighter shell and stiffer suspension.*

1966. Top of the range was the 160bhp 911S, with forged pistons and larger valves, which could do 140mph (225kph). The brakes were now vented but as always unservoed, for better feel. 1966 saw the début of the classic five-spoke alloy wheels, hallmark of the early 911.

In 1967 the 911L replaced the

standard 911 (130bhp, similar trim to 911S) and there was a new base-level 911T with 110bhp. The semi-automatic "Sportsmatic", three speed and no clutch pedal, is little fancied today.

1968 saw introduction of the B-Series models with a 2.2in (5.6cm) increase in wheelbase – for better weight distribution and handling. Meanwhile,

PORSCHE 911 (1964-73)	
Engine	Aircooled flat six
Capacity	1991-2993cc
Power	130-230bhp
Transmission	5-speed manual
Top speed	130-155mph (209-249kph)
No. built	89,256

■ OPPOSITE *The enduring shape of the 911 is much the same today. This is a 911 2.4S from the early 1970s.*

■ ABOVE LEFT *Today's 911, available with two- and four-wheel drive and as popular as ever.*

■ LEFT *In the 1960s and 70s the 911 had considerable rallying success thanks to its power and traction.*

the new 911E model replaced the 911L, and there was now Bosch mechanical fuel injection for between 140bhp (E) and 170bhp (S), although the 110bhp 911T kept its Weber carbs.

The 1969 C-Series models had 2195cc engines for more bottom-end torque. The flat six had larger valves, magnesium crankcase and lower compression; power outputs ranged from 125bhp for the T to 155bhp for the E and 180bhp for the S, which had standard alloy wheels and a rear anti-roll bar. Faster 2.4 cars came in from September 1971, ranging from 130 to 190bhp.

The ultimate early 911 was the Carrera 2.7RS with a lighter shell and stiffer suspension. Launched in Sport, Touring or Racing form, it was built for just one year (1972–73) as a homologation car for Group 4 racing. A bore increase gave 2687cc and 210bhp thanks to flatter forged pistons and Nikasil cylinders. Only 500 were required for homologation, but the car proved so popular that Porsche built more than 1500. These ultimately early 911s, capable of 150mph (241kph), were characterized by a ducktail spoiler, flared rear arches and bold Carrera side decals.

■ ABOVE *The last 59 Carrera RS lightweights had a three-litre engine, giving 230bhp.*

■ OPPOSITE *Early cars had 130bhp, still good enough for a top speed of 130mph (209kph).*

OTHER MAKES

■ PARAMOUNT
The Ford-based sporty tourer Paramount was first shown to the British press in 1950. By 1951, making was taken over by the Meynell Motor Co, before being done by Camden Motors who formed Paramount Cars (Leighton Buzzard) Ltd. The car's price was too high and by 1956, with just a handful built, Paramount was finished.

■ PEEL/VIKING
The 50cc Peel P50 of 1962–66 and the "astrodome" Peel Trident 100cc bubble-car were austere runabouts. The firm then developed the Trident Mini but after two were built the project was taken over by Bill Last, later to make the Trident. He renamed the car the Viking Minisport.

■ PEERLESS/WARWICK
The Peerless was created by British special-builder and engine-tuner Bernie Rodger. Two alloy-bodied prototypes were built in 1957. Manufacture started in Slough,

Berkshire in 1958, with backing from hotelier Jim Burns and John Gordon. After the demise of Peerless Cars, Bernard Rodger Developments was set up in Horton, Buckinghamshire, to continue Peerless production. Gordon stayed at the retail outlet of Peerless Motors and worked on the Gordon GT, which became the Gordon Keeble.o

■ PIPER
Originally, Piper offered sports-racing and Formula 3 cars. A separate enterprise developed the dramatic GTT with its space-frame, square-tube chassis and Ford engines. Plans for V-eight-powered road and competition cars were shelved but GTT/P2 production continued until 1974.

■ POWERDRIVE
Another of the late-1950s crop of British economy cars, the Powerdrive had a 322cc motorcycle engine and gearbox and a three-seater roadster body with twin-tube frame. It survived until 1958. Low road tax, insurance and fuel consumption were the attractions. It is *not* related to the similar Coronet three-wheeler.

RELIANT

■ BELOW *Tom Karen of Ogle gave the Scimitar its distinctive shape, based on the original Scimitar Coupé.*

■ RELIANT SCIMITAR GTE

Today's sporting Estates come from BMW and Volvo, but it was Reliant of Tamworth – a marque synonymous with the three-wheeler – that originated the genre in 1968. Its trend-setting Scimitar GTE inspired imitators worldwide.

The Scimitar GTE (Grand Touring Estate), based on Reliant's existing Ford three-litre V-six engined Scimitar coupé, had a trendy rising waistline and a wedge-like profile which skilfully hid the 36 cu ft of load space, accessible through a stylish one-piece glass hatch supported on spring struts. The full four-seat GTE was the first car to have rear seats that folded *separately*, an arrangement copied by almost all hatchbacks. Styled by Tom Karen of Ogle (responsible for the Scimitar coupé and Robin three-wheeler), like every other Reliant the GTEs body was moulded in rust-resistant glassfibre while retaining a steel box-frame chassis for strength and rigidity. Ford's big pushrod three-litre V-six engine in such a light car meant the Scimitar was fast – it could do 120mph (193kph) – and reliable. Frugal overdrive cars did 27mpg. The Scimitar was soon the darling of the English country-house set, an image boosted when Princess Anne received a GTE as a

Christmas gift in 1970.

In 1975, Reliant introduced wide-bodied SE6 cars. These softer, more comfortable Scimitars – built to enter the executive market – never recaptured the elegance of the 1968 original. Cheaper mass-market imitators were eating into the market the GTE once had to itself. By the early 80s, Reliant were losing heart, ravaged by recession and unable to find investment to bring the GTE up to date. The last car was built in 1986.

■ LEFT *The most desirable of the Scimitars was the narrow-bodied SE5A, here on alloy wheels.*

■ ABOVE *The Scimitar GTC was a convertible version of the late 70s, designed to rekindle some showroom interest in the Scimitar.*

SCIMITAR GTE (1968–86)	
Engine	Ford V-six
Capacity	2994-2792cc
Power	135bhp @ 5500rpm
Transmission	4-speed manual
Top speed	121mph (195kph) (SE5a)
No. built	15,273

RENAULT

■ RENAULT 16

Today, the front-wheel-drive hatchback is the mainstay of the family-car market in Europe, but when Renault introduced its 16 in December 1964, the concept of a five-door saloon was very new. With its rear hatchback door and fold-down rear seats, the 16 was unparalleled when introduced, even if you didn't appreciate the slightly awkward styling.

Front-wheel drive gave it excellent roadholding while long-travel, all-independent suspension ensured a soft, absorbent ride on even the roughest of French roads. Disc front brakes were also to its credit, and even on a modest 1470cc the original 55bhp 16 could touch 90mph (145kph). It was an instant hit and had a long production life, finally giving way to the Renault 20 in 1979.

The 16TS of 1968 was a higher-performance 1565cc, 88bhp version of the car giving 100mph (160kph), though the ultimate 16 was the TX of 1973 with power increased to 93bhp. Five speeds made it an ideal motorway cruiser, while electric front windows were a rare luxury on a family car in the mid-70s. You could spot a TX by its four-headlamp nose and sports wheels.

Enthusiasts are now beginning to rediscover the excellent qualities of this ground-breaking saloon, which is now a rare sight.

RENAULT 16 (1964–79)	
Engine	In-line four
Capacity	1470/1565/1647cc
Power	55-93bhp
Transmission	4/5-speed manual 3-speed auto
Top speed	90-105mph (145–169kph)
No. built	1,846,000

■ ABOVE *In 1964-65 the rear hatch was the ultimate in family car practicality, but today we wouldn't accept the high loading sill.*

■ LEFT *With its 16 of 1964, Renault invented the five-door hatchback. Every major manufacturer has since copied it.*

■ BELOW LEFT *The 16 was no beauty, but its looks were honest and distinctive. Later TX models had four square lights.*

■ BELOW RIGHT *With its long wheelbase and high roof-line the 16 was a generous five-seater with comfortable long-travel suspension.*

OTHER MAKES

■ RELIANT

A development of the Raleigh Safety Seven three-wheeler, the first Reliant three-wheeler car was a girder-forked and handlebar-steered van. It gained an Austin Seven engine in 1938, and the following year Reliant took over production of the Austin engine. In 1953 came the Regal, Reliant's first production passenger car. Ten years later, Reliant introduced its own all-alloy engine – by which stage it had moved into four-wheeler production with the Sabre. It made its name, and began a new genre of sporting estates, with the Scimitar GTE of 1968.

RILEY

■ RILEY RM SERIES

By the time the RM series appeared in 1945, the great days of Riley had passed. Founded in 1898, the Company made its reputation in the 1920s and 1930s with a series of well-built saloons and thoroughbred small sports cars. It forged a fine racing record too, but, by the late 1930s, finances were looking shaky and the Nuffield organization took the helm in 1938.

Even so, the immediate post-war cars managed to retain their individuality: RMA and RMB models had a classic high-cam four-cylinder engine, torsion-bar independent front suspension and elegant fabric-topped, timber-framed, steel-bodywork bodies. The 1½-litre RMB could manage 75mph (120kph) the 90bhp – later 100bhp – 2½-litre RMB a highly respectable 95mph (152kph) with long-geared cruising at about 85mph (136kph).

With the longest stroke of any post-war British production car, the RMBs were extremely torquey, too. They handled well, though heavy steering at low speeds was a constant source of criticism.

For enthusiasts, the ultimate RM variant will always be the RMC, an open, three-seater roadster with sweeping, rakish lines. This was built to capture American sales (hence the column gearchange). A fold-flat screen

■ ABOVE *The cars were built with either a 1.5 or 2.5-litre high-camshaft four-cylinder engine, the latter giving a top speed of 95mph (152kph).*

■ RIGHT *Built for the American market, 507 RMCs were sold, along with a further 502 four-seater drophead RMDs.*

■ OPPOSITE *The most desirable of the RM Rileys was the three-seater roadster with its cut-away doors.*

■ BELOW *The rare drophead version, now highly prized by collectors.*

and lowered bonnet line were other recognition points. 507 were built, plus a further 502 four-seater drophead RMDs which had more conventional lines.

Last of the RM line were the 1952 RME (1496cc) and RMF (2443cc) with full hydraulic brakes, a hypoid back axle and bigger rear windows. For the run-out 1954 model year the styling of the RME underwent subtle changes: no running boards, streamlined headlight

■ OPPOSITE *The saloon RMA and RMB were very elegant cars with their distinctive fabric roof covering.*

RILEY RM SERIES (1945–1954)	
Engine	In-line four
Capacity	1496/2443cc
Power	54-100bhp
Transmission	4-speed manual
Top speed	75-100mph (120-160kph)
No. built	RMA 10,504/ RMB 6,900/ RMC 507/RMD 502/ RME 3,446/RMF 1,050

■ RIGHT *Handling of all the RMs was good, particularly the 1.5-litre with its lighter steering.*

pods and rear wheel spats.

By that time the flagship RMF had been replaced by the unfortunate Gerald Palmer-designed Pathfinder, which had nothing but the traditional four-cylinder Riley engine to recommend it.

After the death of the RME in 1955, there were no more thoroughbred Rileys; instead the famous jewel badge was progressively debased on a succession of badge-engineered BMC saloons until the end of the 60s.

■ ABOVE *The RM Series Rileys were built until 1955. They were replaced by the much less satisfactory – but much more modern-looking – Pathfinder.*

OTHER MAKES

■ ROCHDALE

The first complete car produced by the British firm Rochdale was the 1960 grp-monocoque Olympic, but they had been producing glassfibre bodies for the specials market since 1952. The MkVI was followed by the F-type, C-type, ST, GT and Riviera bodyshells. Volume production of the 100mph (160kph) Olympic had ceased by the mid-60s, but the last Olympic shell was sold in the early-70s.

■ RODLEY

The Leeds, Yorkshire-built Japanese-engined Rodley was another short-lived baby car from the 1950s, although it did look more serious than some of its contemporaries. Production was supposed to reach 50–60 a week, but few were made in the car's short production life of just over a year. The firm disappeared in 1955.

ROLLS-ROYCE

■ ROLLS-ROYCE SILVER CLOUD

The Rolls-Royce Silver Cloud and the virtually identical Bentley S-Type were revealed in 1955. Beautifully proportioned, exquisitely constructed and near-silent in operation, they were everything the traditional Rolls buyer could have hoped for.

This was Crewe's second "standard steel" car after the post-war Dawn and R-Type, with an off-the-peg factory body rather than a made-to-measure hand-crafted aluminium item in the pre-war tradition. Mulliner Park Ward, James Young and others all built exquisite special bodies on this chassis, and there was a long-wheelbase version of the standard body with an extra four inches (10cm) of rear leg room and a division. The traditional Rolls and Bentley radiator grilles were retained – these and a few badges and items of insignia were

D 444

■ **FAR LEFT** *Mulliner's famous Continental style was carried over from the R-Type but was phased out in favour of more modern coach-built styles.*

■ **NEAR LEFT** *The Flying Spur Bentley had a lightweight aluminium body on the Continental chassis. This is an S3 V-eight.*

the only differences between the two otherwise identical cars. They rode on a substantial, and resolutely separate, traditional box-section chassis with independent front suspension and rear damper rates that could be altered from the driving seat to suit whatever type of road you were thinking of taking your Bentley or Rolls down. The interior was nothing if not luxurious, with superbly crafted leather seats and a magnificent walnut dashboard.

The engine in the Cloud and S1 was basically the same 4.9-litre power unit carried over from the previous R-Type (and Silver Dawn), except that it had a new aluminium cylinder head and twin SU carburettors. Transmission at the start offered a choice of either four-speed synchromeshed manual or four-speed Hydramatic automatic, manufactured under licence by Rolls from General Motors in the USA. In fact, after just 18 months, the manual option was dropped,

and Rolls never encouraged owners to order it anyway. While the engine was incredibly refined, it wasn't really that powerful – the maximum speed was 106mph (170kph). It was Rolls-Royce's policy never to reveal specific power outputs but the estimated 178bhp had 40cwt (2032kg) to pull along.

The S-Type, known retrospectively as the S1, and the Silver Cloud 1, were built until 1959, with 3,072 Bentleys being made against 2,238 Rolls-Royces.

■ BELOW *The cut-away shows the Cloud's old-fashioned separate chassis, big drum brakes and aluminium V-eight engine.*

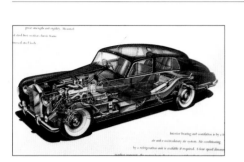

■ LEFT *The Cloud as it appeared in 1955 with single headlights and a six-cylinder engine. The V-eight Cloud II looked identical.*

ROLLS-ROYCE SILVER CLOUD AND BENTLEY S-SERIES (1959–65)	
Engine	Straight six and V-eight
Capacity	4887/6230cc
Power	N/A
Transmission	4-speed manual
	4-speed auto
Top speed	106-116mph
	(170-186kph)
No. built	Cloud 1/S1 3,107/2,231
	Cloud 2/S2 2,417/1,932
	Cloud 3/S3 2,044/1,318
	Plus 671 Clouds I/II/III

■ ABOVE *The Bentley version was technically identical – only the grille and badges were changed.*

■ ABOVE *Park Ward's famous Chinese Eye Continental, here in convertible form – the ultimate in open car luxury.*

Bentley/Rolls fans today are split on whether the S1 Series are better than the later V-eight-powered SII and SIII cars, the latter having a lower bonnet line and quad headlamps reckoned by some to spoil the cars' looks. The V-eights are far more powerful – good for nearly 120mph (193kph) with a likely 200bhp and far more torque on tap – but not as refined and quiet. American-inspired (some say by the Chrysler hemi), this alloy engine was the unit Rolls had wanted for the car all along. It's just that it took, in typical Crewe style, an awfully long time to make perfect. Rolls engineers started work on the unit in the very early 1950s, intending that it would be one of the world's best. It survives in vastly updated form in today's Rolls and Bentley cars.

To own and drive a Bentley is a satisfying and ethereal experience as long as you don't want blistering performance and can afford the expensive maintenance. These days, it's cheaper to buy but costly to restore.

■ NEAR RIGHT *For lightness, the body of the Continental models was finished in aluminium; the factory saloon came in steel only.*

■ FAR RIGHT *The HJ Mulliner convertible, heavier but just as beautiful as the Continental versions.*

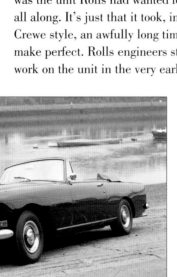

ROLLS-ROYCE

■ BELOW *The Shadow was also produced as a Bentley T1. Again, only the grille and the badges were different.*

■ OPPOSITE *The Shadow II of 1977 with its rubber-faced bumpers, air dam and smaller radiator grille.*

■ ROLLS-ROYCE SILVER SHADOW

If the boxy shape of the 1965 Silver Shadow was something of a shock for Rolls-Royce traditionalists after the flowing lines of the Cloud, there were much more revolutionary changes under the skin: all-independent self-levelling suspension, disc brakes and a monocoque structure came as a powerful retort to critics who accused Crewe of falling behind the times. In one fell swoop Rolls-Royce had entered the modern era.

Built by Pressed Steel at Oxford, the main bodyshell was steel while doors, bonnet and bootlid were aluminium. The all-round independent suspension by coil springs with wishbones at the front and single trailing arms at the back had hydraulic height control at

both ends, a system supplied by Citroën. At last disc brakes all round replaced the big drums used on the Cloud.

The 6.2-litre V-eight engine and GM Hydramatic four-speed automatic gearbox – made under licence by Rolls – were standard and carried over almost unchanged from the outgoing Silver Cloud. With a 115mph (185kph) top speed, a 0-60mph (96kph) time of 10.9 seconds and a standing quarter-mile covered in 17.6 seconds, the Shadow

■ ABOVE *The long-wheelbase Shadow II – badged Silver Wraith – with its trademark Everflex roof.*

■ LEFT *The Silver Shadow was announced in 1965, the first modern Rolls-Royce for many years.*

■ RIGHT *The alloy Rolls-Royce V-eight is whisper quiet and super-smooth but not particularly powerful by big luxury car standards. This one is a Camargue.*

■ ABOVE *The Camargue was the Rolls-Royce flagship from 1975 until the mid 80s. It was one of the most expensive cars in the world.*

■ BELOW *The styling was less happy from the rear, even if it did echo the lovely Fiat 130 coupé.*

was a fast car. Fuel consumption was good by Rolls standards, indulgent by everyone else's: between 12 and 15mpg on a run. There was, as usual, a Bentley version of the new car, called the T-Series or, retrospectively, the T1. The differences, however, were limited to a 'B'-winged radiator grille, badges and small items of trim. With the advent of the monocoque range, Bentley sales fell dramatically – only eight per cent of the Shadow I/I1 cars were Bentleys, compared with 40 per cent of the previous Cloud/S-Series cars.

Changes came slowly until the engine was enlarged to 6.75 litres in 1970: three-speed torque converter transmission replaced the four-speed fluid flywheel transmission in 1968; 1969 saw a long-wheelbase version of both cars, while air conditioning and a safer American-style dashboard came as standard. The Shadow II models of the mid 70s had rack steering to tighten up

ROLLS-ROYCE SILVER SHADOW (1965–80)	
Engine	V-eight
Capacity	6230/6750cc
Power	N/A
Transmission	4/3-speed
Top speed	117mph (187kph)
No. built	20,000 plus

■ ABOVE *The square-cut nose of the Camargue was never quite as Pininfarina intended.*

the soggy handling, rubber bumpers and an air-dam, plus Crewe's impressive split-level air-conditioning system.

Because there was no separate chassis, coach-built versions weren't possible. However, Rolls's subsidiary, Mulliner Park Ward, announced the Silver Shadow coupé in 1966 and a year later a convertible. Both were built at MPW's north London factory and adopted "Coke bottle" shapes for waistlines to look more handmade. Both were renamed Corniche in 1971. There were even a few two-door Shadow saloons, specially made by coachbuilder James Young.

Rolls-Royce Silver Shadow and Bentley T-Series cars were made in much larger numbers than any previous models: by the time they were replaced by the Shadow II/T2 cars in 1977, 20,000 of all types had been built. Today's Silver Spirit uses much of the technology pioneered on the Shadow.

ROVER

■ BELOW *The 3.5-litre Rover in saloon and coupé form (nearest camera) was one of Britain's best-loved luxury cars, built from 1967 to 1973.*

■ ROVER P5

There was nothing to replace the Rover P5 as a ministerial barge when production stopped in 1973. No other British car being built in the 1970s had the same air of solid worth and self-effacing dignity. They were still doing sterling service when Margaret Thatcher arrived in Downing Street in 1979 to begin her 11-year tenure. The elderly saloon was held in such esteem that a batch of the last cars were kept in storage and used for high-ranking cabinet duties well into the 80s. For years they were a regular feature for news bulletins, sweeping into Parliament and Buckingham Palace or pulling up outside No. 10. Harold Wilson had a

■ ABOVE *The P5B had a new Buick-derived aluminium V-eight engine. Rostyles wheels mark the car out as a V-eight model.*

■ LEFT *The P5 was previously offered with a less powerful three-litre straight-six engine. This is a MkIII coupé.*

ROVER P5 3½-LITRE (1967–73)	
Engine	V-eight
Capacity	3528cc
Power	185bhp
Transmission	3-speed auto
Top speed	110mph (177kph)
No. built	20,000

■ LEFT *The 3.5-litre V-eight could do 110mph (177kph) with acceleration that surprised some sportscar drivers.*

■ LEFT *For many years the 3.5-litre saloon was favoured transport for British government ministers: Harold Wilson had a special pipe rack fitted to his. A batch was set aside at the end of the production run for Goverment use, and the cars could still be seen in the 1980s.*

special ash-tray fitted to his to cater for his pipe. Even the Queen had a 3½-litre saloon: rumour has it that it was her favourite car and that she could often be seen driving it around Windsor.

Dispensing at last with the separate chassis of the P4, the three-litre of 1958, or P5 (post-war design number 5), was a Rolls-Royce for the middle classes. With modern but dignified styling by David Bache and a traditional interior with African cherry wood on the dash, thick Wilton carpet under foot and leather almost everywhere else, this was

an Edwardian drawing-room on wheels, perfect for the power brokers of the 60s.

At first, nobody really minded that the three-litre, joined by a hunch-roofed coupé version in 1962, was a bit slow, its soothing refinement being all that was asked of it by most owners. By the mid 60s, however, mere gravitas was not enough. Even on the gravel drives of leafy suburbia, the corpulent three-litre's lack of urge – it struggled to reach 100mph (160kph) as an automatic – was becoming embarrassing. Enter the Buick V-eight engine, a left-over from

General Motors's brief flirtation with "compacts" in the early 60s and acquired by Rover as an end-of-line bargain in 1966. Packing 184bhp (the last three-litres gave 134), it was a perfect fit under the P5's bonnet. It gave this stately boardroom barouche – renamed the 3½-litre in 1967 – speed and a new lease of life.

Suddenly the P5 was the car it always should have been. With a reasonable price tag Rover could barely keep pace with demand, which remained strong until its death in 1973.

■ NEAR RIGHT *A neat toolkit was fitted in a slide-out tray in the centre of the dash.*

■ FAR RIGHT *The "Office", with its huge wheel and neatly grouped instrumentation. Power steering was standard on the V-eight.*

ROVER

■ ROVER P6

The Rover 2000 – P6 – was the first young man's Rover. Bristling with new technology, it was ideal for the new breed of thrusting executives who wanted big-car ambience with sportscar manners in something a little more compact. Here was a 100mph (160kph) saloon, ripe for the dawn of Britain's motorway age, that didn't appeal exclusively – as did most prestige cars (and every previous Rover) – to grey-templed men in Homburg hats.

It was an immediate hit, lavishly well-reviewed around the world: *Car and Driver* magazine said it was "the best sedan ever presented in the pages of this magazine", while American safety campaigner Ralph Nader paid the 2000 the ultimate compliment when he cited it as a prime example of "how all cars should be built". It inspired many inferior imitators in the genre it created, and sold, by Rover standards, in huge numbers – not only to young executives but to all the old-style Rover customers too: doctors, bank managers, lawyers and every other shade and shape of

■ LEFT *In the early 1960s the 2000 set new standards of safety and driver appeal in the two-litre executive class.*

■ BELOW *The ultimate P6 was the 3500S with its V-eight engine and manual gearbox.*

■ LEFT *The 2000 TC had twin carbs, Rover's answer to the standard 2000's lack of urge.*

■ ABOVE *The 2000 was a firm favourite with young executives as well as bank managers and doctors. Wire wheels are a rarely seen option.*

middle-class professional bought the 2000 in their thousands, just as, today, they buy BMWs.

For the first time, Rover were selling safety with the 2000, long before it was fashionable. With its muscular "base unit" cage (a steel skeleton to which all the unstressed outer panels were attached), four-wheel disc brakes and well-padded interior, this was a great car in which to have an accident. Best of all, in the 2000 you stood a good chance of avoiding an accident in the first place. The DeDion suspension at the back followed race-car practice, so the 2000 didn't just ride softly but had prodigious grip, more than enough to keep the new overhead-camshaft four-cylinder engine in check. It easily equalled the superb 3.5-litre V-eight transplant thanks to which the P6 turned into a real Jag-eater in 1968 (and was much favoured by the police as a Jag-catcher).

If the P6 2000 didn't go like any past Rover, then it certainly didn't look like one either: David Bache's shape did full justice to the modern mechanisms underneath. This was a crisp, restrained

ROVER P6 (1963–77)	
Engine	4-cylinder
Capacity	1978cc
Power	90-124bhp
Transmission	3-speed manual
	3-speed auto
Top speed	104mph (167kph)
No. built	329,000

car, modern without being gimmicky, which resisted all later attempts to tart it up. The Rover 2000 was one of the great saloons of the 60s, a car as mouldbreaking in its class as the Mini.

■ ABOVE *The shape of the 2000 was by Rover's David Bache; its crisp, restrained lines were influenced by the Citroen DS – look at the rear of the roof-line.*

■ BELOW *Rare options on this TC are the wooden steering-wheel and extra round gauges.*

■ ABOVE *The 3500S was easy to spot thanks to its sports-wheel covers. All were Series 2 models with plastic grilles.*

■ RIGHT *The only way of spotting a TC was by its badges.*

SAAB

■ SAAB 96

Saab – Svenska Aeroplan AB – built its last 96 in 1980, but the roots of this tough, rally-winning saloon can be traced back to 1945 and the 92. A teardrop-shaped aerodynamic saloon with a two-cylinder two-stroke engine driving the front wheels (through a three-speed box with freewheel), the 92 model was current from 1950 to 1956 as Saab began to diversify from its aircraft-making interests. The 93 which followed it had a three-cylinder two-stroke engine, providing up to 55bhp in twin-carb GT form and improved coil-spring suspension with a conventional dead-beam axle at the rear to cure the once wayward handling.

The definitive Saab 96 was launched in 1960. The most noticeable feature on the outside was its larger wrap-around rear window, while under the bonnet was a bigger 841cc two-stroke giving 38bhp

SAAB 96 (1960–80)	
Engine	2-stroke 3-cylinders/ V-four
Capacity	841/1698cc
Power	38-65bhp
Transmission	3/4-speed
Top speed	79-95mph (127-152kph)
No. built	547,221

■ ABOVE *Front-wheel drive gave the 96 sure-footed handling and the free-wheel saved on fuel costs.*

■ ABOVE *The definitive 96 was launched in 1960 with its wrap-around rear window.*

■ ABOVE *The solid, low-slung shape of the 95 estate has been likened to that of a brick-built bungalow.*

■ ABOVE *The interior of the desirable Sport with its extra dials and stylish wooden steering-wheel.*

in standard form. For enthusiasts, there were the 65bhp Sport and Monte Carlo models with triple carburettors and front disc brakes. Other goodies included a four-speed gearbox and full pressure lubrication, eliminating the need for the usual petrol/oil mix in the fuel. Top speed was a very creditable 90mph

(152kph), and it was in this form that the car proved such a rally winner in the hands of Erik Carlson.

For those with more utilitarian needs there was the 95 Estate, introduced before the 96 and always using the four-speed gearbox. Saab stuck with the two-stroke until 1968, but by then the V-four

engine, bought from Ford of Germany, was selling strongly. It gave Sport and Monte Carlo performance but with much better economy.

Good handling and solid build quality were the most endearing qualities of this tough little classic, of which many examples survive to this day.

■ OPPOSITE *The shape of the 96 can be traced back to 1945 and the original 92. It lasted until the mid-1970s.*

■ BELOW *The badge shows Saab's heritage as a plane maker.*

■ BELOW *The two-stroke engine was replaced by a Ford V-four in the mid 1960s.*

■ BELOW *The 96 was a famous rally winner, most notably in the hands of Eric Carlson.*

OTHER MAKES

■ SIATA

Siata of Italy had been modifying cars, mainly Fiats, since 1926 and made its first production vehicle, the Amica, in 1949. Most Siatas were Fiat-derived, including some handsome V-eight-engined Vignale-bodied coupés, and the firm lasted until 1970, pooling resources with Abarth from 1959 to 1961. Its last model was the Fiat 850-based Spring of 1968–75.

■ SIMCA

Simca was founded in France in 1934 by HT Pigozzi to make Fiat cars under licence. The first uniquely Simca model, the Aronde, appeared in 1951, and such was its success that the firm started its policy of acquiring other makes, taking over Unic in 1951, Ford France in 1954 and Talbot in 1958. In 1958, Chrysler bought a minority stake in Simca. By 1963 this was a controlling interest, preceding the change of name in 1970 to Chrysler France SA. The last Simca cars, Horizon and Alpine, were built in 1981.

■ SINGER

Singer made its first car in 1905, and by the late 1920s it was Britain's third largest car maker. The first of a long line of OHC engines was launched in 1926, and the Le Mans Nine and 1.5-litre were credible sportscars in the 30s. A dull post-war range, the SM1500, sealed the firm's fate and in 1956 the ailing concern was taken over by Rootes. Henceforth, Singers were to be badge-engineered Hillmans and the last Singer-badged car was built in 1970.

■ SKODA

The first of the Czech-made Skoda cars were seen in 1925. Early products were conventional but the mid 1930s saw a range of more advanced offerings. Following the Second World War, after which the firm became state-owned, products were essentially evolutions of pre-war designs, until the arrival of the rear-engined Renault-inspired 1000 series in 1964. Once the butt of endless jokes, Skoda is now part of the Volkswagen group.

■ STANDARD

By 1906, three years after its formation, Standard was marketing Britain's first inexpensive six-cylinder car. A small car, the Nine, helped to circumvent increasing financial problems in 1928. After the Second World War, the firm acquired Triumph and two years later introduced the famous Vanguard, spearheading the export drive. This was the sole Standard model until the 1953 launch of the Eight. Leyland took over the Standard Triumph in 1961, and the Standard name was quietly dropped from passenger cars in 1963.

■ STEYR-PUCH

Before 1939, the Austrian firm Steyr made some interesting cars, some designed by Ferdinand Porsche. From 1949 onwards, there were no home grown models, only licence-assembled Fiats. Latterly the high-performance 650TRII was based on the 500. Steyr now produces four-wheel-drive (4WD) vehicles and systems and collaborates with Chrysler, VW-Audi and Mercedes-Benz.

SUNBEAM

■ SUNBEAM TIGER

The sunbeam Tiger, introduced in 1964, was in essence nothing more than a V-eight-engined version of the four-cylinder Alpine whose pretty, open body dated from 1959. As with the AC Cobra, the initial engineering was carried out

■ ABOVE *Brochure artwork shows the rare MkII Tiger with its bigger 4.7-litre engine.*

■ BELOW *The 4.7-litre MkII had 200bhp, up from the 164bhp of the 4.2. The roll-bar is non-standard.*

■ TOP LEFT *The Sunbeam Tiger is often modified by its owners.*

■ BOTTOM *An egg-crate grille was another MkII recognition point. When Chrysler bought Rootes, the car was killed because it used a rival Ford engine – and no Chrysler V-eight would fit.*

■ BELOW *The body shell of the Tiger was a direct carry-over from the Alpine. The cars were assembled by Jensen.*

by American Caroll Shelby, but all subsequent work was done by the parent company Rootes. Out came the four-cylinder 1592cc engine and in went a Ford V-eight of 4.2 litres along with a new "top loader" four-speed gearbox and beefed-up final drive.

This much bigger engine required extensive re-engineering under the bonnet and a stiffened-up shell. Rather than clog up the higher-volume Alpine

production lines with the new car, Rootes subcontracted the job to Jensen. Located just up the road in West Bromwich, in the West Midlands, Jensen were famous for their own big V-eight GT – the CV8 – and were already producing the big Healey models for BMC.

With a leap from 97 to 164bhp, the Tiger was a very different kind of car from the modest little Alpine, though they

SUNBEAM TIGER (1964–68)	
Engine	V-eight
Capacity	4260-4727cc
Power	164-200bhp
Transmission	4-speed manual
Top speed	120-125mph (193-201kph)
No. built	6,495 MKI/571 MkII

■ LEFT *The powerful Tiger with its relatively light bodywork was a natural in racing and rallying, though it was never fully developed.*

looked identical apart from discreet badging. Top speed was 117mph (187kph), with 0-60 (96) in 9.5 seconds, the enormous torque rendering the gearbox almost superfluous. The Tiger was no car for the novice, however: the rack-and-pinion steering – somewhat hastily contrived – wasn't of the highest quality, and the Hillman-derived suspension was never really adequate for the power now on tap, even with the Panhard rod and optional limited-slip diff. Still, it was good value and sold well in America. It wasn't offered in Britain until 1965.

Its life was cut short when Chrysler took a controlling interest in Rootes: the new regime didn't like the idea of a car using an engine from its Detroit arch-rival. Thus, the axe came down on the Tiger, but not before Rootes had produced 571 MkII models in 1967-68 with a bigger 4.7-litre engine from the Mustang. This version had wider gear ratios and was easily identified by its body stripes and egg-crate grille.

Today these exciting cars are much sought after as a cheaper alternative to the AC Cobra.

OTHER MAKES

■ SUNBEAM-TALBOT
Sunbeam-Talbot was a marque invented in 1938 by the Rootes brothers. The cars were derived from contemporary Hillmans and Humbers, but in most instances carried individual coachwork. The "90" models of the 50s were surprisingly good sports saloons. In 1954 the Talbot suffix was dropped.

■ SUNBEAM
The first British manufacturer to win a Grand Prix, Sunbeam made its first car in 1899. In 1920 it became part of the Sunbeam-Talbot-Darracq combine, and after the collapse of STD it was bought by Rootes in 1935. The name was dormant from that point until 1953, when the sports version of the Sunbeam-Talbot 90 was re-launched as the Sunbeam Alpine. The Alpine and Rapier of the 60s were good sellers, but the name faded away in 1976 with the Hunter-based Rapier fastback.

■ SWALLOW
Originally part of Jaguar, the Swallow Coachbuilding Co (1935) became part of the giant Tube Investments organization during the Second World War. Its sportscar, the Doretti, was destined mainly for the American market. It used Swallow's spare capacity but was dropped because parent company TI (Tube Investments) decided they could not go on supplying sportscar manufacturers producing a rival product.

■ ABOVE *Just 571 MkII Tigers were built. Body side stripes were another recognition point.*

■ LEFT *The big V-eight was a tight fit under the Tiger's bonnet – overheating was a problem.*

TATRA

■ TATRA 603

First sight of the 603, Tatra's bold rear-engined V-eight saloon, came in 1957. There had been no Tatra passenger cars since the demise of the flat-four Tatraplan in 1954, but the new 603 kept the tradition of an air-cooled V-eight rear mounted in a six-seater saloon, the last in a line of streamlined Tatras that started with Ledwinka's Jaray-styled T77 in the 1930s.

The 603 took its name from its hemi-head V-eight, a 2.5-litre unit with pushrods and twin Jikov down-draught carbs (Weber copies) first seen in a single-seater Tatra racer in 1950. Twin belt-driven scavenge-blowers did the cooling, with vents let into the rear wings plus a thermostatically-opening grille in the bumper. Alloy build meant low weight (373lb/169kg), but with a low 6.5:1 compression ratio it packed just 100bhp, denying the 3240lb (1470kg) car sparkling acceleration. On the other hand, top speed was 100mph (160kph), testimony to the car's slippery shape: the floorpan was virtually flat with no exhaust or propshaft to impede clean air flow.

■ ABOVE *The Tatra 603 as it looked from the mid 1960s onwards, though many earlier cars were modified.*

■ LEFT *The 2.5-litre V-eight engine was air-cooled and gave 105bhp in its latest form. Twin blowers can be seen in the lower part of the picture.*

TATRA 603 (1955–75)	
Engine	Aircooled V-eight
Capacity	2472cc
Power	95–105bhp
Transmission	4-speed manual
Top speed	100mph (160kph)
No. built	22,422

■ LEFT *The unmistakable front end of the 603. Luggage lives in the front with the fuel tank.*

■ ABOVE *The rear view shows the split rear window and remnants of the dorsal fin seen on earlier Tatra models.*

■ BELOW *Late 603s like this had disc brakes all round, and all were good motorway cruisers with a high top gear.*

Drive went through a four-speed transaxle with column shift, and early 603s used big hydraulic drums with advanced twin circuits. Dunlop discs, built under patent, didn't arrive until the mid-60s. At the back, trailing arms with coil springs were no surprise, but for the front of the 603 a new suspension system was schemed, a form of MacPherson strut with trailing swinging arms to save space in the big front luggage compartment.

In looks, the 603 couldn't have been anything but a Tatra, somewhere between Jaray's classic brave-new-world modernism and fashionable Detroit

■ ABOVE *Although little known in the West, the Tatra marque is one of the oldest in the world. New Tatras are still available.*

kitsch. At the front, three lights peered from behind a one-piece glass panel, giving the 603 the look of a bullet-nosed diesel express train. At the back, the roof line swept down sharply into the engine cover, the panoramic back window split by the remnants of an embryonic dorsal fin that was left off at the last minute.

Through the 60s, Tatra made gradual changes. They toned down styling with a new split, four-light nose. The 603-2 of 1967 had a wider grille with lights spaced farther apart in a glassfibre panel. Accidents or factory refits meant

that many earlier 603s gained this later front-end look. Miniature chrome fins evolved on the rear wings, the over-riders were tamed and the car lost its bonnet vent. The roof line became slightly more bulbous too, and front-door windows on these later cars had quarter-light vents. The 603H engine of 1969 gave 105bhp and used electronic ignition, still a rarity on western cars. Initially fitted only at the front, by this time servo discs were used all round. Production ended in 1975 as the 603 began to give way to the four-cam, Vignale-styled 613.

■ ABOVE *Cooling air is sucked in through a hole under the bumper.*

■ RIGHT *The 603 was a full six-seater, favoured transport of government officials.*

TOYOTA

■ TOYOTA 2000GT

Toyota launched its beautiful 2000GT as an image-building loss leader. Its birth was convoluted. It was Nissan, not Toyota, who in 1963 had originally commissioned the styling from Graf Goertz, the New York-based industrial designer, best known for his 503 and 507 BMWs. Yamaha built a running prototype, but Nissan backed out at the last minute, leaving Yamaha free to sell the design package to Toyota. Because production levels were always going to be low, Toyota farmed out the work to Yamaha and the first prototype was presented at the Tokyo show in 1965. The production car stood just 45in (114cm) high on tall, slim 165/15 shod centre-lock alloys. The sweep of its roof and its rounded rear haunches were undeniably influenced by the E-Type, but there was much that was bold and original about this now 30-year-old design with its upswept slash-like side windows, slim pillars and plunging, sensual bonnet line.

Under its seductively curvaceous shell, the 2000GT's hardware lived up to the looks. There were twin-cams (a free-breathing and sophisticated hemi-head design with straight-through ports

■ RIGHT *The beautiful shape of the 2000GT was by Goertz, also responsible for the BMW 507 and, later, the Datsun 240Z.*

■ ABOVE *When it was introduced in the USA in 1967, the 2000GT was priced well above the Porsche 911 and Jaguar E-Type.*

■ ABOVE *Production stopped in 1970, just as Datsun were introducing the 240Z.*

and big valves), a brace of double-throat Mikuni/Solex carburettors and a purposeful six-branch exhaust manifold, one outlet for each cylinder. The gearbox had five speeds, there were four-wheel disc brakes, and the Lotus-like back bone chassis used wishbones all round.

Back in 1965, this was copybook stuff: rare in high-calibre European machinery, unheard of on a Japanese car. There were three optional final drives, but with the 4.375 ratio a 2000GT should be good for 130-135mph (209-217kph), which means

■ OPPOSITE *The 2000GT was probably the first truly desirable car to be built by Toyota: only 337 were built.*

■ RIGHT *There was certainly a touch of E-Type about the 2000GT, but it had a dynamic elegance all of its own.*

TOYOTA 2000GT (1967–70)	
Engine	Straight six
Capacity	1988cc
Power	150bhp @ 6000rpm
Transmission	5-speed manual
Top speed	135mph (217kph)
No. built	337

100mph (160kph) in third and 115 (185) in fourth. The high second will run the 2805lb (1272kg) 2000GT to 70mph (112kph) in 12.7 seconds.

You couldn't actually buy a 2000GT until May 1967. Changes were few in a protracted five-year cycle although, towards the end of its life, Toyota built nine simplified single-camshaft cars with

air conditioning and the option of automatic transmission to stir up interest in North America. Despite an ecstatic *Road and Track* test report on the twin-cam version, only 63 American buyers could be persuaded to part with $6,800 for a 2000GT, a price well above that of more prestigious Porsche and Jaguar competition. Even at that price, Toyota

probably lost money on every one: you only have to look at the specification – and the complex curvatures in the body and glass – to see why. Production ceased in October 1970, just as Datsun were coming on stream with the 240Z. With only 337 produced, the 2000GT is one of the most collectable post-war Japanese classics.

■ ABOVE *The 2000GT had a six-cylinder engine with twin overhead camshafts and a five-speed gearbox.*

■ TOP RIGHT *Driving lights at the front were supplemented by retractable headlights.*

■ BOTTOM RIGHT *The 135mph (217kph) performance was stunning for a two-litre car, but the complex curvature of the body made it expensive to produce.*

TRIUMPH

■ TRIUMPH 1800/2000 ROADSTER

A torquey tourer rather than a true sportscar, the Triumph roadster with its "dickey-seat" fold out was one of the most memorable British cars of the immediate post-war years.

Standard's British boss Sir John Black bought Triumph in 1944 to take on Jaguar, using the Triumph name as an upper-crust sister marque to Triumph and trading on the make's pre-war prestige. Jaguar's boss William Lyons had built his business with the help of Standard, which had provided engines, gearboxes and chassis for his stylish SS – later Jaguar – saloons and sportscars, yet he had brushed aside Black's proposal of a takeover. Enter the roadster, a new breed of Triumph using existing Standard mechanics and calling on engineering skills developed during the

company's wartime experience in aircraft manufacturing. Out of the parts bin came the 1776cc Standard 14 engine and matching gearbox. In fact, the power unit selected was the overhead-valve variant created by Harry Weslake to the order of William Lyons and since 1937 made by Standard exclusively for the SS-Jaguar

■ RIGHT *With just 60bhp the Roadster was grossly overweight, but its looks have a certain appeal today – as does the car's rarity.*

1½-litre. Black had wanted a straight six originally but in a moment of weakness had sold the tooling for Standard's own six-cylinder engine to Jaguar. The transverse-leaf independent front suspension of the Flying Standard Series was used with a Standard Fourteen back axle.

■ ABOVE *The rakish looks of the Triumph Roadster were designed to tempt buyers away from Jaguar: few were convinced.*

TRIUMPH ROADSTER (1946–49)	
Engine	In-line four
Capacity	1776/2088cc
Power	65-68bhp
Transmission	3-speed manual
Top speed	75mph (120kph)
No. built	2,501/2,000

The underslung chassis of the new Triumph was a completely new design, a simple ladder frame made of the 3½in readily available, round-section tubing. In a similar vein, bodying the car in aluminium, over a timber frame, got around the steel shortages of the immediate post-war years. For the

■ BELOW *The two-litre engine from the Vanguard was introduced in 1948, but the top speed was still just 75mph (120kph).*

■ RIGHT *The rear dickey seat was unique on a post-war car.*

■ BELOW *Cabin was functional but hardly sporting in flavour, with seats offering little support. It was a three-seater.*

■ LEFT *Produced between 1946 and 1949, only 4,500 Roadsters were built. The bulbous shape tried to evoke the pre-war Jaguar SS100.*

■ BELOW *With the hood up the cabin looks cramped. Doors are rear-hinged. The long bonnet promises an exciting power unit.*

Roadster's styling, Black wanted something in the style of the SS-100 with big headlamps and flowing wings. He wanted a dickey-seat too, a hangover from the pre-war Triumph Dolomite Roadster coupé. Styled by Frank Callaby, it had a long bonnet with full-bodied front wings, a hunched rear and a cramped-looking passenger compartment.

At the time of its 1946 introduction, the cheap-to-build 1800 was a unique concept, with its bench front seat and its two jump-seats in the capacious boot. It offered a three-plus-two configuration that made it a more versatile package than any other post-war open car.

In 1948, after 2,501 Roadsters had been made, the car received a new wet-liner Vanguard engine along with the Vanguard three-speed gearbox. In this form, a further 2,000 examples were made before production ceased in October 1949.

The bigger-engined car was 0.7cwt (36kg) lighter and with 3bhp more it was better accelerating – 0-60mph (96kph) in 27.9 seconds, against 34.4 seconds for the 1800 model.

TRIUMPH

■ TRIUMPH TR2/3/3A

To challenge MG in the all-important post-war North American export market, Standard/Triumph boss Sir John Black knew he needed a more credible sportscar than the quaint, under-powered 2000 Roadster. With his bid to take over Morgan rejected, he initiated a prototype of an affordable Triumph sportscar.

A Standard Vanguard 2-litre engine was installed in a shortened Standard 8 chassis and clothed by a two-seater roadster body. Called the TS20, it was revealed to muted applause at the 1952 London Motor Show. The runtish looks were not liked, but Black gave the concept of a cheap and cheerful sportscar the go-ahead.

The TR2 revealed a year later overcame the TR1's problems: it featured a simple ladder-type chassis and a longer body with a much bigger boot. A 90bhp 1991cc version of the Vanguard engine with twin carbs was mated to a four-speed gearbox, while suspension was coil spring and wishbone at the front and a live rear axle on semi-elliptic springs.

It could reach 60mph (96kph) in

under 12 seconds, return fuel consumption of 25mpg in daily use, yet still do 100mph (160kph) – or 108 (173) with optional overdrive. This simple, enjoyable small sportscar was lapped up by American buyers and the TR2 quickly became the company's top dollar earner.

The TR2 sired the similar 1955 TR3. It had a bit more power and a new front grille, and a factory hard top was offered as part of an optional GT package. In

TRIUMPH TR2/3/3A (1953–62)	
Engine	In-line four
Capacity	1991/2138cc
Power	90-100bhp
Transmission	4-speed manual
Top speed	103-110mph (165-177kph)
No. built	TR2 8,628/TR3 13,377/ TR3a 58,236

■ RIGHT *The TR3A had a new full-width front grille, a 100bhp engine and exterior door handles.*

■ LEFT *The hole-in-the-wall grille is a trademark of the TR3, produced from 1955. The earlier car had a recessed grille.*

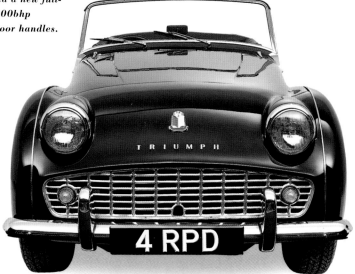

■ LEFT *Cut-away doors and a pinched waist are hallmarks of the TR2 and 3. Wire wheels and overdrive were optional.*

■ BELOW *The basic shape of the TR2 was first seen on the unlovely TR1 at the 1952 Motor Show. The look was much improved on the production cars.*

■ ABOVE *The functional interior featured a big steering-wheel, bucket seats and plain, but comprehensive, instrumentation.*

■ ABOVE *Though somewhat crude, the TR2 and 3 had a reputation for toughness.*

■ ABOVE *Smiths dials gave temperature and oil pressure information. Engines were comparatively low-revving but had good pulling power.*

1956, it became the first mass-produced car with front disc brakes. Triple overdrive and a token rear seat became available at the same time. The 1957 TR3a was the last of the cutaway-door TRs with a full-width grille, door handles and a 2138cc engine. The TR3b was a version with full synchromesh gearbox of the later TR4, produced for the American market only.

Although the TR4 that came next had smoother Italian styling, mechanically it followed the same rugged principles. Indeed, the basic TR chassis survived, albeit with independent suspension, until the TR6 came to an end in 1976.

■ LEFT *Late TR3s had the biggest 2138cc engine and the full synchromesh gearbox later found on the TR4.*

TRIUMPH

■ ABOVE *The TR4 and 5 were designed by Michelotti of Italy. This is a six-cylinder TR5 with fuel injection.*

■ TRIUMPH TR4/5/6

Launched in 1962, the Triumph TR4 was the first "pretty" TR sportscar, with a roomier Michelotti body and a smattering of creature comforts. Under the skin, though, it retained all the solid, proven qualities of the 2 and 3. It had a big-banger 2.2-litre wet-liner four, giving 100bhp (and ample torque), and the reassurance of a simple, solid rear axle for predictable handling, improved on the 102mph (163kph) TR4 by wider wheel tracks and rack-and-pinion steering. An all-synchromesh gearbox was another innovation.

Inside the car, the cockpit was roomier and occupants enjoyed face-level ventilation. The TR4 featured an early form of the Targa roof, later adopted by Porsche on the 911, with a removable panel (Surrey top in Triumph parlance), and had wind-up side windows. The TR4 answered criticisms of poor roadholding and a rough ride on the early TR4 with a new independent rear suspension system, a semi-trailing link system first seen on the Triumph 2000 saloon.

Calls for more and smoother power were answered in 1967 by the TR5 with a 2498cc six-cylinder engine. Boasting the notoriously troublesome mechanical

TRIUMPH TR4/56 (1962–76)	
Engine	Straight six
Capacity	2498cc
Power	150bhp
Transmission	4-speed, optional overdrive
Top speed	119mph (191kph)
No. built	91,850

■ ABOVE *The TR6 was mechanically almost identical to the TR5 but restyled by Karmann.*

Lucas fuel-injection system, this 150bhp car was capable of 120mph (193kph). It was a short-lived variant, supplanted 15 months later by the TR6. Mechanically, little was changed, but the TR6 had a crisper, more modern body courtesy of Karmann of Germany. The TR line had traditionally enjoyed a strong following

in the USA and so it was with the TR6 which continued in that market until 1976 in detuned carburettor form.

By that time the controversial wedge-like TR7 was getting into its stride. Never as well loved by enthusiasts as its rugged forefathers, it was the last and numerically most successful, TR of all.

■ FAR LEFT *On 150bhp the TR5 was good for nearly 120mph (193kph). The six-cylinder engine was also found in the 2.5 PI.*

■ NEAR LEFT *The TR6 was the last of the traditional TRs, with a separate chassis and a straight-six engine.*

■ RIGHT *To overcome engine problems, many owners substituted the Rover 3.5-litre V-eight for the Stag's 3.0-litre unit with its inherent snags.*

TRIUMPH STAG

British Leyland had a world-beater in the Triumph Stag – making its poor execution, dodgy reputation and untimely demise more tragic. First seen in 1970, this four-seater convertible looked good with top up or down, the strength-giving roll bar skilfully blended into the profile by Michelotti to become part of the character of the styling, rather than detracting from it.

The Stag's brand-new 2998cc V-eight engine produce 145bhp, which in manual overdrive guise made this 2810lb (1275kg) luxury four-seater good for 116mph (186kph) with 60 (96) coming up in 9.3 seconds. Automatics were good for about 110 (177) and fuel use in both versions was about 20mpg. With struts up front and semi-trailing arms behind, the Stag had neat, conventional handling but always lacked the well-bred poise of its German contemporary, the Mercedes SL.

It lacked the German's reliability, too. Overheating was the initial snag, usually triggered by a blocked radiator which was sensitive to silting (in the service schedule Triumph omitted to mention

TRIUMPH STAG (1970–77)	
Engine	V-eight
Capacity	2998cc
Power	145bhp @ 5500rpm
Transmission	4-speed manual overdrive 3-speed auto
Top speed	116mph (186kph)
No. built	25,939

■ ABOVE *The one-off prototype Stag three-door coupé of the mid 1970s.*

■ RIGHT *MkII Stags had body stripes, chrome sill covers and optional alloy wheels. The roll bar gave effective protection in an accident and helped the rigidity of the body.*

■ ABOVE *Though it had a family resemblance to the 2000/2500 saloons, the Stag shared no body panels with them.*

the need for a yearly coolant flush and new antifreeze). A blown head gasket usually followed and, at the same time, the thinned-out, overheated oil that resulted from a boil-up did little to protect crank bearings. A worn timing chain on a neglected engine also gave trouble: left too long, the chain would wreck the valve gear. Initial sales were healthy but, as word got around about the engine, it bombed. The V-eight was not used in any other car. The last Stags, MkIIs with detail changes, were built in 1977.

These days, specialists seem to have the Stag's engine problems licked. Now with uprated radiators, hardened cranks and regular 3000-mile (4800-km) oil changes, the engines can have a long life. It is tragic that Triumph got the engine so wrong first time around, because the rest of the car is quite well sorted.

The Stag was a great idea. Indeed, it still is, if the car's continuing popularity, almost 20 years after its death, is anything to go by.

TVR

■ TVR GRANTURA & VIXEN

The first TVR Grantura sportscars were built in Blackpool in 1958, using VW suspension on a tubular backbone chassis, clothed in a pretty glassfibre body and powered by a choice of Ford, BMC and Coventry Climax engines. By 1962 the MkIII Grantura had evolved, a crossover model mixing quaint early styling elements with the increased chassis sophistication of the later cars.

There was no longer a choice of engines – it came with MGA power, take it or leave it – and best of all it had a new chassis, eschewing the ultra stiff-riding VW trailing-link design for a proper factory-fabricated double-wishbone and coil-spring suspension. Although still built from 16-gauge steel tube, the frame – with a slightly longer wheelbase – was more rigid, good enough to live on into the early 1970s until introduction of the "M" series. The cast-alloy front suspension uprights are unique to TVR, and although the diff internals are MG, they sit in TVR's own cast-alloy housing.

The look was familiar: the stub-tailed coupé shape dated from the first 1958 Grantura and had a Perspex wrap-around rear window, Ford Consul front screen, blistered wheel arches and low, almost Porsche-like bonnet, a one-piece

■ LEFT *Early TVRs came with a variety of engines, from small Coventry Climax units to monster 4.7-litre Ford V-eights. The bodies were always glassfibre, while the shape, based on a rugged tubular backbone chassis, dates back to 1958.*

■ LEFT *TVRs came ready built or in kit form for the do-it-yourself enthusiast. The rear window is perspex, the front screen from the Ford Consul.*

moulding hinged at the front.

With such a relatively light engine, mounted well back, the Grantura felt delicate and well balanced on the road. The Spitfire-sourced rack was light and accurate, and the braking progressive and powerful with Girling discs at the

front but no servo assistance.

By 1967, the Grantura had become the Vixen, via the 1800S and 1800S Mk IV. The former introduced the squared-off 'manx' tail with the bigger rear window and MKI Cortina rear lights: the latter merely heralded detail refinements

■ ABOVE *The wide transmission tunnel was a hallmark of early TVRs, along with a slightly home-made look to the fixtures and fittings.*

■ ABOVE *The early manx-tailed Grantura: the basic shape – with changes – lived on until the 1970s.*

■ ABOVE *The bonnet has a hint of Porsche 356 about it and forms almost the entire front of the car, giving good access to the engine bay.*

■ FAR LEFT *Even with the smaller engines, the top speed of the early cars was over 100mph (160kph).*

■ LEFT *The Ford 4.7 V-eight made the TVR into a very desirable car.*

to the suspension and interior. The sausage-bonnet Vixen was essentially a Ford Cortina GT-engined version of the 1800S, using a lighter 88bhp crossflow unit with matching all-synchromesh Ford gearbox.

The Vixen S2 replaced it after just 12 months, using the longer-wheelbase chassis developed for the Tuscan V-eight SE. That meant larger doors, wraparound MkII Cortina lights, a new bonnet bulge and lots of detail changes. Also, it was the first TVR in which the body was bolted, rather than bonded to the chassis. You could still buy it as a kit, though the new Lilley management didn't encourage do it yourself builders, and by the turn of the decade, new purchase-tax rules wiped out the kit market anyway.

Despite a high price, the Vixen made a credible MGB GT alternative in its day and sales figures proved it: 746 were produced before the 1600M took over as the small-engined car in the TVR range in 1973.

TVR VIXEN S1 (1968–69)	
Engine	4-cylinder
Capacity	1599cc
Power	88bhp
Transmission	4-speed manual
Top speed	106mph (170kph)
No. built	117

OTHER MAKES

■ TALBOT-LAGO

After the 1920 formation of the Anglo-French company Sunbeam-Talbot-Darracq, Darracq cars became known as Talbots in Europe and Darracqs in England to avoid confusion with the British Talbot firm. Major Anthony Lago took over Darracq's Suresnes works in suburban Paris after the 1935 STD collapse and set to making a new line of six-cylinder cars. After 1945, car sales were hit by high taxation, shaky finances and a misguided model policy, although the flagship Grand Sport was the ultimate touring car of its day. The company was absorbed by Simca in 1959.

■ TRABANT

The now famous Trabant was a product of the IFA grouping, a nationalized consortium of all car plants in the German Democratic Republic (DDR). It was a smaller sister to the 686cc Zwickau P70 of 1955-59, which was a development of the preceding IFA F8 – a DDR version of the pre-war twin-cylinder DKW Meisterklasse. It features a separate chassis, rot-free glassfibre bodywork and smoky two-stroke engines, though later cars had VW Polo power.

■ TRIDENT

The sleek Fiore-style Trident has a troubled history. Unveiled at the 1965 Geneva Show as a TVR, the body moulds were bought by TVR Dealer Bill Last when TVR hit financial trouble. He set up his own manufacturing operation in Suffolk and the firm produced cars in Woodbridge and then in Ipswich. Trident folded in 1974, but the car made a brief reappearance in 1976 before the firm folded finally in 1977.

■ TURNER

Jack Turner built small glassfibre-bodied, tubular-framed sportscars with various proprietory engines ranging from the 803 A30 engine to the Climax unit used from 1959 with up to 90bhp. Fast and agile, they were among the best British cars of their type. However, they could never compete with the mass-produced Soprite/Midget and the company went into voluntary liquidation in 1966.

■ UNIPOWER

The mid-engined Unipower was conceived by BMC works driver Andrew Hedges and racing driver/power-boat racer Tim Powell. A small, high-quality GT coupé capable of up to 120mph (193kph) with the biggest Mini-Cooper power-pack, it was built at Perivale, Middlesex, from 1966 to 1968 by Universal Power Drives, makers of fork-lift trucks and forestry tractors. A new company, Unipower Cars Ltd, took over but folded in 1970.

VAUXHALL

■ VAUXHALL CRESTA

Few cars are more evocative of late-50s Britain and its popular obsession with all things American than the Vauxhall PA Cresta. This was Vauxhall's answer to the Ford Zodiac, obviously inspired by the products of Vauxhall's American parent, General Motors of Detroit. Small fins sprouted from rear wings. Front and rear screens had a heavy "dog-leg" wraparound. Optional whitewall tyres and two-tone paint only emphasized the heavy American influence.

Launched in 1957, the PA Cresta (and its cheaper, less well-equipped sister the Velox) leaned heavily on the E

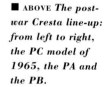

■ ABOVE *The post-war Cresta line-up: from left to right, the PC model of 1965, the PA and the PB.*

VAUXHALL CRESTA PA (1957-62)	
Engine	Straight six
Capacity	2262/2651cc
Power	78-95 bhp
Transmission	3-speed, overdrive and auto
Top speed	90-97 mph (145-156 kph)
No. built	81,841/91,923

■ BELOW *Some brave drivers campaigned the Cresta in rallying: this model is an Army team car.*

■ ABOVE *The styling of the PA was very transatlantic, with fashionable rear fins, wrap-around screens and two-tone paintwork.*

■ BELOW *This is a pre-1959 PA with the distinctive three-piece rear window and egg-crate grille.*

■ ABOVE *Inside the car, bench seats, white steering-wheel and column gearchange added to the American flavour.*

■ ABOVE *Rust ravaged many PA Crestas, so fine survivors like this one are rare.*

■ LEFT *PA engines were straight sixes with up to 95bhp for a top speed of over 90mph.*

Series mechanically, though they were physically bigger cars. The smooth, understressed 2262cc pushrod six remained, now producing 75bhp for a top speed of more than 90mph (145kph). The three-speed, column-shift box was all synchromesh now, but the PA retained the leaf-spring rear axle and soft wishbone and coil-spring suspension of its predecessor.

For 1959 the wrap-around rear screen became one-piece and there was a new grille, along with the option of an estate car model, built by Friary (the Queen had one for many years). The best of the bunch was the 1960 model with a bigger 2.6-litre, 96bhp engine. Other recognition points were bigger wheels and fins. Two-pedal "Hydramatic" control or dual overdrive for the manual box broadened the car's appeal. Servo-assisted front disc brakes were another welcome improvement.

Sales remained strong right up to the model's death in 1962. By then, fins were somewhat *passé* and Vauxhall had a cleaner looking Velox and Cresta on the stocks, the PB. The Cresta name finally died with the PC model, discontinued in 1972, but the PA remains the best-loved and most collectable of this breed of big Vauxhalls.

■ LEFT *In 1962 the PA Cresta was replaced by the PB, with a bigger engine and cleaner, more modern styling. This is the 3.3-litre PB, one of the fastest accelerating family saloons of its day.*

OTHER MAKES

■ VANDEN PLAS

Guillaume Van den Plas, originally a Brussels wheelwright, entered the coach-building market in 1884. In 1913, a British licensee was appointed, and in 1923 this offshoot, always known as Vanden Plas, moved to Kingsbury, in north-east London. Many high-class British cars such as Alvis and Bentley received Vanden Plas bodies. In 1946, Austin took over the firm and from 1960 it became a BMC marque in its own right, producing up-market versions of the 1100, the three-litre and finally the Allegro. It was famous for its large formal limousines, too, such as the big Austin Princess-based four-litre and the Daimler DS420. The works closed in 1979.

■ VOLGA

The post-Second World War Volga M21/22 was a product of the USSR's giant Gorky auto works. It was a big tough saloon (or estate) with a conservative technical specification, poor performance and dated styling; one of the few highlights was a vast tool kit. In Russia, it served as a taxi and transport for middle-ranking officials.

VW

◼ VW BEETLE

The Volkswagen Beetle, born out of
Adolf Hitler's desire to provide low-cost
motoring for the masses, needs little
introduction. Its rounded shape and air-
cooled throb are familiar around the
world. Although the last German-built
cars came out of the Wolfsburg factory,
Lower Saxony, in 1978, the model is still
in production in South America. Total
sales stand at 21 million (it overtook the
Model T's 15 million in the early 70s), a
figure unlikely to be beaten.

Ferdinand Porsche designed the
original rear-engined, air-cooled design,
although very few were actually built
before 1939. Production started again in

◼ LEFT *The most
familiar car of all,
the Beetle, dates
from well before
the war. It soon
gained a
reputation for
reliability and
good quality.*

◼ BELOW *The
Beetle's shape and
engineering were
conceived by Dr
Ferdinand
Porsche.*

◼ ABOVE *The split-screen models are the
most collectable of the lot. Early cars had
non-synchromesh transmissions and feeble
50mph (80kph) performance.*

VW BEETLE (1945–77)	
Engine	Flat four
Capacity	1131–1584cc
Power	25–50bhp
Transmission	4-speed
Top speed	50-84mph (80-135kph)
No. built	21,000,000

1945 with a very basically specified
1100cc model with a non-synchromesh
gearbox, cable brakes and very little
brightwork. In America, the model
started a small-car revolution as
millions of drivers, looking for a cheap
second car, fell in love with the Beetle's
good engineering, practicality and
economy.

The size of the flat-four pushrod
engine grew from 1131 to 1200cc in the
50s, and the range expanded with the
pretty Karmann Ghia sports models and
a cabriolet with its pram-like hood.

Calls for a faster, more modern-driving
Beetle were answered in the mid 60s
with the 1300 and 1500 models, which
gained an all-synchromesh box and
could be had with disc brakes and even
a semi-automatic transmission.
Ultimately, however, VW's reliance on
one basic model had a serious effect on
sales in the later part of the decade.
Buyers began to tire of the noisy, slow
Beetle. The 1961 1500 amounted to
nothing more than a dressed-up version
of the original car, and even the big four-
door 411 with its fuel injection didn't

■ LEFT *The 1300 and 1500-engined cars of the mid-1960s answered calls for more performance.*

fool many buyers: under the skin it was still pure Beetle.

Salvation for VW arrived in the form of the water-cooled, front-engined Golf in 1974, a benchmark for front-wheel-drive hatchbacks two decades ago, though the Wolfsburg-made Beetles continued until 1977.

Today, the Beetle is a cult machine and the older cars, particularly the "split window" model from the early 50s, command high prices, while the 60s and 70s models are still plentiful and cheap.

■ ABOVE *The Beetle has long been a cult favourite with customizers all over the world.*

■ BELOW *The car's good traction makes the Beetle an ideal choice as a beach buggy.*

■ ABOVE *The Karmann Ghia was a luxurious sporty version of the Beetle: sadly VW never gave it extra performance.*

■ RIGHT *One of the most sought-after Beetles is the convertible, also by Karmann.*

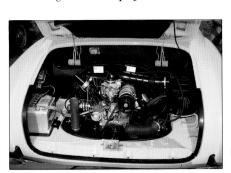

■ ABOVE *The flat-four aluminium engine was noisy but ultra-reliable and was responsive to tuning.*

VOLVO

■ LEFT *An early P1800 – with cow-horn bumpers – in the foreground, an 1800ES in the background. Mechanically the cars were identical to contemporary Volvo saloons.*

■ VOLVO P1800

The initial production of Volvo's stylish Ghia-designed P1800 coupé was somewhat convoluted. The steel bodies were tooled-up for and built in Britain by Pressed Steel in Scotland and then sent to Jensen of West Bromwich who, with chassis parts supplied from Sweden, assembled the complete cars.

Although not a sportscar in the true sense of the word, the high-waisted P1800 was a good, long-legged cruiser, and with its overdrive gearbox had a respectable top speed of more than 100mph (160kph). The 107bhp engine was the familiar twin-carb in-line four unit (B18) with a four-speed transmission sending the drive to a coil-spring live rear axle. Servo-assisted front disc brakes were standard, enhancing handling qualities which were safe but uninspiring. All the

P1800's mechanics were shared with the contemporary "Amazon" 120 Series saloons. Handsome and practical, the P1800 quickly gained popularity despite a high price tag, and its profile was further raised by its weekly appearances in the television series *The Saint*, driven by the show's star Roger Moore (who also owned one in real life).

Volvo were never very happy with the quality of the Jensen-built cars, and in 1964 they shifted production over to

VOLVO P1800, 1800S, 1800E & 1800ES (1960–73)	
Engine	4-cylinder
Capacity	1778/1986cc
Power	90-125bhp
Transmission	4-speed manual 3-speed auto
Top speed	102-115mph (163-185kph)
No. built	P1800 6,000/ 1800S 23,993/ 1800E 9,414/ 1800ES 8,078

Sweden. With more power and detail trim differences (the cow-horn bumpers of the Jensen-built cars were replaced by conventional items), the car became known as the 1800S. The engine became a full two-litre with 115bhp in 1968 and from 1969 gained fuel injection, upping the power output to 125bhp. There was an automatic option on this version and an "E" can be spotted by its alloy wheels.

The final flowering of the design was the 1800ES, Volvo's answer to the Reliant Scimitar GTE. With its extended roof line and rear hatchback, it was a useful small-load carrier with a good turn of speed – 115mph (185kph). However, by the early 70s Volvo were beginning to lose interest in their aging sportscar and stopped production.

■ ABOVE *The ES was Volvo's answer to the Scimitar GTE but proved short-lived. Top speed with injection was 115mph.*

■ ABOVE *The ES had leather seats and was a comfortable long-distance express, especially with overdrive.*

■ ABOVE *Both versions had ample luggage capacity, useful in their role as long-legged GT cars.*

■ ABOVE *The famous profile of the P1800 was from Ghia of Italy and dated from the 1950s. Early cars were built in Britain.*

■ LEFT *The 6/80 was a prestige car in its day, with a surprising turn of speed from its six-cylinder engine.*

WOLSELEY

■ WOLSELEY 6/80

Born into a grim post-Second World War world starved of new cars, the six-cylinder Wolseley 6/80 – and its four-cylinder sister the 4/50 – headed the Nuffield range for 1948.

Based on the M/0 Series Morris saloons, the basic monocoque hull looked like an overgrown Morris Minor (basically what it was), but in 6/80 form it shared the 13in (33cm) longer wheelbase of the Morris Six. A bold grille and twin spotlights gave it a more

WOLSELEY 6/80 (1948–54)	
Engine	In-line six
Capacity	2215cc
Power	72bhp
Transmission	4-speed manual
Top speed	85mph
No. built	24,886

■ ABOVE *A sight to fill the hearts of criminals with fear in the 1950s. The Wolseley badge lights up.*

■ ABOVE *The interiors were luxurious: drivers needed the big wheel to get to grips with the handling.*

up-market image. The 6/80 shared its straight-six overhead-cam engine with the Morris Six, at 72bhp a heady six horsepower stronger than the Morris.

Its best feature was its interior, with leather seats, wooden dashboard and the rare luxury of a heater as standard equipment. Less impressive was the steering, a Bishop cam system which was both vague and heavy and no doubt somewhat off-putting in a car that was actually quite powerful for its day: the 6/80 could pull 85mph (137kph) easily.

It was the performance of the big Wolseley that attracted police forces all over Britain in the late 40s and early 50s – even today the model is synonymous with 50s law enforcement. If you watch late-night TV, the cars are hard to miss, with bumper-mounted bells ringing and a tense driver battling with the car's wayward handling.

By the end of the decade, the 6/80 was struggling to keep pace with the new breed of Jaguar-driving criminals, though remarkably, with production having ended in 1954, the last cars were still in use in 1961.

■ BELOW *The shape owed a lot to the Morris Minor and shared panels with the Morris MO Series.*

OTHER MAKES

■ WARTBURG

Like the Trabant, the Wartburg was a product of the nationalized East German combine IFA. An evolution of the preceding IFA F9, which was a DDR-built version of a 1940 DKW prototype, it was manufactured at the former BMW plant in Eisenach, Thuringia. The 312 and later 353 Knight were front-wheel-drive two-stroke saloons sold in the West at low prices, but the cars found few friends: handling was poor and the economy unremarkable at 25mpg.

■ ZAPOROZHETS

Clearly inspired by Western designs, this Soviet minicar, made in the Ukraine, was first seen in 1960 and survived three decades with only one restyle. It retained its rear-engine configuration to the end and had an unusual air-cooled V-four engine. A prototype front-wheel-drive replacement was shown in 1987 but the NSU-like ZAZ 966 was still listed in 1990.

INDEX

Page numbers in *italic* refer to the illustrations

Abarth, 83
AC Ace, *10*, 23, 32, 40, 66-7, *66-7*
  Cobra, 32, 40, 51, 63, 68-9, *68-9*
air suspension, 29
Alfa Monza, 22, *23*
Alfa Romeo, 13, 24, *25*, 47, 61
  Giulia, *33*
  Giulietta Berlina, 41
  Giulietta Sprint, 34, 41
  Montreal, *35*
  Spider, 58, 70, *70*
  2000 coupé, 35
Allard J2/J2X, 71, *71*
Alvis, 43
  TD/TE/TF, 72-3, *72-3*
Amphicar, 83
Armstrong Siddeley, 83
  Star Sapphire, *41*
Aston Martin, 10, 11, 37, *56*, 60
  DB MkIII, 40
  DB2/DB2/4 and DB MKIII, 40, 59,
    74-5, *74-5*
  DB5, 59, *59*, 76-7, *76-7*
  V-Eight, 78, *78*
Audi, 43, 83
Austin, 31, 83
  1100, 42
  A35, 40

A40, *33*
A90 Atlantic, 79, *79*
  Seven, 12, 23, 56
  Westminster, *50*
Austin-Healey, 49
  100, 40
  3000, 49, 80-1, *80-1*
  Sprite, 40, *41*, 48, 82-3, *82-3*
Austin/Morris 1800, *29*
Auto-Union, 30-1
Automobile Association (AA), 56

Bentley, 10, 11, 12, 22, 24, 33, 36,
  36
  Continental, 84-5, *84-5*
  S-Type, 39
Bentley, WO, *17*
Benz, 12
Berkeley, 95
Bertone, 34, 35, *35*, 41
BMW, 29, 38
  3.0 CSL, 43, 51, 90-1, *90-1*
  328, *22*, 32
  503, *32*
  507, 33-4, 86-7, *86-7*
  635 coupé, *63*
  2002 Turbo, 88-9, *88-9*
  M3, *62*, 63
bodywork, 32-7
Bollée, 24
Bond, 95

Borgward 2.3, *40*
Bosch, 24
brakes, 30-1, *30*
Bristol 401, 92, *92*
  V8s 407-411, 93, *93*
British Motor Corporation (BMC), 13,
  43
BRM, 47
BSA, 13, 36
Bugatti, 11, 13, 24
  Type 35, 22, *23*
Buick, *38*
  Riviera, 34, 94-5, *94-5*

Cadillac, 33, *33*, 42
  Eldorado Biarritz, 97, *97*
  Eldorado Brougham, 29, 96, *96*

camshafts, overhead, 12-13, 24
Chapman, Colin, 17, *17*, 23, 27, 42,
  46, 47
Chevrolet 13, 41
  Bel Air, 34
  Camaro, 43, 51
  Corvair, 100-1, *100-1*
  Corvette, 24, 37, 40, 41, 51, 63
  Stingray, 98-9, *98-9*
Chrysler 58, 31
  300, 42
  Airflow, *12*
Cisitalia 202, 32, *32*, 102-3, *102-3*
Citroën, 11, 13, 19, *57*
  2CV, 13, *13*, 57, 62
  DS, 14, *14*, 23, 31, 33, 39, 41, 106-
    7, *106-7*
  SM, 14, 35, 108-9, *108-9*
  Traction Avant, 14, 15, *14*, 36, 37,
    104-5, *104-5*
Citroën, André, 16, *16*
Clément, 24
Collins, Peter, 46-7
Connaught, 109

Cooper, 47
Cooper, John, 50
Cord, *12*, 13
Costin, 109
Cosworth engines, *26*

Daf, 117
Daimler, 30
  Majestic Major, 112-13, *112-13*
  SP250 "Dart", 110-11, *110-11*
Datsun 240Z, 15, *15*, 114-15, *114-15*
De Tomaso, 43, 117
Delage, 117
Delahaye, 117
Dellow, 117
Dodge: Charger, 116-17, *116-17*
  Viper, 62-3, *63*

Duesenberg, 23, *23*
Dunlop Maxaret brakes, 12
DWK, *39*, 117

Edsel, 118-19, *118-19*
Elva, 119
endurance rallies, 53
engineers, 16-17
engines, 24-7, *24-7*, 61

Facel Vega Facel II, *34*, 120-1, *120-1*
factories, 18-19, *18-19*
Fairthorpe, 143
Falcon, 143
Ferguson Formula, 12
Ferrari, 11, 22, 37, 47, 62
  166, *10*
  250 Berlinetta Lusso, 34, *34*
  250 GT, 23, 34
  250 GTO, *42*, 43
  275 GTB, 122-3, *122-3*
  308 GTB, 43
  330 GT, *19*
  Daytona, 43, 126-7, *126-7*

Dino 206/246, 35, 43, 124-5, *124-5*
F40, *62*
Spider, 34
V-twelve engine, 26
Fessia, Antonio, 16
Fiat, 18
  124 Spider, 131, *131*
  130 Coupé, 35, 132-3, *132-3*
  500, 14, *14*, 41, 128-9, *128-9*
  600, 41
  850 Coupç, *19*, 130, *130*
  Topolino, 29, *36*
films, 58-9
Ford, 18-19, *18*, 32, 43
  Anglia, *19*, *38*
  Capri, 142-3, *142-3*
  Consul, 28, 29, 32, 37, 39, 41, 134, *134*
  Cortina, 42, *43*
  Escort, 48, 49, *49*, 51, 63, 136-7, *136-7*
  GT40, *47*
  Lotus Cortina, 135, *135*
  Mustang, 51, 58, 138-9, *138-9*
  Pilot, 57
  Popular, *38*
  Prefect, 38
  Thames, *56*
  Thunderbird, 140-1, *140-1*
  Transit, 57
  V-eight engine, 27
  Zephyr, 32, 41, 50, *50*, 134, *134*
  Zodiac, *40*, 50, 57, 59, 134, *134*
Ford, Henry, 18
four-wheel drive, 12
Frazer Nash, 28, 143
front-wheel drive, 13
fuel injection, 24

General Motors, 24, 34
General Post Office (GPO), 57
Giacosa, Dante, 17, *17*
Gilbern, 145
Ginetta, 145
Girling disc brakes, *30*, 31

Glas, 145
glass-fibre bodywork, 37, 60
Goertz, Albrecht, 33
Gordon Keeble, 144-5, *144-5*
Grand Prix, 46-7
GSM, 145

Hawthorn, Mike, *46*, 47, 50
Healey 100/4, 33
Heinkel, 147
Heron, 147
Hill, Graham, 50
hill climbs, 53
Hillman, 147
Hispano-Suiza, 23
Honda S800, 146, *146-7*
Hotchkiss, 147
HRG, 147
Hudson Super Six, 32, *32*
Humber, 147
hydraulic tappets, 24-5

Invicta, 149
Isetta bubblecar, 38, 56, *60*
Iso Grifo, 148-9, *148-9*
Issigonis, Alec, 16, *16*, 41

Jaguar, 11, 12, 22, 24, 43, 56, *59*, 61
  C-Type, *10*, 31
  E-Type, 23, 34, 42, 59, *59*, 154-5, *154-5*
  MkI, 50
  MkII, 50, 58, 59, 152-3, *152-3*
  MkVII, 40-1, *51*
  MkX, 158-9, *158-9*
  S-Type, *58*, 59
  XJ6, 35, 156-7, *156-7*
  XJS, 43
  XK, 25
  XK120, *22*, 23, 32, 150-1, *150-1*
  XK140, 31, 150-1, *150-1*
Jensen 541, 31, 161, *161*
  FF, 12, 31, 160, *160*
  Interceptor, 160, *160*
Jowett, *52*, 161

Kieft, 161
Kimber, Cecil, 22

Lagonda, 162, *162*, 181
Lamborghini, 62
  350GT, 163, *163*
  Espada, 35, 166-7, *166-7*
  Islero, 59
  Miura, 59, 164-5, *164-5*
Lanchester, 181
Lancia, 61
  Aprillia, *12*, 32
  Aurelia B20 GT, 32, 168-9, *168-9*
  Delta Integrale, 62, 63
  Flaminia, 33, *33*, 41
  Flavia, *13*, 29, 41
  Florida, 33
  Fulvia, 29, 49, 170-1, *170-1*
  Lambda, 36-7
  Stratos, *34*, 49, *49*, 172-3, *172-3*
Land-Rover, 38-9, *39*, 56, *56*
Lea-Francis, 181
Lincoln Continental, 34, 174-5, *174-5*
Lloyd, 181
LMB, 181
Loewy, Raymond, *33*
Lotus, *47*, 53
  Cortina, 42, 50, 56, 57
  Elan, 37, *37*, 42, 59, 180-1, *180-1*
  Elise, 63
  Elite, 34, 37, *37*, 60, 178-9, *178-9*

Europa, *35*
  Seven, *15*, 23, 176-7, *176-7*
Lotus/Ford twin-cam engine, 27
Lyons, William, 16-17, *17*

MacPherson struts, 28, 29, *29*
Marauder, 187
Marcos, 187
Maserati, 37, 47
  250F, *25*, 47
  1500 Berlinetta, 32
  Bora and Merak, 185, *185*
  Ghibli, 35, 182-3, *182-3*
  Khamsin, 184, *184*
mass production, 18-19, *18-19*
Maybach, 30
Mazda, 27
  Cosmo, 186-7, *186-7*
  MX-5, 62, 63
Mercedes-Benz, 29, 30-1, 47
  220S, *40*
  230/250/280SL, 190-1, *190-1*
  280SE 3.5 Coupé, 192-3, *192-3*
  300, 29
  300SEL, *28*
  300SL, 24, 33, 188-9, *188-9*
  600, *28*, 29
  Gullwing, 23
  W154 "Silver Arrow", *47*
Mercury Cougar, 59
Messerschmitt, 38, *39*, 195

Metropolitan, 195
MG, 22, 24, 34, 40, *53*, 63
  Magna, 31
  Magnette, *28, 41*
  MGA, 196-7, *196-7*
  MGB, *43*, 198-9, *198-9*
  Midget, 19, 41
  TC/TD/TF, 194-5, *194-5*
Michelin X tyres, 13
Mini, 13, *13*, 14-15, 19, 23, *25*, 41, 42, *49*, 50, 56, 62, 63, 200-1, *200-1*
Mini Cooper, 23, 42, 59
Mini Minor, 34
Minijem, 203
monocoque bodies, 37
Monteverdi, 203
Morgan, 19, 27
  4/4, 40, 202-3, *202-3*
  Plus 8, 204-5, *204-5*
Morris, 207
Morris Minor, 39, 56, 57, 206-7, *206-7*
Moskvich, 207
Moss, Stirling, 46-7, *46*, 50

navigational rallies, 53
Nobel, 209
NSU, *27*
  Ro80, 35, 42, *42*, 208-9, *208-9*

Ogle, 211
Oldsmobile Toronado, 210-11, *210-11*
Opel, 211

Panhard 24CT, 212-13, *212-13*
Paramount, 219

Peel/Viking, 219
Peerless/Warwick, 219
Pegaso, 23
  Z102 and Z103, 214-15, *214-15*
Peugeot 205 GTI, 63, *63*
Pininfarina, 32, 33, *33*, 34, 35, 41
Piper, 219
police, 56-7
Porsche, 41
  365, 216-17, *216-17*
  911, *22*, 23, 24, 29, 43, 57, 62, 218-19, *218-19*
  917, *47*
  flat-six engine, 26-7
Porsche, Ferdinand, 16, *16*, 38
Powerdrive, 219

rallying, 48-9, 53
Range Rover, 13, *35*, 57

Reliant, 221
  Scimitar GTE, 23, 35, 220, *220*
Renault 4, 57
Renault 16, 221, *221*
Renault, Louis, 30
Riley: 1.5, *27, 28*
  RM Series, 222-3, *222-3*
road runs, 52
Rochdale, 223
Rodley, 223
Rolls-Royce, 12, 33, 36
  Silver Cloud, 39, 224-5, *224-5*
  Silver Shadow, 31, 226-7, *226-7*
Rover, 43
  3.5, 59
  P4, *28, 40*
  P5, 228-9, *228-9*
  P6, 230-1, *230-1*
  V-eight engine, 24, 25-6
Royal Automobile Club (RAC), 56
rust, 60, *61*

Saab 96, 232, *232-3*
saloon car racing, 50-1, 53
Sayers, Malcolm, 34
self-levelling, 13
Siata, 233
Simca, 233
Singer, 233
Skoda, 233
sprints, 53
stage rallies, 48-9, 53
Standard, 233
  Vanguard, *27*, 38, *38*
Steyr-Puch, 233
stock car racing, 51
Studebaker, 34, *33*
styling, 32-5
Sunbeam, 235
  Tiger, *24*, 234-5, *234-5*
Superleggera bodies, 37, *37*
suspension, 28-9, *28-9*
Swallow, 235

Talbot-Lago, 247
Tatra 603, 236-7, *236-7*
television, 58-9
Toyota 2000GT, 59, 238-9, *238-9*
Trabant, 247
trials, 52
Trident, 247
Triumph: 1800/2000 Roadster, 240-1, *240-1*
  Herald, *36*, 41
  Spitfire, 41, *60*
  Stag, 245, *245*
  TR2, 33, 242-3, *242-3*
  TR3, 27, *27*, 31, 242-3, *242-3*
  TR4/5/6, 244, *244*
Turner, 247
TVR Grantura & Vixen, 246-7, *246-7*
tyres, 13, 31

Unipower, 247

Vanden Plas, 59, 249
vans, 57
Vauxhall: Cresta, 248-9, *248-9*
  Ventura, 51, *51*
Volga, 249
Volvo P1800, 58, *58*, 252, *252*
VW: Beetle, 29, 37, 38, 39, *39*, 62, 250-1, *250-1*
  Golf GTi, 23, 62, *62*

Wartburg, 253
Wolseley, 18, 56
  6/80, 253, *253*
  1500, 26

Zaporozhets, 253